I-CHING
AND
TRANSPERSONAL PSYCHOLOGY

Marysol González Sterling

Introduction by José Argüelles, Ph.D.,
author of *Earth Ascending*

SAMUEL WEISER, INC.

York Beach, Maine

First published in 1995 by
SAMUEL WEISER, INC.
P.O. Box 612
York Beach, ME 03910-0612

Passages from the "Commentary" to *Milton: A Poem by William Blake* (Boulder and New York: Shambhala and Random House, 1978) are used by permission of the authors of the "Commentary," Kay Parkhurst Easson and Roger R. Easson.

LIBRARY OF CONGRESS CATALOGING-IN-PUBLICATION DATA

González Sterling, Marysol.
  [I Ching y psicologia transpersonal. English]
  I-Ching and transpersonal psychology / Marysol González Sterling.
      p. cm.
  Includes bibliographical references and index.
  1. Divination. 2. I ching. 3. Transpersonal psychology--Miscellanea.
  BF1770.C5G6613   1995
  133.3'3--dc20   95-35060
                                             CIP

ISBN 0-87728-836-4
MG
Cover art copyright © 1995 John Rosenfeldt
Illustrations in the text by M.G. Sterling except the illustration on page 174 by A. de Diego.

Typeset in 10.5 point Garamond

Printed in the United States of America

01 00 99 98 97 96 95
10 9 8 7 6 5 4 3 2 1

The paper used in this publication meets the minimum requirements of the American National Standard for Permanence of Paper for Printed Library Materials Z39.48-1984.

Table of Contents

The explanation of the philosophical contents of the I-Ching and its metaphysical reference to the electromagnetic resonance of Heaven, the gravitational resonance of the Earth and the biopsychic resonance of the human being. Explains the difference in the arrangement of the trigrams of Fu-Shi's Earlier Heaven and King Wan's Later Heaven, as the world of thought and the world of the senses, the compensatory polarities and the temporary contradictions of matter.

An explanation of the process of transformation contained in the trigrams, as well as those which express inner and outer changes. The stages of formation of the human being and the Yin-Yang rhythm according to the arrangement of the trigrams in the world of the senses; the environment before birth in the Receptive, conception in Fire, youth in Lake, adulthood in Wind, maturity in Mountain, death and post-death in The Creative.

I-Ching as instrument to connect with the Higher Self and to synchronize oneself with the Here and Now. An explanation on how to use the yarrow sticks, how to obtain hexagram and changing lines, how it changes to another situation through changing to another hexagram. How to divide the hexagram in time and see the root of the first hexagram through the nuclear trigrams. The thought behind the situation created the first hexagram. How to use stones or coins to obtain the answer. How to use a diagram that describes how a circumstance has been created and how that circumstance progresses via its complementary polarity. The meaning of the lines that don't change, given the circumstance mentioned in the first hexagram. The consecutive numbering of the hexagrams, their reversibility and the non-reversibility of karma. The space and time relationship of the different stages of the hexagrams. Advice to help with the interpretation of the Book of Changes, The I-Ching. References to the meaning of the language of the original text.

PHASE 4

Through the moon phase of the day of birth, one obtains a hexagram; the karmic steps through which it passes in micro and macro cycles in order to reach its polarity. The meaning of the evolutionary position of each line in the hexagram. List of hexagrams with alternative names. Reference to the meaning of the superior and the inferior human in the original texts. Reference to the psychic process and its connection with the trigrams.

PHASE 5

Explanation of the philosophy of Jung's psychology, the meaning of the anima-animus and shadow. The physical, vital, astral, and mental bodies, and the psychological preparation for death. How one integrates one's androgynous self and manifests one's unique and creative individual self.

PHASE 6

The difference between the mental, astral, vital, psychic, and physical bodies compared with the brain frequencies of the delta, theta, alpha, and beta states, also compared with double lines of the I-Ching.

PHASE 7

The process of psychological maturity of the individuation process according to the sequence in the opposite direction of the human being's rhythm in the world of thoughts. Receptive darkness (Earth); trust in material darkness and the arrival of Light (Mountain); the absorption of light and the projection of darkness to the outside (Water); the deepening of darkness and the dispersal of light to the outside (Wind).

PHASE 8

The penetration of light and the explosion of darkness (Thunder); the revelation of light and the centering of darkness upon recognizing it (Fire); the integration of light, inner space and the expulsion of darkness (Lake); Creative luminosity (Heaven). The luminosity of the Self.

*Above all, I am grateful that the Taoist Wisdom from the
Chinese ancestors still prevails today.*

*And that Carl Gustav Jung saw that the I-Ching actu-
ally outlines the psychological archetypes of light and
darkness.*

*This has helped me to navigate the synchronicity of
Heaven and Earth.*

*Most of all, I am grateful to José Argüelles and
Geraldyne Lewis Waxkowsky for their inspiration
and guidance deciphering the clues of so many shared
experiences, and to my old friend, Matts Höjer, for
teaching me the I-Ching some twenty years ago.*

I-Ching: Heaven, Human Beings, and Earth

A Metaphysical Treatise for Transpersonal Psychology

A human being is a galactic agent, a cosmic vibratory root. Heaven is the galactic order of being from which this human agent draws its inspiration and power. Earth is the plane in which this agent is allowed to grow and act.

What is the purpose of human action? To establish the foundations of galactic culture. What is galactic culture? Galactic culture is the universal stream of being, capable of infinite forms of expression and infinite levels of attainment. Galactic culture is to the Earth plane what light is to color. The human being is the prism through whom the light is broken down into its full Earthly spectrum.

In the present world situation, humans have lost sight of their cosmic mediating role. Instead of being prisms of light, they are prisoners of matter. This is a complex reality which now threatens the future of human evolution.

The purpose of transpersonal psychology is to help lift us out of the anarchic mire of parochial, ego-obsessed thought and culture into the light of higher possibilities. Because the I-Ching corresponds to the structure and order of DNA, it is one of the few Earthly touchstones upon which we can base the possibility of galactic culture. In this way, the I-Ching has crossed the great water of time and history to become a key transpersonal tool.

Marysol González Sterling understands the I-Ching from both a planetary and transpersonal perspective, as a guide to the larger, more universal order of galactic culture. Her book offers numerous keys useful for sorting out individual processes within a larger, transpersonal matrix of understanding. By concentrating on the interrelationship of the symbols—the trigrams and hexagrams—one is able to establish an objective foundation for human behavior.

Her insight into the relationship between the psychic order and the external world, as described by the mandala pattern, is creatively useful as well as aesthetic. This is an important point, since a total aesthetic is the beginning foundation of galactic culture. A total aesthetic is the quality of attention which an individual brings to all matters of life.

The synergy of humans turning together in harmony makes galactic culture a possibility for this planet. Marysol González Sterling's understanding of the I-Ching allows us to approach this possible moment with complete clarity and an integral aesthetic that enters us into the galactic metaphysic: Heaven, Human and Earth. In this way, her work may become one of the foundation stones of universal understanding and compassion.

—José Argüelles, Ph.D.
Day of the Lunar Warrior

According to the I-Ching

Heaven is expressed through the action of the circle. The human being (the Self) bases its physical and psychic expression on the base of the triangle and turns both vision and action toward the upper vertex, toward Heaven. On Earth, we express mobility within the receptive immobility of the Earth Square.

In the lines, we can see the mobility of humankind's action in Heaven and, if we watch closely, we can see the movement in the figures, and also their colors. This shows the freedom of action we have in the dream world and in our thoughts. On Earth, human beings move through the senses, and are oriented toward North, South, East, and West.

The effect of Heaven on the human being.

The effect of Earth on the human being.

The Human Being Between the World of Light and the World of Darkness

Human beings are creatures of the galactic universe. We are rational and instinctive beings who can think about the meaning of our life; while our feet are strongly magnetized to Earth, our minds can wander through Heaven. Human beings are placed between Heaven and Earth; we feel the instinctive, organic impulses, and at the same time we think, perceive, we are impressed; we project ourselves and create our vision of Heaven, transforming matter.

When we perceive the response reflected by the material world, we become aware of the duality in everything, penetrating its contradictions and discovering the relativity in the whole of Heaven and Earth, day and night, full and empty, light and darkness, Sun and Moon, life and death, awake and asleep, matter and dreams, man and woman, thoughts and actions, past and future, conscious and unconscious, color and sound. It all dances in soft and dense vibrations around us, and we discover there is a third one: ourselves—alone. It all happens from within, it is all integrated from within, it all converges within and is polarized within. It all depends on ourselves; we finally become aware that each human being becomes that central point, that individual consciousness, integrating in the present moment all the polarity we experience in our time-space relationships.

It all constitutes a reflection of the Self in the present. The unit is alive, it interacts and moves in a world that grants us life and takes it away. Everything depends on the harmony of the particular inner pulsation arising from the tone or vibrational octave that integrates and makes everything that our dream world dreams real. We are aware of our experience and of our temporal creation.

Human beings are experimental entities who can separate from their own nature through cognition, and are therefore cut off from their own sacred power to create and evolve. Being cosmic creatures, humans can only return to the source of their eternity by being aware of their own vehicle, which, in turn, makes them aware of their disharmonies and, at the same time, of the only parcel the cosmos has granted us: the nature of the planet Earth.

The union of Heaven and Earth is the sacred power and the gift of creativity which reveals the meaning of the human being and of every creature on this planet.

As we join the heavenly dreams with the transformation of physical matter, human beings create our world, a world centered upon self-awareness and upon ourselves, forgetting that, with each small act and thought, we are imitating the cosmic creation. Strangely, we are so immersed in ourselves that we lose our way and perceive only darkness; our opaque external body interacts with other opaque bodies, flowing and defending ourselves. We are immersed in a dance that weaves a unique and irreparable vibrational resonance. Nothing ever is or happens the same as anything else. Everything is similar and relative. Everything is heavy and painful until we discover that all is within and that there is only the Here and Now.

In Chinese culture, Heaven is the circle of the infinite, Earth is the square that centers matter, and humans are the triangle that mobilize everything; all that is above is below and the below is above, inverting reality and recreating it again and again. Cycle after cycle, one concentric spiral after another, we find the center, the vertex of each thinking molecular unit of the planet, each human being.

No matter how many times we draw the circle, the square, or the triangle, never will they be the same, for each moment is unique and irreplaceable, just as each human being is irreplaceable.

Each cell of the planet Earth's brain contains within itself a series of vibrational impulses that are unrepeatable, although they appear similar. They imitate the constant pulse of that primeval polarity with all the richness of multicolor vibrational multiplicity that we perceive each moment of our lives. Thus, Chinese thought reveals the mutability and the basic changes in nature through which the wider range and infinite array of possibilities becomes manifest in the realm of phenomena.

When the two worlds unite, the world of the compensatory pulsating polarity and the world of temporality[1]—the senses of awareness in the present moment—we achieve the most basic synthesis of the universe and of our own nature. All becomes a revelation and reveals the miracle of creation.

---

1. Will be explained in depth later on.

For Chinese sages, geomantics is the mother of all sciences; observation, participation in life, knowledge, and divination of the nature of our planet Gea or Gaia. In their desire to communicate the basis of thought with the capacity to expand from the most simple to the most infinite, they created the I-Ching, the "Book of Changes," which still deciphers the wisdom of human life, and contains the base of the binary system discovered by modern science. It also includes the genetic code, the DNA, the foundation and inherited genetic framework that decodes the origins of every living being on this planet. The double spiral deciphers a single harmonic octave and unites the forces of Heaven and Earth through each individual.

The basis of the study of the Chinese sages is the union of light and darkness. The active principle of the spirit, which they call "Yang," is the light of heaven, the thought element, the world of dreams and of thought. And the passive principle of physical matter, which they call "Yin," is the darkness of the Earth, of organic density, of the temporal, the world of senses and instinct. The one (Yang) is represented by a straight line, meaning the masculine principle, and the other (Yin) by a broken line representing the passive receptive feminine principle.

In the I-Ching, Yang is represented ▬ and Yin ▬ ▬, but we can also represent it as a space of darkness or of light: Yang ○ and Yin ●. Yang □ △ and Yin ■ ▼. Both are visually representative of their deep meaning: Yin—receptive feminine sexuality and the darkness of dense matter, earth and water; Yang—masculine sexuality, active, creative, the light and void of the air and the Sun.

The Yin and the Yang in the life of the human being appears as a dark triangle pointed downward because of the Yin gravity, the pull of earth and water, the expanding spiral and the centrifugal forces of the universe. The Yang, a white triangle pointed upward due to the electromagnetic force of heaven, of the Sun and the air, a concentrating spiral and the centripetal forces of heaven.

The human being represents the wood element, the most adaptable and manageable, the organic element of Earth endowed with the consciousness of Heaven. It is the most flexible and sensitive element on the planet Earth, and in that high fusion of the organic and the psyche, it represents an independent being with a very high level of creativity and even freedom. Thus, we have the awareness of the microcosm through the energy of our thoughts, which are the most permanent and creative source of the spirit, while our organic aspect is an earthly temporal one.

As responsible existential beings, the thoughts and connections of the planet evolve constantly and adapt to survival, through a constant resistance created by the necessary tension between Heaven and Earth when they merge into life. Flexibility and friction is the fluid of life, and it moves in a single direction from past to present to future.

Our matter does not go backward, but our minds have the freedom of the microcosm to be in the past, in the present, or in the future. We are biologically aware of a limit between the personal and the collective, but our emotions betray us, for we feel everything around us, and often cannot tell whether it belongs to us or not, whether it arises from our own personal sensation or not. It separates us from—and integrates us into—the world, and does not understand the constant dissatisfaction and lack of fulfillment derived from the awareness of the duality "I/others." We perceive a projection unaware that it is the mind's inner film and it baffles us, for we cannot conceive how it can be, since we have not chosen our parents consciously, we do not remember how we decided to live in an insomnia of amnesia and ignorance of our true primeval self.

We don't remember our dreams and, without them, it would be impossible for us to live in organic matter; without the sleep that recharges the spirit, our bodies would grow weak and we would experience that inner projection of feeling like a rag, a puppet of our own visual distortions. We need to trust the Earth and the spot that has been granted to us each night for our sleep, as well as administer wisely the nourishment the Earth provides.

Awareness starts to become distorted in the process of conquest and control of the material world, which in turn controls us as an obsession would, in the process of assuring our appetites and pleasures. What really happens is that we take our inner world and spirit for granted, trusting inwardly that it exists eternally, while focusing attention on temporary, ephemeral, and unendurable things. The material world becomes the challenge and the difficulty that must be overcome, leading to a greater separation from the awareness we trusted in and which has the purpose of facilitating real access to the conquest of the physical world. This separation between mind and body causes more and more blocking in the material world, either on account of illness or of the difficulty in finding real happiness and real pleasure, which is basically a spiritual state manifested through matter when not torn apart.

We find it hard to understand that suffering does not exist in the spirit, except in the case of trespassing our essential principles and causing imbalances that hurt the spirit and that only manifest physically. When humans feel at one with their spirits, physical pain and spiritual peace help us feel things as they are, and we don't need to project our expectations on them.

When spirit merges with matter, light with darkness, Yin with Yang, four possibilities arise, as we can see in figure 1. Two Yang lines, 2 Yin lines and 2 Yin-Yang lines; Yin above, Yang below, or vice versa. 2 x 2 = 4. This is the basis of all multiplicity from the essential polarity of the universe. We exist because of the merging of two sexes, man and woman, which are also fruit of another man-woman union.

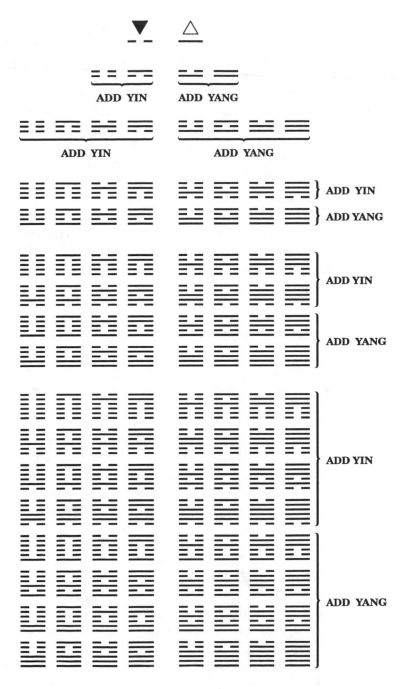

Figure 1. Yin and Yang progression.

So, we have received our genetic makeup from our parents' parents, two men and two women. It is impossible to exist without this, and everything in our lives will also be divided according to this same basic formula—a double duality that baffles us if we don't learn to transcend it.

The number where movement begins is the 3, for it is here that multiplicity begins, and it is the unit of that duality. If we add that humans exist as the third factor uniting the polarity of Heaven and Earth, the real movement and evolution begins at this third unifying point.

Continuing with figure 1, if we add a third line to the four basic possibilities, four times a Yin line underneath and four times a Yang line underneath, we obtain eight possibilities. These are the eight basic mutations of nature, the trigrams of the I-Ching.

The creative Heaven, the light ☰, in polarity with receptive matter, the Earth, darkness ☷; the Water in light within material darkness ☵, in polarity with Fire, dark matter at the core that is surrounded by light ☲. Thunder, which is an upwards explosion, from light to its dark material manifestation ☳, in polarity to Wind, luminosity that descends and spreads out over Earth ☴; the Lake, light radiant as a mirror underneath the darkness of matter ☱, in polarity to the Mountain, material darkness resting under the light of Heaven ☶.

Starting with these eight possibilities of change, when we add Yin or Yang lines underneath, we get sixteen forms made up of four lines each, and as we repeat the procedure adding one more line, we get thirty-two possibilities with five lines. Finally, if we repeat again and add Yin and Yang lines underneath, we get sixty-four basic possibilities of mutation or change. These are called hexagrams, and are made up of two trigrams, one above and one below. They make up the original mutability in nature which is interchangeable. This is also the way the chess board is formed, 8 x 8 = 64, as well as the genetic DNA code of life on this planet. It is the numeric base of a totality which can multiply among each other innumerable times.

We will now study the eight trigrams in greater depth, looking at their relation in the inner changes of Heaven, the inner changes of Earth, and the resulting synthesis as external changes in the human being and in nature. In figure 2 (pages 8 and 9), we define each line, the lower line of the trigrams corresponds to the gravitational pull of the Earth, the closest and most temporal; the upper line of each trigram corresponds to the electromagnetic force of Heaven, the farthest and most permanent; the center line of each trigram corresponds to the human being, who tries to relate to both and act as a bridge between them. In the trigrams, this relationship Heaven-human being-Earth is the perfect one, and the passive Yin center line or the active Yang line is the adequate position for the human being in order to fuse the forces of Heaven and Earth in the changes and transformations indicated by the trigrams.

In the creative, the human being activates Yang, the energy of light reflected on Earth, and elevates it toward the spirit of Heaven.

In the receptive, the human being becomes empty to receive the solar energy of the Yin upper line from Heaven and helps it descend and penetrate into the darkness of Earth to fertilize it.

In fire, the human being opens up, receiving the active light of Heaven and its active reflection on Earth. Central Yin line—letting ourselves be consumed by the transforming energy of fire. Fire arises also from the Earth, just as water rains and falls from Heaven.

In water, the human being becomes active—central Yang line—in order for the creative spiritual principle to fuse with the solar energy, the Yin from Heaven and the material receptivity of Earth. Humans pray for the fertile rain from Heaven, to wash and purify us with its blessing.

In thunder, the human being receives the energy released by the Earth— Yin central line—and takes on the spirit to awaken the power of Heaven's thought in matter.

In the wind, the light from Heaven descends and mobilizes the dispersion of the Earth. Since the human being accepts it actively—Yang central line—it takes on spirit to disperse and facilitate the thought of Heaven in matter.

In the lake, the human being activates—Yang central line—so that the spirit rests on the energy of the Earth and reflects the light from Heaven in order to penetrate the Earth, and receives the warmth of the Sun's light—Yin above— that evaporates the water and recycles life in the form of rain. Lake is also clouds in the sky.

In the mountain, the human being rests receptively, merging into the passive peacefulness of the Earth—Yin central line—to reach and observe, to integrate and assimilate the light and warmth of the spirit of Heaven.

When two trigrams merge and two of these permutations combine, we obtain sixty-four mutations, or hexagrams. Through each of these duplicated changes, one for Heaven and one for the Earth, we obtain all the possibilities and alternatives of permutations in our universe. Since we are in between the Earth and the Heavens, we have the mission of integrating both by attracting the creative consciousness of Heaven and modeling the receptive Earth, which opens up and is only resistant enough to maintain life.

Those six lines of a hexagram are divided in various forms, both in space and time. In time, the first lower line refers to the most present moment right now, and escalates time as it progresses upward; the last line, the upper sixth, refers to the last moment and the last step in time. In space, it refers to the union of

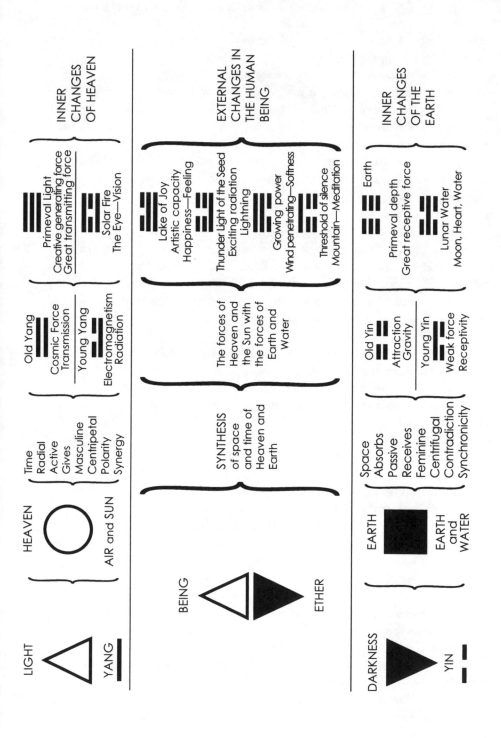

LIGHT

HEAVEN

YANG

AIR and SUN

Time
Radial
Active
Gives
Masculine
Centripetal
Polarity
Synergy

Old Yang
Cosmic Force
Transmission
Young Yang
Electromagnetism
Radiation

Primeval Light
Creative generating force
Great transmitting force

Solar Fire
The Eye—Vision

INNER
CHANGES
OF HEAVEN

BEING

ETHER

SYNTHESIS
of space
and time of
Heaven and
Earth

The forces of
Heaven and
the Sun with
the forces of
Earth and
Water

Lake of Joy
Artistic capacity
Happiness—Feeling

Thunder Light of the Seed
Exciting radiation
Lightning

Growing power
Wind penetrating—Softness

Threshold of silence
Mountain—Meditation

EXTERNAL
CHANGES IN
THE HUMAN
BEING

DARKNESS

YIN

EARTH

EARTH
and
WATER

Space
Absorbs
Passive
Receives
Feminine
Centrifugal
Contradiction
Synchronicity

Old Yin
Attraction
Gravity
Young Yin
Weak force
Receptivity

Earth
Primeval depth
Great receptive force

Lunar Water
Moon, Heart, Water

INNER
CHANGES
OF THE
EARTH

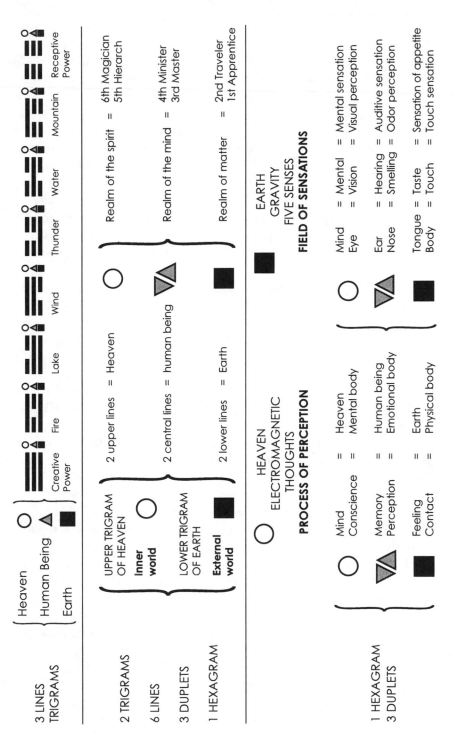

Figure 2. Defining the trigrams.

Heaven and Earth, while the central space belongs to the human being, placed between the top line of the lower trigram—on top of the Earth—and the lower line of the upper trigram—Heaven—for it is below Heaven.

Likewise, in the union of the trigram of Earth with the trigram of Heaven, human beings find themselves in the two central lines which is where Heaven touches Earth, and the mission entrusted to humans is to understand the revelation of Heaven through our thought and consciousness and integrate it in the Earth through our creativity and the harmony of our body. All we have to do is adhere to the clarity of the thoughts of Heaven and flow with the senses of the Earth, without stagnating either.

Human beings, in our escalade [ascent] from the point closest to Earth to the point farthest in Heaven, go through different stages of learning, mastery, and excellence in our behavior, which plays a role in both psychological and spiritual maturity.

The first stage is the beginner's stage; when it is Yin, we are accepting the teachings indicated by the state determined by a specific hexagram. When it is Yang, we are looking for those learning experiences actively. The second line indicates the travelers, Yin when caused by external elements, and Yang when activated by an internal search. In the third line, it is the teacher, Yin, receiving the capacity to be so, and Yang teaching. In the fourth line, it is the official who gives orders—Yang—or who receives orders—Yin. In the fifth line, we are the leaders who create situations—Yang—or who let them happen—Yin. In the sixth line, we are the magicians who transform—Yang—or are transformed—Yin.

Moreover, each line of a hexagram, when referring to something earthly and temporal, fills a space in the realm of sensation, and when referring to something mental and permanent, to perceptions and thoughts, each line fulfills a mission in the different levels of psychological perception and maturity.

Through the mutations of the lines of each hexagram, whether it be a line that changes into its opposite, 2, 3, 4, 5 or 6 lines, it can change into the other sixty-three hexagrams. Therefore, multiplicity becomes innumerable and slowly reaches the variability of alternative life experiences present to us. The I-Ching is the book that shows us the way of Tao, with all the detours, crossroads, and knots that make up life's experiences. It presents us with what we call obstacles—which are really challenges to our wisdom—and inspires us to recognize when to yield and when to act without hesitation when we see the knot opening or the path clearing up. Weaving that fabric requires excellence in intention and pureness.

In Chinese philosophy, life is a fabric woven by innumerable patterns which, as they mingle, multiply their possibilities, and at times seem to condition us temporarily. When we enter into a "world of knots," we can only counteract with the action of untying them, or by being aware of the steps that have taken us into that tangled situation. Meanwhile, and at the times when we've achieved an untangled past, we have a clear conscience and freedom, but only for a while, until we encounter the next challenge, when we must achieve a special wisdom to turn it around and make it a mental and spiritual benefit for us.

Taoist wisdom shows us how to acquire moral excellence, impeccability in our actions, and adaptability in any situation in life, showing us that material reality is only temporary. The only permanent thing is what we have learned from our temporal experience in the world of physical sensation.

The I-Ching is a magnificent guidebook of psychological maturity and transcendence of our confinement and excessive trust in matter; therefore it is an excellent transpersonal tool.

The I-Ching is the instrument of the wisdom of living the present moment in synchronicity. It teaches us to connect with the Source of universal wisdom. It is a psychological computer through which we find the answers to all that happens, since it helps us to gain a clear view of the doors into and out of the difficulties created by a misunderstanding of life. The I-Ching is a system of equations—and of unforeseeable situations—which find the formula of the most perfect solutions and the alchemy to merge with the forces of Nature and Spirit.

The psychological guidebook that the I-Ching offers us is an ideal way to clear up distortions in our perceptions and clean up obstructions in our senses in order to reflect brightly the divine purpose of our personal existence and maintain a healthy, radiant, translucid, and transparent body, not needing to block the light when it penetrates into the body, nor cover up what we perceive and project with the mind and feel with our senses. A compensatory reality—a polarity—helps us to find our center, the third state of the constant mobility of the present moment, or the perception of time as relative.

The relativity of time is a reality of heaven and spirit; it refers to a permanent Yang state, even if it seems impermanent, since the possibility of ignoring time comes from the misunderstanding arising when we enter the temporal world of Yin, the reality of space. Depending on this union, we perceive time as stretched out or compressed, a minute seeming like an hour or vice versa. Astrophysics shows us that traveling a few days at the speed of light in space can be translated into many years in terms of the original time-space. When we look at the stars in space, the distortion of time perception depends on macro—or microcosmic space. We see the stars now as they were hundreds of thousands of years ago.

The I-Ching presents us with a threshold to perceive the structure of all forms of change. It is a matrix that moves through space with the right perception of time; it allows us to see the light of those synchronistic messages (or sig-

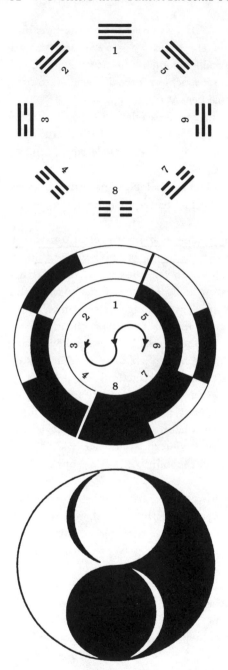

1. Creative Sky
2. Lake
3. Fire
4. Thunder
5. Wind
6. Water
7. Mountain
8. Receptive Earth

The biopsychic resonance rotates in both directions, uniting Heaven and Earth.

The symbol of Tai-Chi, "The Great Supreme," compared to the lunations.

Figure 3. The human being.

nificant coincidences) that help us solve anything that arises in daily experience. The reason for this is that we contact our higher being, our inner being—the essential consciousness that knows everything through its contact with the center of our galaxy—and the principle of each of our individual and unique existences.

The texts of the I-Ching can also be used as a guide, for they help us meditate, reflect on, and know the answers to all that happens to us at certain moments. When we ask a question, an oracular spiritual connection takes place in the same way as if we were asking a wise man. It provides a way of looking at absolute totality in detail, and shows us what the higher human and the lower human in us would do.

It helps us understand the duality of life within ourselves so that we can choose to concentrate on the voice and the vision best suited for any given subject. By understanding the world around us, and allowing for the union of the spiritual and material world, we connect to the planetary universe and to the body and its senses.

I recommend reading the translations of the I Ching published by Richard Wilhelm, Thomas Cleary, or Jacoby de Hoffman. This treatise on Chinese wisdom was written down thousands of years ago, and although its translation can limit our full understanding of the mentality of the times, observations are so keen that they take into account the essence of every situation which inspired it and revealed its wisdom.

We can understand duality by experiencing the union of the two worlds we live in—material and spiritual. The difference between temporal contradictions and the compensatory polarity is in the circular possibilities that come from the eight trigrams, the eight states of change.

The first circular arrangement was created by Fu-Shi and is called the Earlier Heaven. It is the beginning of the universe, which only exists at first in a state of dreams and thoughts. It later materializes, and this shows in the Later Heaven created and studied by King-Wen, where the positions of the light-darkness pulsation create distortions of the senses into contradictions.

The arrangement of Fu-Shi's Earlier Heaven is called the world of thoughts (the axial world), where the axes are clearly marked by the compensatory polarity existing between a trigram and its contrary (a 180° configuration). What above is Yin, below is Yang, and what below is Yin, above is Yang; what on one side is light, on the other is darkness; what appears as active creativity meets passive receptivity at its complementary axis. Therefore it is named the world of compensation, the world of the psyche, with its relativity in time, where nothing exists in material form because it is immediately and perfectly compensated, thus avoiding the distortion, resistance, and tension that create knots in the existence of material reality.

The pair of complementary opposites in the perfection of the creative heaven, the energy of the spirit, are: Heaven ☰ and receptive Earth ☷ , inert matter that awaits the impulse of the creative spirit; the Fire of mental revelation ☲ ; the Water ☵ of feeling emotions, instincts and desires; the Wind ☴ as the descent of the intellect into the senses; Thunder ☳ as the explosion of desires and the detachment from matter; the Lake ☱ as the reflection of light on Earth; and the Mountain ☶ , material tranquillity recognizing its spiritual purpose (figure 3, page 12).

In the world of thoughts, nothing happens in matter, but the compensatory axial world reacts and counteracts immediately to whatever happens on each side. Although nothing seems to happen in the world of matter or of the conscious senses, the psyche exerts a slow but constant influence on the senses and eventually expresses itself in matter (see figures 4 and 5 on pages 15 and 16).

The latter arrangement of the trigrams of Heaven by King-Wen refers to the world of senses and to the effect of the temporal distortion of time when it relates directly to a specific space, ignoring the totality or eternity of the world of dreams. In this configuration, the polarity of light and darkness in the trigrams is maintained in Fire and Water, referring to the alchemical formula that photosynthesis endows matter with animated life when the light of the spirit (Fire) penetrates the water and nourishes it with life and sensations. Fire refers to the moment of conception and Water refers to the principle of life in the womb that nourishes and softly gives birth to all life in matter.

This configuration of the trigrams refers to the temporal rotation and to the rotation of Earth around its own axis (figure 4). Like everything else, it returns to its starting point. Matter reflects the roundness of Heaven; it imitates the universe in its circular totality, but as it passes through its various stages the divine purpose of nature starts to distort. It starts with the presence of Heaven in the human being and moves through the understanding of the Mind of Fire (since the trigram of Fire is placed South) where the creative Heaven is located in Fu-Shi's arrangement (figures 5 and 6 on pages 16 and 17).

The human receptivity to receive (central Yin line) the light of Heaven and of Earth in Fire, illuminates mind and understanding, and projects us in an opposite and alchemical polarity: Water. Here humans creatively activate (central Yang line) and penetrate the action of Heaven (two Yin lines, one above and one below) and of Earth: the photosynthesis of life.

We feel instincts and start to move to materialize a vision, but in that movement, we enter into temporal contradictions due to the natural resistance each element has according to its rhythm and speed of change. When we move, we lose contact with Heaven and the mind gets confused. The mind no longer reflects luminosity; it becomes a blurred mirror; actions cause reactions—the law of Karma. In movement, as we focus attention on the objects and obstacles of material life, we lose the purpose and essential inspiration of the mind in contact with Heaven.

Visually, this is evident from the position of the Later Heaven of the trigrams in the world of senses. On one side of Fire and Water is creative Heaven and receptive Earth, the principles of light and darkness that separate understanding

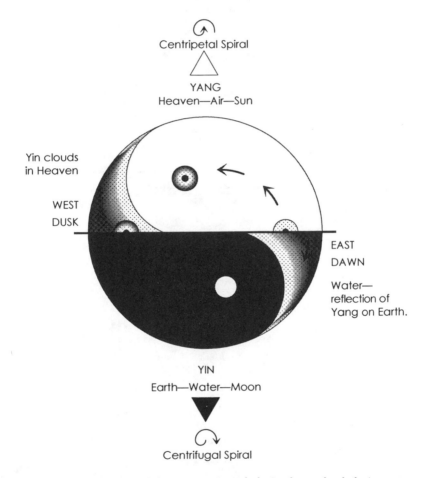

Figure 4. Apparent movement of the Sun is counterclockwise due to the clockwise movement of the Earth's rotation. The action of the Sun on the waters of the Earth evaporates the water, transforming it into clouds, being Yin in Heaven, and the reflection of the sunlight on the Yang water on the Earth.

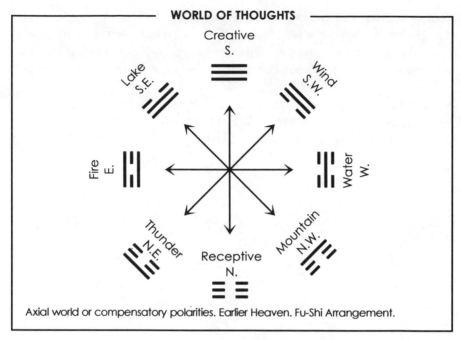

WORLD OF THOUGHTS

Axial world or compensatory polarities. Earlier Heaven. Fu-Shi Arrangement.

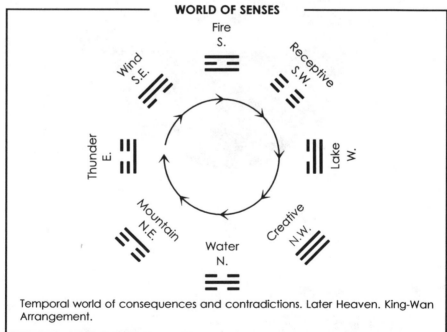

WORLD OF SENSES

Temporal world of consequences and contradictions. Later Heaven. King-Wan Arrangement.

Figure 5. The world of thoughts and senses in the symbolism of the I-Ching.

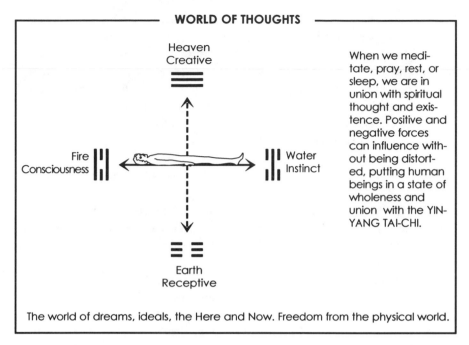

WORLD OF THOUGHTS

Heaven
Creative

Fire
Consciousness

Water
Instinct

Earth
Receptive

When we meditate, pray, rest, or sleep, we are in union with spiritual thought and existence. Positive and negative forces can influence without being distorted, putting human beings in a state of wholeness and union with the YIN-YANG TAI-CHI.

The world of dreams, ideals, the Here and Now. Freedom from the physical world.

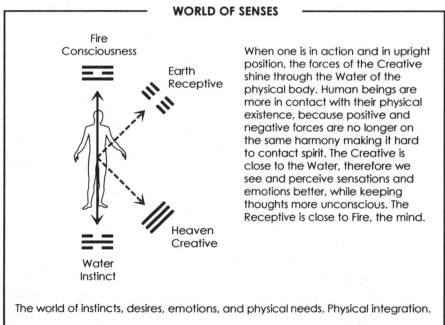

WORLD OF SENSES

Fire
Consciousness

Earth
Receptive

Heaven
Creative

Water
Instinct

When one is in action and in upright position, the forces of the Creative shine through the Water of the physical body. Human beings are more in contact with their physical existence, because positive and negative forces are no longer on the same harmony making it hard to contact spirit. The Creative is close to the Water, therefore we see and perceive sensations and emotions better, while keeping thoughts more unconscious. The Receptive is close to Fire, the mind.

The world of instincts, desires, emotions, and physical needs. Physical integration.

Figure 6. The world of thoughts and senses in relation to the human being.

from the polarity of intellect-instinct. This, in human beings, becomes the concept of duality and the mind-body split.

There is a strange polarity in east and west that becomes a contradiction. It is represented in Thunder, which takes its place at the east of Fire in the Earlier Heaven of thoughts and in opposition to the Lake, which should reflect on the Earth the creative spirit of Heaven. This distortion transforms movement into a circle, a clockwise rotation around a central axis, similar to that of the Earth.

King-Wen's Later Heaven has been misunderstood, for it represents a similar distortion, or error of perception, as the temporal destiny of humans condemned to a world of matter. The only complementary polarity maintained is that of Fire and Water. This is an alchemical formula par excellence, to avoid one neutralizing the other; everything has to rotate or circulate. On the other side of the Earth is the Mountain that rests and looks up to Heaven, elevating its material being. Opposed to creativity is the Wind, which is the way Heaven descends to Earth, penetrating its spirit softly within nature.

There is an opposition between Thunder and the Lake, and the relationsihip is shown by the fact that Thunder is a Yang line with two Yin lines on top, while the Lake is the opposite: two Yang lines below and one Yin line above. When they are placed in a circle and read in one direction, they seem to be polar complementaries. This isn't so, because they are to be read from the center. The bottom line is the one at the center of the circle. Contradiction and opposition are basic clues, for Thunder is a manifestation of Earth in Heaven through electromagnetic interaction of the clouds and their various electric charges, while the Lake is the reflection of Heaven on the Earth. Possibly this contradiction is related to the way life is formed: the discharge of Heaven produces the photovoltaic fusion of the energy of the spirit in the peaceful waters of the Lake.

In fact, they represent another form of polarity, such as Fire and Water, where the phenomenon of life is depicted. The peaceful Lake, with the action of the sunlight, evaporates and ascends, forming clouds, which in turn discharge in Thunder, inciting Heaven to manifest its spirit and providing life to inert matter. Rain is one of the supreme gifts of life on planet Earth.

Once the light and energy of Fire provoked by Thunder has taken life in Water and in the Lake, everything else has to circulate so that the high density energy knot produced does not dissolve, as would be the case in the world of dreams and thoughts, of complementary polarity. In Fu-Shi's arrangement, it appears in its most perfect form, and therefore doesn't need to densify to manifest itself; all movements are counteracting phenomena. While in the King-Wan arrangement, everything that circulates, rotates, and forms a world more dense with energy which in turn produces what we call life and physical manifestation.

These arrangements of trigrams represent the way in which our lack of psychological harmony crystallizes and forms an energy knot responsible for illness.

In the temporal distortion that makes everything spin, from the moment that an idea penetrates the mind in Fire, receptive darkness receives it to be materialized, but often the idea is lost and forgotten in the darkness of the Earth. If the revelation is strong enough, it maintains its vision and enters into the joy and the peace of the Lake in order to carry it out. It sees—in the creativity of Heaven— the way to manifest an idea into matter and in the senses, indicated by Water. If we forget the receptive Earth, the original idea becomes distorted in the Lake, pleasures become priorities, and the result is a misunderstanding of the vision of the creative, distorting the spiritual purpose. Humankind penetrates into the Water with instincts, desires, and wild passions, and the body becomes attached to material appearances and the physical world, trapping the spirit in a senseless battle and in endless suffering by separating the spiritual soul from the body. This eventually may cause illness.

Human beings are seldom aware of the imbalance that crystallizes and stagnates in the Mountain. It explodes in sudden imbalances of pain in the next roar of Thunder, until the Wind makes us understand the need to be mentally conscious—to allow ourselves to hear the body. If a revelation is honored and we know how to bring it to the world of senses, it is nurtured by Water, it crystallizes and materializes in the Mountain. With Thunder, it attains life and purpose with nonattachment and we understand how to develop that idea through the Wind. The mind of Fire can then produce other creative revelations and materialize anything that helps the spirit evolve through matter. Creative revelation keeps us from sliding back spiritually because of stagnation, distortion, or disharmony.

Becoming aware is an inevitable law. Human beings who live in a world devoid of meaning, wrapped up in short-lived pleasures that produce premature physical disharmony and illness, don't bring happiness. This is the means the divine law uses to make us aware of Self and our divine purpose. Once the idea is nurtured by Water, it penetrates the senses, and the Mountain looks to Heaven to find the solution to difficulties encountered along the way. Thunder and Wind are the bridge that mobilizes and activates organic life. It represents the Chinese Wood element, which compares to the ether or plasma element, where something has attained life and is able to evolve. Wood is vegetable life, adaptable and moldable.

The birth of something is always in Thunder and therefore takes place in the East, where Fire lies in the Earlier Heaven of thoughts, and where we see the sun rise at dawn. Likewise, where the sun sets in the West lies the Lake, maintaining an inner light by reflecting Heaven during the darkness of the night.

The symbol of the last supreme, represented by the Tai-Chi, shows the correspondence between the polarity of Thunder and Wind in the arrangement of Fu-Shi, the Earlier Heaven. In figure 3 (page 12), we see the Yin lines of a broken stroke in a space filled with darkness, and the Yang lines in a space of white light. Beginning at the revelation of the creative Heaven and rotating, like tornadoes in the sky, toward the left (counterclockwise), after passing through the reflection of the creative essence on the Lake, the conception of Fire inside the Lake leads to birth in Thunder. When it explodes, it reaches its opposite, the Wind—an awareness that reverses rotation as the idea penetrates in water. The caring that nurtures the Mountain looks up to Heaven in meditation and finds a way to enter the receptive darkness of the Earth and materialize it.

This is how the Tai-Chi circle is formed. It represents our biopsychic resonance integrating the psyche and the biological body, moving with the rhythm and pulsation of the universe. Everything is born, everything dies, and everything is reborn. Here, the symbol of Tai-Chi is compared to the cycles of the lunar phases: from full Moon to new Moon and to full Moon again, reminding us that the constant pulse of the universe is maintained by the reflection of the Sun's light in the darkness of the night.

The change in rotation produced by the human beings when we unite Heaven with Earth in the world of the thoughts (Fu-Shi's arrangement), being already a materialized entity, can only move in a circle, imitating the forward spin, like the Earth and the horizon. The reverse spin is the apparent movement of the Sun in Heaven and is due to the distortion of reality in the terrestrial world of time even though we do not perceive its movement. Humans can only live the polarity in the great leap from Thunder to Wind. In figure 4 (page 15), we see how the apparent clockwise movement of the Eastern horizon gives the impression that it is the Sun that moves around the Earth, not the opposite. We already know the truth: the solar system is in fact heliocentric, not geocentric. This distortion of perception is based on the fact that we are on the Earth, our personal macrocosm.

The Earth and its gravitational force become a gravitational resonance. The silent and constant pulse is created by the influence of the Moon on the Earth; the resistance of both forces slows down the Earth's rotation, and the Sun warms the surface of the Earth for 24 hours. The balance of life is maintained and nurtured throughout its whole surface; the influence of the Moon on liquids and tides softens and caresses the surface of Earth, allowing life to exist inside the water and from the oxygen in the air.

There are evolved beings that live outside the water and these beings understand the duality (or polarity) of the creative Heaven and the receptive Earth. The Earth's gravitational resonance, with its expansive and slow frequency, densifies things and influences human beings. The biopsychic resonance can reach enormous speed and knows the subtleties of the electromagnetic resonance of Heaven. All that exists has been created in the mind.

All that exists in nature and in our earthly environment has been created first in dreams, just as the human being has been created in the consciousness of the mind of something or someone larger than we are. The adventure for every human being is finding an answer, as small as it may be, to this enigma: Who has created us? And why do we experience everything in such a strange way?

Our destiny depends on our understanding of this revelation, as small as it may be. This understanding grants us creativitiy in the spiritual world of thoughts and dreams, as well as creative energy to carry out our ideas in the material world.

In figure 7 we see the placing of the world of thoughts within the infinite circle of Heaven with its apparent backward movement. Backward in time, as when we look at the starry sky and see a reality millions of years old, which is the time it takes for light to travel the enormous cosmic distance to reach the Earth.

It is those stars that suggest human beings' first intelligent questions and the reason behind their destiny. It is through this apparent distortion of time (and

Sky • Lake • Fire • Thunder • Earth • Mountain • Water • Wind

Figure 7. The Heaven. Electromagnetic Resonance.

Sky • Lake • Fire • Thunder • Wind • Water • Mountain • Earth

Figure 8. The human being. Biophysical Resonance.

of the sky) that human beings find solutions to almost all their earthly growth and to the relativeness of appearances.

In figure 8 we see the shadow of human beings in the world of the psyche, the change of rotation we accomplish when we are aware, through the revelation of Thunder and the intelligence of Wind. What seemed permanent is merely temporal. Everything depends on our skill to unite both forces: the psychic one that flows through the electromagnetism of everything around us, and the physical one that drags itself by gravitation and keeps us attached in the macrocosmic planetary density. Psychic growth depends on exercising consciousness and the freedom of our microcosm; thoughts transcend the physical and temporal reality of a bodily microcosm destined to complete its mission in a certain time and limited space.

The microcosm of thought is formed of subtle particles that escape the limits of time. They escape the confinement of the law of gravity and can be launched with skill and dexterity to distant worlds, out of the Earth, to obtain the necessary revelations to spiritualize our human earthly life. This knowledge is achieved through meditation. It is achieved by skilled magicians who use evolved consciousness to cross the temporal limits of time and causal space.

Skill and training in the world of dreams and thought changes our perception of space and stretches time in the here and now. We can reach for the liberating revelation that transforms everything that exists at that moment in our time-space. Mind changes alchemical laws and purifies metals into gold so that the light of Fire burns within the darkness of Water.

In figure 9 we see the world of senses. This is the path human beings use to bring ideas to manifestation. Everything is born in the mind, and when we observe this, we become aware that thoughts are projected outward, either because of our own actions and understanding, or because of unconscious misunderstanding. Our thoughts return, or are reflected in our surroundings and we experience hardships. These hardships are the projection and impression of our own ignorance, of the vicious circle in which we live, and they represent the cyclic movement of life. Most of all, mind represents our earthly confinement and our constant desire to return to the starting point. Figure 9 shows the gravitational resonance of Earth. Everything returns to its origin and is born again with Thunder. If we are able to elevate our consciousness so that we can perceive the immortality of Heaven, it becomes a transforming vision.

When people think that matter is more durable, they are carried away by passion and imbalance. The biological clock becomes distorted and the organic being becomes more dense. It drives people to struggle against a growing heavi-

Thunder • Wind • Fire • Earth • Lake • Sky • Water • Mountain

Figure 9. The Earth. Gravitational Resonance.

THE HUMAN BEING IN MEDITATION
AND REST IN THE WORLD OF THOUGHTS

The center maintains its balance of perfect polarity, producing harmony and compensation in all areas of life, in spirit and in dreams.

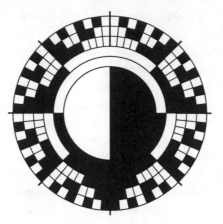

The inner trigram represents the rhythm of the electromagnetic field of resonance: Heaven. The outer trigrams represent the rhythm of the biopsychic resonance field: the human being.

THE HUMAN BEING IN MOVEMENT
IN THE WORLD OF THE SENSES

The center is distorted and divided into triangular pieces due to the action of human beings upon matter. Divided even in our heartbeats, on one side there are 16 Yin and 16 Yang, and on the other it is sub-divided in 8 Yin , 8 Yang, 8 Yin and 8 Yang. We completely distort our inner projection toward the outside.

The inner trigram represents the rhythm of the Earth's gravitational resonance field. The outer trigrams represent the rhythm of the biopsychic resonance field, the human being.

■ **YIN** - Darkness   □ **YANG** - Light

Figure 10. The 64 hexagrams of light and darkness.

ness, as if gravity has an even greater force in dragging us to our death, to our complete surrender to the Earth. However, with the mind people are also able to alleviate the weight—not only of psychological but also of physical suffering. It seems, then, that the gravitational pull lightens and the materialist feels lighter, sometimes even reaching the point of bodily levitation. Levitation happens to schizophrenics, where the imbalance of the psychic and physical world causes an extrasensorial state. When this happens, the psychic world is so intense that it is only experienced in the cycle of Heaven (figure 7, page 21). Without the resistance and tension of the cycle of Earth (figure 9, page 23), the body does not become ill to become aware of its imbalance, but experiences the psychic imbalance by blocking the cyclic causality of the body. Imbalances do not really exist on the physical plane but only in dreams and thoughts.

The example of levitation in schizophrenics is not often revealed by psychiatrists because they have no explanation for it, so it is kept a professional secret. Intense extrasensorial experiences which are not assimilated endanger the balance of the tension-resistance between Heaven and Earth in life. Levitation might explain mystical experience in a transpersonal sense, for the extrasensory finds expression and creativity in matter. It does not upset the balance of the delicate harmony human beings can achieve between the world of Heaven and the world of Earth.

In figure 10 we see areas of light and darkness—all the hexagrams of the I-Ching in both worlds. There is an electromagnetic polarity and perfect harmony in the center of the world of thoughts—Fu-Shi's arrangement—contrasting with the distortion and central disharmony in the world of senses—King-Wan's arrangement—which causes tension and resistance that creates knots and densifies energy by turning it into physical matter.

In the center of the drawing is placed the lower trigram. That is what makes the difference between one world and the other. The pulse of light and darkness maintains a harmony in the world of thoughts. It becomes a temporary distortion in the world of the senses.

The pulse of light and darkness in the three external spheres belongs to the higher trigram of Heaven. It is the same for both worlds and maintains the pendular movement of human beings in Heaven. It begins in the creative Heaven; it jumps from Thunder to Wind and changes its spin to end up in the receptive Earth.

Every pulsation is a rhythm, a vibration, a music which we can grasp through our senses. Thoughts are vibrations of silent sounds, ultrasonic sounds we cannot hear, but which penetrate through the pores of our skin. Thoughts are able to break the cyclic pattern or vicious circles that attract repeated karma and disharmony which we initially created with our own thoughts.

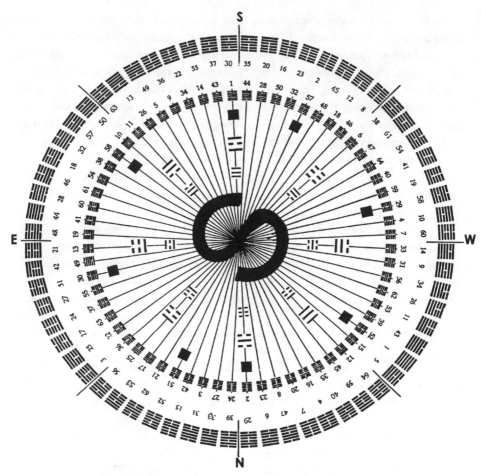

Interior Hexagrams and Trigrams; The world of thoughts.
Exterior Hexagrams and Trigrams; The world of the senses.

Figure 11. The Geomantic Compas. The hexagrams with a double trigram are marked with ■. The hexagrams in the inner circle reveal the thought pattern that leads to the physical reality of the hexagram in the outer circle of the world of senses.

That's why in figure 11 we have the geomantic compass, where we can search, in the external circle of the world of the senses, for the inner thought which has caused a material reality. The hexagrams corresponding to our thoughts are in the interior circle and reveal our inner psychological state at the root of our physical reality. For example, Hexagram 2: receptivity, or the natural response of the senses in the outer circle, corresponds underneath to Hexagram 57, the soft and intelligent penetration of the Wind within the thoughts of the interior circle. Both hexagrams are made up of double trigrams marked by a square.

Behind the adherent luminosity of Fire—Hexagram 30—in the world of senses, lies the hexagram of the highest creative clarity in the world of thoughts—Hexagram 1.

Behind Hexagram 18—deterioration and decadence—we find in thought Hexagram 54—the marriagable girl or the subordinate; the thought that lets itself be dragged away to its destiny without exercising free will leads to decadence in the world of the senses.

In addition to these two worlds that belong to the electromagnetic resonance of Heaven and the gravitational resonance of Earth, there is another arrangement of the hexagrams. This is a consecutive numbering that belongs to the biopsychic resonance of the human being. The causality of the relationship of the microcosm of thought with the macrocosm of human materialization are paired in two hexagrams referred to karma, to the action and reaction between both worlds, constantly going from microcosmic spirals to a macrocosmic one, from centrifugal to centripetal and vice versa.

Mastery in uniting both worlds is the task of every human being, for everyone is imprisoned by the causal laws of karma in this macrocosm. At the same time, we all have the possibility of freedom for the microcosmic particles of our thoughts are not constricted by the laws of gravity.

Numeric consecutivity represents the consequences of Karma, the reactions to actions. Four consecutive pairs of the numbers in the hexagrams are irreversible, while most of them are karma-reversible[2] (see figure 17, page 73, in Phase 3).

To explain the progressive meaning of the hexagrams that express the totality of development in the universe and in our lives, my work is inspired by the book written by Diana Ffarington Hook, *I-Ching and You*,[3] and *The Taoist I-Ching*, translated by Thomas Cleary.[4] (See figure 12 on page 28.)

Hexagram 1, containing six Yang lines, is the most powerful and positive of the whole series, while its complement, Hexagram 2, contains six Yin lines and is the most negative. Yang is the creative force, always pushing forth toward the new, and toward a more perfect manifestation, and Yin is the opposition it encounters. The creative Yang life is stronger and overcomes the opposition, making all forms adapt each other to that which diminishes. Heaven is firm, Earth is flexible. The two first hexagrams are the foundation on which all the others are based, and therefore more has been written about them than about the rest. It is

---

2. This will be studied at the end of Phase 3.
3. Diana Ffarington Hook, *The I-Ching and You* (London: Routledge & Kegan Paul, 1973). See pp. 38–42.
4. Thomas Cleary, trans., *The Taoist I-Ching* (Boston: Shambhala, 1986).

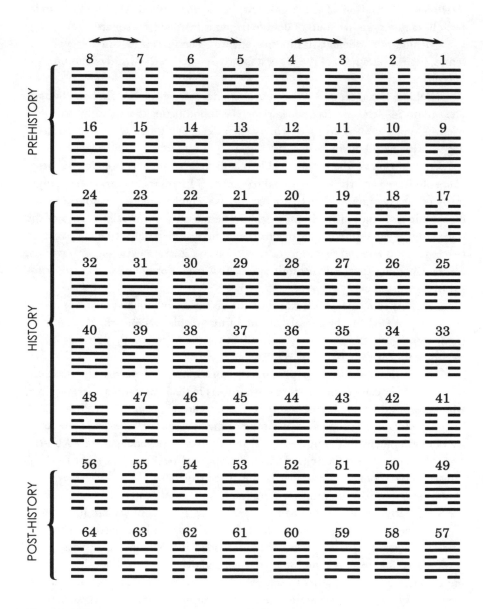

Figure 12. Hexagrams in consecutive sequence. They turn around, the upper line comes down and the lower one comes up. Includes the historical correspondences of the hexagrams and human life on Earth according to the book, Earth Ascending, *by José A. Argüelles.*

important to spend some time studying these, as it will be helpful to understand the others.

In representing man and woman, they remind us of Adam and Eve. In the beginning God created Adam, the positive male, Hexagram 1, and then Eve, Hexagram 2, the receptive, the negative female. Eve is the symbol of woman, which is not necessarily negative, but rather indicative of the weakness or frailty due to emotions. It also seems to represent the genitals of both, one closed line for male and an open line for female.

In Hexagram 3 there is a new birth: the Yang—Hexagram 1—enters into the Yin—Hexagram 2—and in changing it, produces something else. This does not necessarily refer to a human baby, but possibly to a work of art, an invention, etc. In other words, the results are produced as a consequence of the inspiration of Heaven entering the mind of man (the trigrams Thunder below and Water above).

In difficult beginnings, we see without our bearings, which gives us entrance to a lack of clarity, darkness that brings adulteration and attachment. Hexagram 4 shows a lack of skill or coordination, and is like a baby who cannot focus the eyes or use his or her legs correctly. It also represents ignorance, as one experiences in embarking on a new adventure (Water below, Mountain above).

Hexagram 5 refers to nutrition, the first thing that makes a baby cry. Minds must also be fed, as well as endeavors (Heaven below and Water above). Waiting to grow, one does not go forward, and in contending, one is not friendly. Hexagram 6 reveals contention, for where there is food, people are likely to fight. This represents the confused mind, broken in two separate directions. It also emphasizes the importance of resolving things correctly from the beginning, to avoid the development of strife (Water below and Heaven above).

Hexagram 7 shows the revival of multitudes (Water below, Earth above). Practicing obedience in the army is the way to prepare against misery, and this brings accord and union. Hexagram 8 indicates the link between the multitudes (Earth below, Water above).

Hexagram 9 indicates the restriction the multitude is subject to in its union (Heaven below, Wind above). They are subjected to small nurturance, which is poverty, and brings Treading not to stay in a lowly position. Hexagram 10 shows the advisable ceremonies which are the consequence of the restriction (Lake below, Heaven above).

Finally, humanity reaches prosperity. Hexagram 11 indicates a peaceful way of life that leads (Heaven below, Earth above) to a state of stagnation due to the lack of challenges in life. Tranquillity is opposite to the Obstruction of Hexagram 12 (Heaven above, Earth below).

This leads in turn to a desire to expand and unite with other people, as Hexagram 13 shows (Fire below, Heaven above).

Sameness with others is closeness, which brings abundance in Great Possession. Hexagram 14 (Heaven below, Fire above) shows the cultivation of union, things finally belong to us. When people have all that is great, they must not become spoiled. As is indicated in Hexagram 15: Modesty (Mountain below, Earth above), submission can lead to depreciation in Hexagram 16, which shows how humble people are and assures the awakening of satisfaction; delight can lead to laziness (Earth below, Thunder above).

Once people act through acquired conditioning, there is no fault, and one obtains followers in Hexagram 17 (Thunder below, Lake above). A loss of autonomy brings Degeneration and Hexagram 18 indicates the service given by those who follow one another and work on what has been spoiled (Wind below, Mountain above).

As a result of such service, people become renowned. In Hexagram 19 (Lake below, Earth above), they have much to teach. Those distinguished people are looked upon by others and in turn look upon those who need their help—Hexagram 20. Overseeing leads to observing, which is sometimes giving and sometimes seeking (Earth and Wind).

This leads to have something to eat in Biting Through—Hexagram 21 (Thunder and Fire). However, this brings Adornment that must be achieved correctly through the mastery of arts in Hexagram 22 (Fire and Mountain). Action must be based on understanding and when this is carried out to the end, there is a need to dissolve and strip away some things in Hexagram 23 (Earth and Mountain). This can lead to decay, so there is a need to restore, recover and return some of the elements to togetherness in Hexagram 24. When things reach the end, there is a revival of the correct ways (Thunder and Earth).

That leads us to free ourselves from error through sincerity and fidelity—Hexagram 25 (Thunder and Heaven) and to a timely accumulation of virtue—Hexagram 26 (Heaven and Mountain).

That virtue must be nourished with inward autonomy and outward cultivation in Hexagram 27 (Thunder and Earth), leading us to a process of too much movement and Great Excess in Hexagram 28 (Wind and Lake).

Such extraordinary progress can lead to Danger in Hexagram 29 descending to the depths (Water and Water) and when human beings feel the danger, they hold on to something or someone to rise up again in Hexagram 30 and act with Discernment (Fire and Fire).

The second section begins with Hexagram 31 (Mountain and Lake), dealing with the attraction of opposite sexes and sensing what is needed to continue life. This brings Hexagram 32: Perseverance, which shows how marriage should endure (Wind and Thunder).

Nevertheless, nothing lasts forever, and Hexagram 33 indicates the Retreat to withdraw from the inaccessible (Mountain and Heaven). But this one does not endure either, for it is followed by a state of Great Power as a strong activity outside and stillness inside in Hexagram 34 (Fire and Earth). This vigor results in an advance of Progress in Hexagram 35, producing the illumination of sunrise which also leads to sunset (Earth and Fire). When one advances, it is sure that one will be hurt—Hexagram 36 (Fire and Earth). In Darkness, one has to be careful, if not, a wounded being will vulnerate the Family's established order in Hexagram 37 (Fire and Wind). Families' hierarchy encounter misunderstandings and Disparity in external matters in Hexagram 38 (Lake and Fire), and this in turn leads to difficulties that cause Halting in Hexagram 39 (Mountain and Water). When difficulties that cannot endure forever reach their end, there is a feeling of relief, satisfaction, excitement and Liberation in Hexagram 40 (Water and Thunder).

With this relief comes the loss as a natural Reduction in Hexagram 41 (Lake and Mountain), and when the loss continues, finally the increase occurs in Hexagram 42. The increase must happen or else there will be Dispersion, in Hexagram 43 (Heaven and Lake) of the strong parts from the weak. This separation leads to a new rejoining in Hexagram 44 (Wind and Heaven). Meeting is encounter, the weak meets the strong, which leads to a new compilation, Gathering the masses in Hexagram 45 (Earth and Lake). The compilation of good human beings in high places provokes an upward advance and a rising to high places in Hexagram 46 (Wind and Earth). Such advance continues until fatigue sets in—Hexagram 47 (Water and Lake). Travail is a matter of encountering the inner weakness. This drawback makes us go back to the lower earth, and so we get Hexagram 48, indicating a well (Wind and Water) as a place to encounter and reach mastery over the lower Earth.

Obviously this will bring a state of Change as provoked by Hexagram 49 (Fire and Lake) and nothing changes things more than cooking—Hexagram 50 (Wind and Fire). Change gets rid of the old, and a Cauldron obtains the new. All this indicates being set in motion in Hexagram 51 (Thunder and Thunder). Thunder is arising but Mountain is still due that things cannot be continually kept in motion, so Hexagram 52 gives the picture of a gradual slow development (Mountain and Wind) to consummation that leads to Submission and acceptance in Hexagram 53 (Lake and Thunder).

Hexagram 54 (Lake and Thunder) is the moment in which things have reached their right point of togetherness; then the state of grandeur exists in Hexagram 55 (Fire and Thunder). Those who reach the summit of grandeur have nowhere to go, so they seek other transient places to explore, becoming foreigners or Wanderers in Hexagram 56 (Mountain and Fire).

Hexagram 57 (Wind and Wind) shows a voyager acquiring flexibility and adaptability, once arriving home, and feeling joy and Pleasure in Hexagram 58 (Lake and Lake). This pleasure dissipates due to habit and again, separation is needed in Hexagram 59 (Water and Wind) indicating Disintegration. The division creates regulations in Hexagram 60 (Lake and Water), so one does not do anything improper and human beings believe in Truthfulness, created in Hexagram 61 (Lake and Wind) and to enforce sincerity, one has to look into all Small Matters in Hexagram 62 (Mountain and Thunder).

Finally we arrive at the two last hexagrams, which, as the two first ones, are very important. Hexagram 63 (Fire and Water) shows everything is settled in a state of balance or climax, bringing stabilization. It is called "After Completion," because it is close to all that can be obtained in a state of completion. However it is at that time when any little thing can throw everything off balance, and this hexagram warns us that we must be careful. Fire burns inside water, the understanding of intelligence penetrates the senses of instincts.

Hexagram 64 (Water and Fire) "Before Completion," the last of the series, turns the existing conditions around, showing a state of transition, for again, the intellect is above and the instincts below. Everything is again unsettled, and therefore, there is no end, only transformation and cyclic change. The fire of intelligent understanding is above and the water of instincts is below. None of the I-Ching hexagrams indicate death, there is no absolute end. This hypothesis proves survival and can be interpreted on the spiritual and mental plane as well as on the physical plane.

In this sequence there is another polarity that occurs when hexagrams are paired in even with uneven numbers: they are the same hexagram, only turned around completely; the top line comes down and the bottom line comes up, between the uneven number and the following pair, 1 and 2, 3 and 4, 5 and 6, 7 and 8, for example 9 (☲) and 10 (☲) . Between one number and the following consecutive one it is as if we looked at the hexagram from the bottom or from the top, except the irreversible hexagrams: HX 1, 2, 27, 28, 29, 30, 61 and 62.[5] (See figure 17 on page 73.)

The study of the relation between the hexagrams gives us an enormous understanding of life and experimental circumstances in matter. It fosters a psychological transpersonal understanding and an awareness of how everything is created in the realm of thoughts. It also makes us more aware of the need to have a clear mind and to stabilize the mind through techniques that can help us create that harmony. Through meditation in action, like Chinese Tai-Chi or sitting meditation, one sees the effect of thoughts on the senses and emotions. That's why it is an essential step for all transpersonal psychology and for overcoming humankind's karmic destiny.

While in matter, we perform movements and we impress ourselves both on space and time, but this really becomes engraved in the fabric of our dream world.

---

5. We will go into this in depth at the end of Phase 3.

Maya, bio-organic physical matter, is nothing but the manifestation of the vibrational phenomenon, the dancing rhythm of our permanent world: dreams.

Our mind-body disconnection begins when we don't remember our dreams; when we don't remember the revelations or warnings that dreams offer about our psychological existence, and when we don't value the true and permanent reality of our dreams. That's why the Oriental culture and the Native-American culture believe that most of humanity is asleep. It is asleep because it doesn't recognize or acknowledge its true owner, and therefore isn't able to connect one reality to another, causing a psychological imbalance. This imbalance eventually manifests in physical disharmony so that consciousness can become aware of the true reality, of Maya, in order that we integrate the dream body with the ordinary and physical reality of things in the fabric woven by our thoughts.

The first goal of transpersonal psychology would be to help people contact their dream world. The first step is remembering dreams and giving people back images that can be analyzed through a creative and artistic means and method, such as painting, drawing, singing and dancing. These images make up the totality of human beings and their environment and project people on the universe and the universe on people. Drawing mandalas, which are a composition of color, form, and inner landscapes, always begins at the center and becomes a circle, and they help people get centered.

Jung studied the relationship between the psyche and the mandala. The mandala image has been used by all spiritual cultures. They are the goal of concentration and the universal transpersonal contact for every individual. Mandalas are a psychological tool which today still have not been adapted to a practical use in transpersonal psychology. We can use any art form; it could be called transpersonal art, for its purpose is the spiritual inner quest of feeling that connects with its unique and creative self. Through it, people become connected to the entire universe, for we each have a particular dance and we move to the rhythm and music of the universe.

The vibration of the voice, body posture and movement in terms of gravitational pull, the qualities of densification perceived in all senses, are the keys to recovering that psychological center which babies open to the world when they are born. The penetration of light in the spirit of the body is accomplished through all the senses, but mostly through the light of its receptive organs—the eyes and the pineal gland. It is said that the coloring of the iris and our vision of the dense material is the psychic vibrational process in every human.

• • •

All phenomena of the universe are manifestations of some idea. Superficial people see small ideas, and people of greater spirituality see greater ideas, making them

Cosmic breathing. Calligraphy by Taisen Deshimaru Roshi.

into prose, poetry, or painting. But, no matter how it is materialized, the inner nature of things, their essential reason, will always be the same—to transcend.

Therefore we must not be content to paint only the external part of things.

The substance of real value lies under all things and can only be contemplated by the eyes of the true being.

Painting is an art that served as a way of cleansing and refining the human spirit in the ancient Oriental world. For painting is like the art of the alchemists, transforming bodies into immortal spirits.

The brushstroke is the backbone of a painting; rocks and trees have no fixed regular form and they have to be established by the brush, moved by feelings and energy flowing through the hand. In such a way, each stroke marks our inner state.

If we paint with firm strokes, both soft and strong, it means we maintain a strong and decided spirit in the actions of our life.

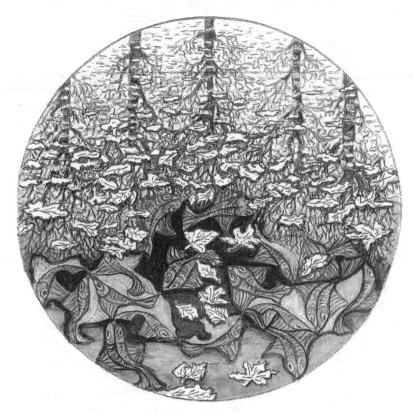

Reflection of the inner and outer worlds.

Blake's . . . vision of physical reality {asserts} that the earth is concave and not convex. We find it very difficult to visualize the concave geography in the world within Milton, because our culture has insisted on the opposite curvature. . . . Blake describes the earth as concave, as a cavern of "labyrinthine intricacy"; this earth is the human skull or body which, if observed from without, is convex but, if observed from within, is concave. . . . Blake insists that the astronomer's model of the earth as "a Globe rolling thro' Voidness" is a delusion, for such would be the model of an earth separated from its perceiver. In a concave model, however, all the earth, the sky, the universe are within man's immediate perception.

Blake's universe is proscribed not by a conceptual framework of geography and terrain, but only by the sensory horizon, the limits of an individual's perception. . . . Blake asserts . . . that it is our interaction with perceived objects which is the essential element of reality.

Blake calls this concavity the Mundane Egg. This concave egg can be seen from the point of view of reasoning perception—the perception that only the body and its senses exist—as a limiting and imprisoning reality. From the viewpoint of the reasoning mind, the labyrinthine concave egg constitutes our reality; its concave shell becomes a sensory horizon. It and all within it constitute the "Limit of Opacity" beyond which our senses do not penetrate. Within the shell or circumference we see, then, a surging chaos, a sensory tumult with which our sensory organs must interact to select and interpret data. . . . In attempting to understand and make sense of this chaos we proscribe a limiting surface upon it, a limiting surface which reinforces the shell as the outermost limit of opacity. In other words, we make the shell more opaque. . . . It is all the opaque surfaces we think we see, all the opaque surfaces a reasoning mind erects in its attempt to know and hence control the universe: the surface of perceived objects, the surface of the body, the surfaces of the earth and the apparent surface of the sky. All the space between the surfaces we think we see beyond and the surface of our body, the empty space we feel we must control, Blake names Udan-Adan . . . "a Lake not of Waters but of Spaces" . . . They are the spaces of error, the regions into which Milton travels to annihilate his selfhood.

{There} are spaces of mercy—spaces which exist so that they may be annihilated continually, spaces within which a spiritual journey is possible. Blake believes that as a consequence of vision from within, the result of the spiritual journey, the spaces of the "dull round" . . . are transformed into energizing, formative spaces, wherein all the component parts of the body and its universe may be formed into human lineaments, the contours of an eternal body. Within these transformed spaces, form and beauty are created. . .

—MILTON: A POEM BY WILLIAM BLAKE
Kay Parkhurst Easson and Roger R. Easson, eds.,
pp. 141–143.

The Trigrams and the Human Being

In order to establish more deeply those changes by progression of the interior and exterior trigrams, we have to study the meaning of each one of them. We know that the integration given to the hexagrams by the ancient wise men of China is essential, whether a trigram is on top or below. For example, in Hexagram 35, the Fire on top of the Earth and the Sun rising at dawn gives an image of rapid progress. It is completely different when Fire is below Earth, the sunset in the evening of Hexagram 36, the darkening of light.

In order that you may easily use this interpretation and learn to comprehend why the wise men of China interpreted it the way it is shown under each hexagram, I will interpret the meaning for each trigram.

The Eight Trigrams

CHIEN

HEAVEN

The creative principle, Yang positive. • The light principle, the active. • Male, active, cold, non-demonstrative. • The Father, King, strong, firm, energy, breathing, the lungs. • The Regeneration process, produces invisible seeds in every form of development. It has grown beyond Earth and rises above it. • Great beginnings: it works in the invisible world with time and the spirit. United, in one direction. Content. Without effort, knowledge through what is easy. Through movement it joins easily what is divided (Yin). • It shares the metal element with the Lake. Symbol of purity. Something shiny that catches the eye. •

Where opposites come together. The time of judgment. The mind and the head. The circle, round. • The union, success, power. Psychologically, it indicates the extreme mental and emotional states. • Determines direction, represents the path and purpose in life. • Originality, individuation, a person by oneself. Totality, perfection. • It belongs to the interior state of change. Shares with Lake the element of Metal.

The receptive principle, Yin. • The principle of darkness, of weakness, passivity.• Divide and separate, the female; inactive; loving; demonstrative, the mother. Must not be a leader or guide; adapted devotionally to CHIEN. Gives in, responds, to do things the simple way. The absolutely simple is possible. • The blood, the night, the winter. The plants disappear and are kept safe from the cold. A kettle to melt and boil things. • Economy, frugality, a support, an anchor, the trunk of the tree. • That from which other things arise. The process of birth. The action of matter in space, completes things. Shapes, the power to transform. The crop, the work of peace, the rise of the human being. Psychologically it causes illness through depression, despair, and melancholy. • Belongs to the interior state of change. • The time of darkness. The space. • God causes things to be of service to others and the main service is in the receptive. The intestines, the stomach. • The earthly nature of the human being. • Balance, justice, fame, and immortality. • The human being must not give too much credit to his or her attributes, which will chain the human to the Earth. • Shares with the Mountain the element of Earth.

The awakening, the excitement, rapid movement. Growing up. The elder son. Lightning and fire. • God manifests in thunder. Tension, energy, moves. • The spirit is manifested in matter. • The path of a superior human being. • One's place in life. • The excitement of power, influential, causing movement and growth. • The beginning of movement, a restless little child. • All new things, expansion, birth. Revelation, clarity of understanding. What returns to life after disappearing. • Rapid and strong growth. The path that leads to the goal or field of activity. Discharges tension. Shocking, electrical, violent, noise, heart attack, earthquake, music, sound. The morning, Spring, feeling active. • The birth of physical existence. The beginning of a project, purpose and direction. Psychologically, it causes illness through a sudden fit of anger and rage. • Belongs to the exterior state of change. • The unexpected, commotion, destruction. • To leave aside that which

Heaven

| Creative | — | Fire | — | Thunder | — | Wind |

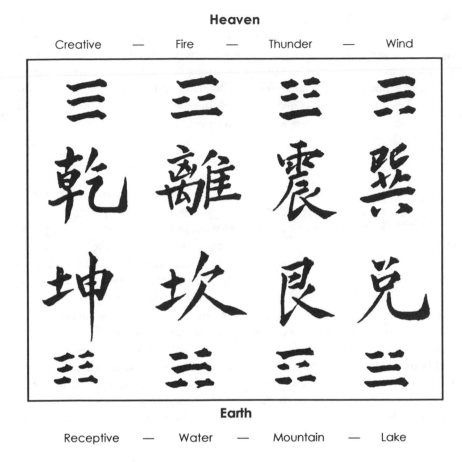

Earth

| Receptive | — | Water | — | Mountain | — | Lake |

Figure 13. The Trigrams of the I-Ching.

is damaged and make room for the new. To change plans. • To overcome the past. • Shares with the Wind the Wood element.

K'AN

WATER

The abysmal, dangerous, and difficult. • The rain, to flow, the brooks, the oceans, the moon, the blood, the patterns of the sea. The emotions, deceptions, hidden things, thieves, the ambush. The time of concentration and work. Resistance. The middle son. The past. To cover, to clothe, penetrating like water and pain. Humid, melancholy. Increases anxiety, madness. The water flows toward that which is true and natural in itself, fills deep places and blocks progress. Does not fear jumping into the precipice. It bends and straightens itself. • Belongs to the interior state. • The kidneys. • To uphold one's duty. Symbolizes the spirit trapped in the physical. • The unconscious, lack of recognition, ignorance, instinctive, possessive. • Love and perseverance, or pleasure and decadence. • Emotions and desires. Psychologically, it causes illness through anxiety, worry, fright, fear, phobias, terror, and tension. • Baptism and purification. • The principle of love fighting against matter to reach the light. • The fetus in the water of the mother's womb. • Represents the Water element.

To relax, to be quiet, meditation, calm, rest. Obstruction, obstinacy, immovable, perseverance. God creates everything according to perfection and completes work in the Mountain. • To sleep, the end of life, older people, maturity, inactivity. The younger son. The time of that which has begun, like the end of a fight. • Contemplation of movement. To wait for growth. Transition between the old and new beginnings. To nourish everything that grows in the vicinity. • The period when the seeds join the new beginnings. • Time of mystery and silence. • The doors, to open, protection, doorman, a narrow path between difficulties. • It belongs to the exterior state of change. • Psychologically, it causes illness through stubborn, obstinate, and imperturbable states of mind. • Meditation, prayer, to relax the mind and body. The barrier or entrance, represents the end of life. • Mysticism, the contact between the inferior and superior being. • That which remains, what remains of the past. • Shares with the receptive the Earth element.

Penetrating air, submissive, gentle, soft, flexible, adaptable, religious. • To wander, spread, disseminate. Indecisive, advances and retreats. The elder daughter. • To work hard and persevere. • To consider quietly. • Initial indecision, to wait, to know later when to advance and when to retreat. • Understanding, the union of love. Make things flow in their own way, develop and grow according to the seeds they contain. • Near gain, purity, and totality. • Psychologically, it causes illness through despondency, grief, sorrow, and sadness. • It belongs to the external state of change. • The indecisive as well as the decisive. The physical and spiritual vitalizing energy. • The renewal of life, the union between spirit and body. • The period of adult life. Liberty, travel, mental growth, spiritual movement. • Everything has a slow influence. • Shares with Thunder the Wood element.

Clarity, intelligence. The Sun. Dependence, attachment to matter until it is consumed. Affection, devotion, adaptable, yielding. Heat, dry, brilliance. The lightning. It shines and beautifies. One sees the other in the fire. The colors. The middle daughter. The future. When power is at its maximum. The moment of conception and attaining the summit of life. The descent of the spirit. Being conscious. • Perception, to clarify, to illuminate. The eye. • The fire that consumes from within. • Psychologically, it causes illness through extreme forms of delirium and hysteria. • It belongs to the interior state of change. • The material, the physical body trapped by the spirit. The conscience. The fire of cleanliness and sacrifice. The illumination and the manifestation of beauty. Lightning, instantaneous intuition. The immediate knowledge. Self-expression, the artist, to create and transform. • Represents the Fire element.

Joy, quiet, calm water. Many strange things may rise from the bottom of the lake, while the surface is so quiet. • Seductiveness, an excess of joy carries danger. Sensual pleasure. To satisfy people and things. Happiness. Satisfaction. The younger daughter. Hard inside, soft outside. Fixed inside, flexible and yielding outside. The lake reflects the sunlight, the creative trapped by the physical water of Yin inside Earth. • Sincerity, innocence. Youth. The fruits fall and open. A reflection of light. • Mirror. • To talk, laugh, drink, smile, taste, eat. • Belongs to the exterior state of change. • Represents knowledge and radiates intelligence. Talking too much and uttering slander is its negative side. • Psychologically, it causes illness through overexcitement and frenzied states of mind. • Association, duality, adaptation. • To achieve some purpose or the awakening of ideas. • Childhood. Dependence, need of support on something stronger. • Shares with the creative the Metal element.

The Trigrams of Interior Changes

They are four, belonging to the internal and essential development of all existence. Besides, they are trigrams that remain the same even if they are reversed. (See figure 2 on pages 8–9.)

K'un—Earth ☷ The receptive.

Ch'ien—Heaven ☰ The creative.

Li—Fire ⚎ The intelligence.

K'an—Water ⚍ The instincts.

These four belong to the interior states and interior life. They represent the evolution of the human being. They represent periods of non-conscious evolution. They also refer to the beginning and end of hexagrams 1-2-63-64, and to all those hexagrams made up of these essential trigrams.

The Trigrams of External Changes

They are the other four, that belong to the distractions and dualities of the external world. (See figure 2 on pages 8-9.)

They are not as balanced as the previous ones. They are the trigrams that change if turned around.

Wind ⚎ , when it is reversed, becomes ⚍ Lake

Mountain ⚎ , when it is reversed, becomes ⚍ Thunder.

That is why they represent our experiences with the world of things and our external growth. The sense we give to our material life and life with others. They refer to all other hexagrams, except those formed by the interior and exterior hexagrams joined together.

With a deeper understanding of trigrams, we have been able to make another consecutive form related to the different stages of human life. This gives us a new rhythmic Yin-Yang pulsation, interesting to study.

In figure 10 (on page 24) we can observe the new Yin-Yang pulsation. Beginning with the receptive and ending with the creative. Opposite to the rhythm of the human being, that begins with the creative, Heaven, and ends in Earth; the Receptive. However, here Earth is ready to receive the spirit, the environmental period of our surroundings and ends with the creative; the Heaven, the period of death and post-human life.

We have divided human experience into eight periods, and have related them to the eight trigrams.

When superimposing these consecutive trigrams, within the King Wan arrangement, a strange outline of eights and spirals is formed. Above all, what we discover is the irregular outline shaped like a circular eight, triangular and ending like a square. This reminds us of the three geometric figures which represent Heaven (with a circle), Earth (with a square), and the human being (with a triangle). The semi-circular outline, shaped like an eight, symbolizes the continual search for spiritual meaning and our struggle with the forces of above and below. In the two triangles, the six-pointed star would symbolize the human course of events on Earth.

This is, in itself, the spiral's constant dynamics and the human attempt to walk, making semi-circular triangles as in the figure 8 or "Lemniscate." It is the unification of both worlds and continuity of relationships. It forms an "Ouroborus" of the eternal snake biting its tail and Heaven, the spirit constantly returning to Earth, to the physical body; it is the eternal return, the reincarnation or "Lemniscate."

In figure 14, we see the King Wan arrangement, belonging to the gravitational resonance of the Earth. In the world of the senses, each trigram represents the physical world through which human beings wind spirally through the time of their existence and formation of being.

Joining both the world of thoughts and the senses, we can see how thoughts support each period of human life (see figures 5, 10, and 11, pages 16, 24, and 26). We start with the beginning of the receptive Earth—in the world of senses it is the environmental period—and it is supported by the spirit of the Wind, soft, the union of love; since this is located in that position in the world thoughts. (See figure 14 on page 44.) It continues in the Fire in the senses during the period of conception, supported by the spirit of Heaven, creative in thought. Then follows the period of the fetus, submerged in Water of the senses, and supported by the receptive Earth, enveloped and protected by the thoughts that shape it and give it life. After, in the period of the birth of Thunder and growth of childhood in the senses, we are supported by the spirit of intelligence, conscious of Fire in the thoughts. In the period of childhood, with the joy of the Lake in the senses, we are supported by the spirit of Water that looks after us and feeds our thoughts. In the adult period, we have the penetrating softness and wisdom of the Wind in the senses, supported by the spirit, the joy and enjoyment of the Lake in the thoughts. In the period of maturity and culmination, the success and solidity of the Mountain in the senses, we are supported by the spirit of Thunder in the thoughts, from which we still obtain the vitality and growth toward spiritual revelation. In the successive period, we enter the stage of death and post-human life. It is the creative invisible beginning of the spirit that is supported and encouraged by the spiritual culmination and serenity of the Mountain, making sure that if our existence has reached the summit of reason, we will return to improve ourselves further when the trigram of the receptive principle is ready again.

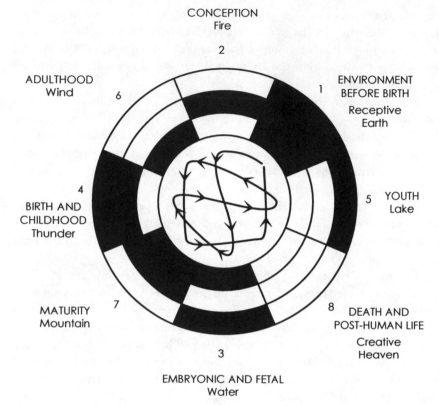

THE PATH OF HUMAN LIFE ON EARTH.

MOVEMENT IN THE WORLD OF SENSES combines the triangle and the square to form a lemniscate.

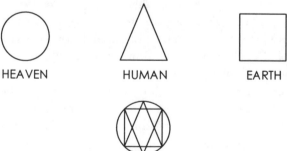

THE HUMAN BEING when uniting the upper and lower forces, forms the square, the hexagon and the circle.

Figure 14. The human being forms Heaven and Earth.

The Stages of Formation in the Human Being

The receptive principle is ready to welcome the soul. The environment already exists for the fusion of the Yang-Yin principles of man and woman.

We transform ourselves from the infinite One of the unending ocean of unity, through the Yin ▼ and Yang △ state of polarization. Antagonistic and complementary forces; the mother's egg and the father's sperm. Both come from reproductive cells that are the result of billions of transmutations of life that began in the infinite ocean of the unknown universe. They have reached the stage of organic life as the primary existence of animal life and are highly charged with electromagnetic vibrations. When these antagonistic and complementary cells combine and join together, each one carries memories of the past and visions of its future.

When fusion exists, the memories and visions are manifested in one organism that successfully accomplishes the undying dream of returning to the path of life, in search of freedom, justice, love and peace.

That fusion, starting in the parental atmosphere, is very important for the spiritual being and the purity of love that it carries. Each one, man and woman, carries his or her Yin-Yang balance or imbalance, but at the time of fusion, when ready to give life, the individual imbalances of either one are fused and complement each other, as if they formed a union of the feminine-masculine harmony and balance; creative-receptive.

The sperm, with its centrifugal spiral, penetrates the egg of centripetal spiral. When both radiate vibrations toward their surroundings making spiral patterns, as one is attracted toward the other within the uterus of the woman, its own movement maintains the spiral pattern and increases the rotation. The spirit traps matter and fire increases, making them turn and burn with vibrations and internal emanations.

Physically, the fertilized egg is the Earth, turning and creating electromagnetic fields and changing the axis periodically. The electromagnetic and gravitational forces received by the mother move up and down the uterine wall. The fertilized egg is continually balanced by celestial and earthly movement. The force that comes down from Heaven goes through the mother's spiritual channel and is fed with the ideas, thoughts, and images of the mother, colliding with the center of gravity that rises from the Earth of the mother, and is fed with emotions, sensations, and instincts. It interacts with the father and his environment, and shapes the brain of the fetus, being reoriented and strengthened by its various images, emotions, and thoughts, providing a new quality of energizing force.

The two trigrams—Fire and Water—represent the intelligent mind and instinctive nature, joining the mind and body with the spirit. This starts happening within the mother's womb, with the father's hereditary contribution.

The period of conception is a repetition of the primary growth in the life of multiple cell organisms. The memories and visions of the parents, contained in the genetic code are cells that grow rapidly.

Each cell is loaded with the same memories and visions, and likewise all of them carry the totality of memories and visions, even the most contradictory and antagonistic ones, to others, as well as other complementary ones.

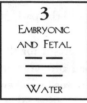

The spirit is trapped by matter, and the embryo and fetus are enveloped by the life-giving waters. During this period, the embryo floats and goes through all the transformations of past cellular lives within the water until becoming amphibious. It develops the organs, the glands, through the vibrations of Yin-Yang spiral patterns that the mother receives, which cover the wall of the uterus. The 266 days are divided into four stages.

First stage: seven days from the moment of fertilization at the time of conception in the deepest part of the uterus. During this period, the fertilized egg accomplishes cell division by rotation and change of axis, in a logarithmic pattern equal to the I-Ching: 1 to 2, 2 to 4, 4-8-16-32-64.

In the second stage: twenty days from the time of conception, begins the formation of the general system. During this period the interior system is formed, which will later develop into the digestive and respiratory functions; the peripheral system, which becomes the central and nervous systems and develops the external and circulatory functions. Each system is not only formed spirally, but also the main central and peripheral internal systems are formed by spiral layers connecting with each one at both ends.

The third stage: sixty days, from the period of formation of the organs and glands, the organs and glands needed in the future are formed: the intestines, gallbladder, the stomach, and also the more compact—like the heart, liver, spleen, and the kidneys.

They are all formed through the Yin-Yang spiral movement of centripetal Yang and centrifugal Yin energy.

The fourth stage: one hundred eighty days from the period of general development until birth. All the systems, organs, glands and structure continue to grow until the 260 days are completed; nine lunar months of the embryonic period.

At all times the spiral movements maintain the balance between the head and the body, right and left, front and back, internal and external, like all systems, organs, glands and circulation. The two tendencies, Yin-Yang antagonistic and complementary, are well balanced, in general preparation for birth. For example, the part of the head becomes more compact and hard, while that of the body becomes more expansive.

The constitution developed during this time is the foundation for the destiny of the next stage—life in the air—and it is essential to know the quality of nourishment received by the embryo, the type of energy received through the mother's activities and what kind of vibrations of consciousness are acquired from thoughts and images through the father, the mother, and the environment. All of this determines the type of life the embryo will have in the next experience in the world of air.

Thunder is the image produced by the energy of the baby's expulsion into life in the air.

After 260 days of life in water and darkness, birth occurs through repeated contractions of the uterus and a flood of water like a storm in the ocean. The new life begins in an atmosphere half dark and half light. The process of birth is a repetition of events that took place on Earth four hundred million years ago: repeated catastrophes and massive floods leading to the formation of the Earth.

In order to adapt to the new life and the atmospheric surroundings, the baby must experience the centripetal Yangnization contraction through a narrow tunnel to come into the great external expansion: centrifugal Yinization.

Life in the air is our human life, leaving behind the placenta and the umbilical cord.

During one year the evolution of life on Earth of amphibians, animals, and monkeys is repeated, until it reaches the human stage, or upright standing position.

The development of sensorial and emotional consciousness develops in centrifugal form in a logarithmic spiral, although there are more sensations of Yin development of the senses and rapid centripetal Yang growth, concentrating in the ability to master the use of the body.

During the first four weeks after birth, our functions are almost all mechanical; in the next twelve weeks, the sensorial perceptions are developed, together with the mechanical functions, and during 36 weeks, approximately, our sensorial consciousness continues to grow. The movements of body growth are also spiral; when bending the body forward, we contract the bodily spiral; when we extend and open the body, we dissolve and expand our bodily spiral.

When we breathe, the inhalation and exhalation form opposite spiral movements, as the air flows through the nasal cavity. When swallowing food and liquid, the downward movement forms an opposite spiral to the movement of discharge of urine and feces.

There are several levels in the growth of consciousness, including mechanical and spontaneous judgment. Nearly all physical movements are governed by autonomous nerves, including the digestive functions, breathing, circulation, excretion, nervous reactions and others. The sensory judgment, and the development of the five senses, touch, smell, hearing, sight and taste, together with the sense of direction and balance, are developed during infancy and the following period of childhood. The refinement in the quality of the sensorial organs and the opening up to life experiences continue. The development of emotional, sentimental, and intellectual judgment also begins in this period and continues into the next: youth.

The lake represents the cheerfulness and joy of youth. Also the enjoyment and appreciation of physical life. It is the period ranging from the straight standing posture to puberty, and physical movement that is more active following a pattern of expansion and contraction. However, we have characterized this period as more Yang due to the two Yang lines pushing upwards toward the Yin. When we start talking, the air circulates outward, forming an expansive spiral pattern as we breathe out; when we inhale, we form a contracting spiral. Likewise, psychological functions as well as several types of thought, develop in spiral form.

Just as we had already begun to develop the emotional and sentimental judgment, it continues to develop to a greater extent in the emotional activity, including the acknowledgment of love and hate, of beauty and ugliness, of excitement and peacefulness, of passivity, of aggression and other mental phenomena. This emotional and sentimental judgment continues to grow until the end of life.

The intellectual judgment begins at age 3, when emotional judgment has already developed. It identifies, counts, forms, organizes, analyses, divides, assimilates, synthesizes and also increases other mental and conceptual activities.

Social judgment appears as intellectual judgment develops, together with the increasing observation of relationships within the family, within society and the country, and eventually the outer world. The determination to have harmonic relationships with others and to improve the social conditions of the community begin to develop, as well as the capacity to recognize well-being and love. This continues to develop in the following adult period but already begins to flower at this time.

The individual's psyche continues to develop in spiral form toward higher dimensions in relation to the external environment and to the imagination. It expresses itself in speculating, calculating, assuming and in a greater intellectual understanding. If we use the right side of the brain, Yin, more, we deal with conceptualization and intuition. If we use the left side more—Yang—the result is a more complex and analytic thought form.

Each type of psychological vibration forms a spiral movement, either centripetal or centrifugal.

The wind is the symbol of this period. As all is molded in the form contained by the seed, it flows naturally and has a mental and spiritual expansion. In the previous period, the Lake, the Yang spirit below supported the Yin physical growth. Here the physical Yin is below and grows upward toward the spirit and the intellect. This is the longest period, going from puberty to approximately age 50. During this time, physical growth is discontinued but not so psychological and spiritual growth. Sentimental and intellectual consciousness continues to grow and develop through experiences with other human beings, moving toward an ideological and philosophical consciousness, toward an understanding of the society and its role in the progress of humanity. Social judgment leads to self-expression. This social consciousness includes respect for tradition as well as a vision of the future.

Ideological judgment develops when we experience the conflicts that constantly arise among people within society. Philosophical and ideological questions arise to reveal what the human being is, what life is, how life should be lived, how society is changing, why the human being is here and toward what destination we should direct our lives. Finally, the understanding of these basic issues of human life inspire us to discover an endless order of the universe and its universal mechanism.

People with a low level of consciousness achieve this judgment at the end of their lives, in maturity instead of adulthood. This causes them not to attain the last judgment which begins at the end of adult life and continues in maturity. This is the Supreme and Cosmological Judgment. After the previous judgment stages have been totally experienced, exercised, and tested, an understanding of the life of the human being and of the universe begins to develop. As one grows, one begins to understand every phenomenon as complementary manifestations of the universe.

Adults reason and base their trust in themselves. They base faith and their emotional state on their experiences and what they have achieved in the past. Children, nevertheless, can draw faith from nothing and can be naïve.

If we have succeeded in giving life a unique meaning and in having a vocation in life, we finally see that there is no antagonist and that all moves and changes according to a universal order. All is balanced and in order with the law of karma.

Our concern for the destiny of humanity continues to grow and later develops into an understanding of the universe, including the visible and the invisible, the material, the spiritual, the mental, the infinite and finite world, why we are here, where are we going, what is our purpose in life, what is love, peace, justice, freedom? Is there a universal order ruling each phenomenon that takes place in this universe?

Due to the fact that these aspects of development grow in spiral form in a Yin expansive direction produced by our human contacts with others, we reflect on the past and plan on the future.

The mountain. It expresses having reached the top and given a new meaning to the world of physical and material experience. It is the period that goes from approximately age 50, to the moment of death. During this period of time, our consciousness increases, expanding our social awareness and our ideological and philosophical understanding, as well as our spiritual development, especially if during the previous period we have achieved individual growth and satisfaction. During this period of life, we can find true happiness to the extent that we develop our cosmological and spiritual consciousness. Our material life, as well as our relationship with other people, adjusts naturally and become established. The Supreme and Cosmological Judgment continues to find a solution to all problems: health, peace, war, poverty, illness, unhappiness, misery, and prosperity in their various manifestations, and we also understand how they have helped us mature and have been the result of our own thoughts, balanced and unbalanced.

The development of such an understanding and consciousness started during the period of human life; our life in the air is preparing us for the coming life in ether, when we leave behind our physical bodies at death and we go on to the following vibrational state of consciousness. Everything evolves toward a greater expansion. Being an embryo in the darkness of the water we go on to the brightness of life in the air, but now the transition is toward a greater expansion, since vibrational life has an even greater dimension. Whether we look at our past experiences and understand them in a clear or confused way depends on the level of conscious judgment we have developed in the previous adult period.

Heaven. It expresses non-material life, the invisible, vibrational life, as well as the maximum contracting Yang movement leading to the last result of matter: Death. However, and in order to reach Yang completely, Yin has to reach its maximum. In the previous trigram, the two lower Yin lines make the Yin separate from the Yang, for Yin tends downward and Yang upward. When Yin descends, it reaches its maximum and finds Yang.

Yin is still the experience of death, but when on the other side, in vibrational life, it is Yang. Death is an accelerated Yin pattern in the process of expanding; then life is accelerated into an active decay of the human body, of physical and material energy. Some parts of the cellular organisms return to their original state of differentiated elements distributed in Water, Earth and Air and other parts of the human constitution—such as vibrations, waves and radiations which have manifested themselves as thought and sense energy—also return and are distributed in their original worlds. What we now call our consciousness remains a massive vibration which continues to exist as "souls" and "spirits" which transfer into several waves and influence people's memory, images, thoughts, and feelings as they tune into their frequency of vibration.

From this level, some go on to a higher dimension of vibrational sphere and others descend to the atmospheric level, merging their vibrations with physical matter of the worlds of Water and Air. Those with a very refined vibrational mass gravitate toward higher levels in the vibrational sphere, awaiting a greater refinement in their next life, changing their vibrational mass into waves and rays.

In this world, all vibrational masses which we call "spirits" have an understanding which differs from physical perception but is similar to the one experienced as spiritual or mental consciousness during our human physical life. From the point of view of our present existence, we can understand vibrational life just as we understand embryonic life: we don't remember it as such, but it is never-

The spiritual journey: flying in the world of thought and diving into the world of the senses.

theless always there. Happiness or unhappiness in this vibrational life depends entirely on the degree of understanding and consciousness attained during the previous physical life of form, just as the destiny of human life depends entirely on the development of embryonic life.

The life of vibrational mass continues to dissolve into waves and rays of the galactic dimension of the universe, from where the body is transferred to the world of radiation. It carries with it thoughts, feelings and images that travel at a speed of millions of light years. Some descend to spheres of vibrational masses and others dissolve further in spiral movement of infinite speed.

All relative nature that is characterized as earlier lives disappears completely and, in a way, reaches the state of non-phenomenon, non-appearance, non-manifestation: universal consciousness or what we call God.

In this infinite world there arises sometimes a Yin spiral movement and other times, it is the path toward matter and physical reality, as forms appear and disappear in the infinite universe. Universal will takes place and manifests itself as images and thoughts in the sphere of radiation, in the spiritual world. Later on it changes into several ideas and relative dreams of the vibrational world, forming a physicalization or reactualization in the lower spheres. Michio Kushi said that a reincarnation is always taking place between each level—as well as a reincarnation at a universal level—in the infinite dimensions of the universe. The memory of each level (or previous life) is taken along, as well as a vision of the future. Memory, and the eternal dream of the dimension of universal reincarnation, is subconsciously carried along throughout each period of life, and we are often not able to recognize it."[1]

We have seen how the trigrams of inner changes pertain to life before birth and to life after death: the receptive, the creative, Earth, Heaven, Fire and Water. However, the trigrams of external change—Wind, Thunder, Lake and Mountain—pertain to the physical life of the human being itself. These trigrams can become one or the other by turning upside down. Therefore, these four periods—childhood, youth, adulthood, and maturity—are interchangeable, making one period more similar to another and attaining further spiral growth forward or backward. Thus, a certain period can be similar to another although distant in time, depending also on the karmic cycles of revision, retribution, or regeneration of karma.

---

1. Michio Kushi, *The Book of Do-In: Exercise for Physical and Spiritual Development* (Briarcliff Manor, NY: Japan Publications, 1979), pp. 17-19; 28-32.

Initiating a spiritual journey requires realization of error and the loving acceptance of the journey and of the teacher.

Spiritual travel includes includes confrontation with error, a testing process. Throughout his journey Milton confronts projections of his selfhood, images of his error, obstacles to the pilgrim's spiritual growth. Among these obstacles, he beholds his own shadow . . . {and} . . . the hermaphroditic reflection of his error. . . . A spiritual journey is always individual. No one person should pretend to offer corporate salvation; "each shall mutually / Annihilate himself for other's good." Each traveler may serve as exemplar, as teacher, but the teacher does not master the student. Such emphasis on mastery would decree the perpetuation of hypocrisy and self-righteousness, those wonders of Satan's holiness Milton surpasses.

Since the traveler must stand open and naked . . . {and} . . . because it requires complete honesty and openness, the journey is painful. Spiritual travel demands sacrifice of all the traveler thinks he is: his old identity, his ego, his comfortable and secure points of reference. Then, in surrendering all he has assumed himself to be, the traveler survives without identity, feeling weak and empty, in uncertainty and chaos, like Milton, "a wanderer lost in dreary night." . . . The spiritual path, Milton senses, requires giving, not getting. Sacrifice and surrender and giving mean a painful renunciation, but they also can be an equally painful openness to love.

—Milton: A Poem by William Blake
Kay Parkhurst Easson and Roger R. Easson, eds.,
pp. 135, 136, 137

How to Use the I-Ching as an Oracle

With the I-Ching, we learn to adapt and fit naturally into the nature of external and internal circumstances. Everything I have presented in this treatise on metaphysics is only for the purpose of understanding how the subconscious can project itself on cards, sticks, or coins, and thus decipher the mesh of fibers in our mind through an oracular system. I advise reading the last phases of this book to gain such understanding.

The Taoist principles are always those of swimming with the current, not against it. This requires a knowledge of the twists and turns of the currents so that we won't feel lost when we run into the unknown. Therefore, the I-Ching shows us about the flow of currents in everything in the nature of the world and of the human being; it helps us understand it and cope with it. The true purpose is self-mastery.

When a situation is favorable we know how to advance gently and joyfully. When it is unfavorable, we know how to move slowly, cautiously, yield, stop or even retreat. This is what the I-Ching shows us and this knowledge makes us imperturbable, allowing us to remain calm in any situation and manage whatever comes. We become flexible and more profound in all aspects, keeping in mind that "good" and "bad" are just words.

Self-mastery requires putting aside all ambition and desire for material gain or fame, while learning to flow with the intrinsic complexity of the Tao and searching for the attributes of the wise, whose happiness comes from doing good to all creatures around them. In order to understand the mystery of reality, we not only need to reflect, we also need vision, the vision of totality. This is a creative skill that the use of the I-Ching helps acquire.

In the old times 50 yarrow sticks were used; they were divided over and over into groups until a reduced and specific number was obtained. The I-Ching requires 50 aquilea or yarrow sticks, each 12 to 24 inches long. If the yarrow sticks cannot be found, 50 regular wooden sticks will do. They must be kept in a closed container in a place that is at least the height of a person's shoulder. The book of the I-Ching, carefully wrapped in clean silk, is kept with the sticks.

The book should never be consulted lightly; if you ask something frivolously or skeptically, it gives a frivolous answer with no sense. One must be completely relaxed in body and mind. It is essential not to think of anything throughout the ceremony except what has been asked.

Supposing we are going to consult the I-Ching and we throw the sticks. The first step is to unwrap the cloth covering the book, lay it out on the table and put the book on top (the cloth protects the I-Ching from impure surfaces). Alongside the book we put a little incense burner and the box containing the sticks. With our back toward the South, kneeling, we make three deep bows, touching the floor with our forehead. Then, still kneeling, we pass the 50 sticks three times through the incense smoke, holding them horizontally and moving our hand clockwise in a circle. One stick is put back in the box and it will not be used anymore throughout the whole ceremony.

We place the 49 remaining sticks on the tablecloth and with the right hand we divide them quickly into two piles. We will call the left pile "A" and the other "B." We take a stick from "B" and put it between the ring finger and the small finger of our left hand. With the right hand we separate sticks from pile "A" in groups of four, until one, two, three, or four sticks remain. We put these sticks between the middle and ring finger of the left hand. Then we begin to take sticks from pile B in groups of four, until one, two, three, or four remain. We put them between the middle and ring finger of the left hand. (This last step can be abbreviated: since the sum of the two remainders must be 0, modulus 4, the second remainder can be easily calculated based on the first.) We will now have in our left hand 5 or 9 sticks. (The possible combinations are: 1, 1, 3; 1, 2, 2; 1, 3, 1; and 1, 4, 4.) All these sticks are placed on the side.

The remaining sticks are grouped and the same division procedure is repeated, beginning by parting them at random into two piles. At the end, 4 or 8 sticks will remain in the left hand. (The possible combinations are 1, 1, 2: 1, 2, 1; 1, 3, 4; and 1, 4, 3.) We put them aside beside the group separated previously.

The remaining sticks are grouped and the dividing process is repeated a third time. In the left hand we will again have 4 or 8 sticks. We put them alongside the previously arranged groups.

The number of sticks remaining now will be 24, 28, 32, or 36. They must be separated into groups of four, that is, we divide by four the total remaining number with an exact number in each group. The quotient will be 6, 7, 8, or 9. These four digits are the ritual numbers indicating the character of the lower line of the hexagram. If the digit is an even number (6 or 8), the line will be Yin (open and receptive); if it is odd (7 or 9), the line will be Yang (continuous). But ritual numbers have even more to say: the numbers 7 and 8 mean that the line (either Yin or Yang) is stable and cannot be altered. The 6 and the 9 indicate a "mutable" line that can be changed into its opposite.

The 49 sticks are grouped again and the whole ritual is repeated to get the second line of the hexagram, starting by the lower line. With four more partitions we get the remaining four lines. On the whole, this division of the sticks is carried out six times for the six lines of a hexagram.

The whole ceremony performed calmly lasts 20 to 30 minutes.

Then we look for the hexagram chosen in the I-Ching and read the accompanying text carefully. The text will answer the question, giving advice in accordance with the situation. If the six lines of the hexagram are stable, that will be the end of the process. But if one or more of the lines is mutable, they are changed into their opposite and the new hexagram is considered. The commentary will say what can be expected in the future—second hexagram—if the advice of the first hexagram is followed. This will now be explained more fully.

After writing the hexagram or the two hexagrams and having read and reflected on the corresponding I-Ching passages, another bar of incense is lit, two or three deep bows are made, the sticks are put back in their box, the I-Ching is wrapped up again and put away along with the sticks.

This is a method of concentration and meditation that imposed an absolute devotion and dedication, synchronizing the person with the currents of Tao. Today such a long process is not necessary and often three coins are used. It will work whichever way we have charged our intention to be. The most commonly used is three heads and two tails or vice versa. We have to make a decision for those coins before consulting with them. It is advisable to keep three coins set aside especially for consulting the I-Ching, mostly because it is hard to purify metal from its previous charge and, although it might work, there can be interferences from previous circumstances and hands that have been in contact with those coins.

Personally, I like to use three stones taken from a river or from the sea with a flat coinlike shape so that they will not fall to one side more than to the other. The advantage of using stones is that the contact with their substance is more pure, and also because stones can be washed with water and can be charged by the Sun.

To decide which side will be heads and tails, we simply take them in our hands, concentrate, and decide which side will appear when thrown. If we decide that when we throw them, they will all be heads, we mark a "2" with a felt-tip pen, and if we decide they will be tails, we mark a "3."

Once we have the sticks, the stones, or the coins ready to consult the I-Ching, we must learn to recognize the best moment to ask a question. It is important to be able to turn to the I-Ching at a given moment to clarify a particular situation although we might already know the reasons and the circumstances of what has happened to us. This will help to ask a question as to what is being manifested and what one is learning spiritually. Taoist philosophy is a guide and counselor that always helps us be in contact with the laws of nature, with the here and now, helping us transcend karma and escape the wheel of fortune and misfortune.

This is a necessary complement for the transpersonal psychologist and for the psychological astrologer. Astrology provides the knowledge of the situation but, at certain times, little information as to the resolution of the problem. It is far superior to a tarot reading because it contains the Taoist philosophy, an inspired guide for all ages whose answers have multiple interpretation levels and are useful for initiates as well as for beginners.

Many make the mistake of believing the I-Ching will give a precise response to their question, when, in fact, what the Book of Changes does is put us in contact with our subconscious who knows the answer, and upon reading the text, we give ourselves the answer.

The I-Ching should be consulted with ritualistic respect using the right questions and in the right frame of mind. If this is so, it will always answer with unequaled accuracy.

In order to deal with this subject with due respect, one must keep in mind two components: 1) an objective contemplation and an internal assimilation attracting mental capacities in the processes of the outside world; and 2) plunging into the depths of the inner world through meditation, vision, and contemplation through which we learn to know ourselves and to penetrate into the heart of the universe, focusing on the depths of our subconscious.

It provides the knowledge that all patterns and developments of destiny are subject to the strict law of cause and effect and are programmed in a system of 64 potential states, with six possible emphases which, when interchanged, automatically multiply with each other into infinite possibilities within that base of 64 states.

I advise people to consult the I-Ching in silence, with the reverence and respect it deserves; to have nearby some object that connects us with the person or situation we are asking about. With a few moments of meditation, emptying the mind for a while, one is ready to formulate the question adequately, asking for guidance, not for a precise answer.

It's important to write the question in a notebook so you can go back to it later, since often the answer is not understood until the situation has materialized.

Then you can go back and read the answer instead of having to ask again. Very often, when you consult the same subject, the same hexagram appears every time; that convinces skeptics, but is not a respectful use of the sacred book. Having the question written out helps understand the answer, for often people make the mistake of interpreting without realizing how, exactly, the question had been formulated.

We need also to define and write down the time between the beginning and the end of the consultation, taking into account the time we need to make the decision or use the guidance of its Taoist wisdom; for example: 1 month, 1 year, 6 weeks, 3 hours, 7 months, etc.

Once we have reflected on the most appropriate and profound way of asking what we want to know, and once we have taken note of the question and the time and we are sure it is the best way to word the consultation, we are ready to throw the stones or coins to obtain the response, always keeping it in our minds and our hearts. We throw 6 times for the six lines of the hexagram.

Several people can consult the I-Ching together, provided they have talked about it in advance and agree on how to formulate the question. If there are 6 people, each one throws for one line of the hexagram, agreeing that the first person to throw will be the one closest to the circumstance or person consulted on. If there are three people, each one throws twice. If there are four people, the last two lines are tossed in pairs. If there are five people, it gets more complicated, but they can always join hands and all together toss for the last or the first line. If there are many more, they join in groups of three, each group tossing the pebble or coin to form a line.

Once we have these basic rules, either in group or individually, the stones or coins are tossed six times, one for each line forming the hexagram. The first line is the lower line and, going upward, the top line of the hexagram corresponds to the last toss, interpreting heads of the coin or stone as the number 2 and tails as the 3—the stones or pebbles have been previously marked. Since we have three coins or stones, we have four possibilities:

2 + 2 + 2 = 6	—x—	great Yin
2 + 3 + 3 = 8	— —	small Yin
3 + 3 + 3 = 9	—o—	great Yang
3 + 2 + 2 = 7	——	small Yang

The even numbers are Yin lines and the odd are Yang lines. The big Yin and the big Yang, the 6 and the 9, are mutable lines; we will now explain them.

The first toss is marked at the bottom and the last at the top. For example:

```
6th   8  =  — —
5th   9  =  —O—
4th   7  =  ———
3rd   7  =  ———
2nd   6  =  —X—
1st   7  =  ———
            49
```

Once we have written the hexagram, we look at the chart that is usually at the back of the Book of Changes. In this case we have the trigram Tui (the Lake) above, and the trigram Li (Fire) below; joining both sets of lines, vertical and horizontal (figure 19 on page 89), where they both join, we get the number corresponding to that hexagram, which here is 49: the Revolution.

This hexagram reveals the situation or circumstance of the moment. The whole text might be meaningful—or perhaps only a couple of sentences, the image, or the judgment. It can also be read in the interpretation of the second book if you have the translation of the original text by Richard Wilhelm and Baynes, which I definitely recommend, although it might be harder at the beginning for users not adept at symbolic interpretation. Some people find it very useful to start with the version used in *The I-Ching Workbook*, by R.L. Wing,[1] but the symbolic magic of the original version favors a personal outlook.

The whole text of Hexagram 49 is read, together with lines 6 and 9—great Yin and great Yang—which are the specific answers; the lines are situations which mutate to give another hexagram. They are the guides to transform that circumstance into another expressed situation in the second hexagram that will be obtained. In this case, in Hexagram 49, we would read line 6 in second place and 9 in fifth place. These lines are not only specific advice on how to change the situation into another pertaining to the second hexagram to be obtained, but also refer to the time in which that advice should be followed or the situation would be revealed. Therefore, before the toss, we define the time when we need to know the answer or the guidance of the Tao. If we divide the whole hexagram by that time, the first line is the most immediate and the last the most distant in time.

If the whole hexagram is divided into 6 days, each line corresponds to each

---

1. R.L. Wing, *The I-Ching Workbook* (New York: Dolphin/Doubleday, 1979). Also see *The Illustrated I Ching* (New York: Dolphin/Doubleday, 1982).

day; if it is 3 months, each line represents 15 days; if it is 12 months, each line affects 2 months, and if it is an odd number such as 15, it is divided by 6: 15/6 = 2.5, two and a half days for each line approximately. In the example of Hexagram 49, we would divide it by 12 days so that the second line would refer to the third and fourth day, and the fifth line to the ninth and tenth day after the consultation.

We can obtain as an answer a hexagram with no 6 or 9, that is, with no mutable lines. This would show only the circumstance and give no advice as to how to change it. The reason for this could be either that it cannot be changed, that there is no need for change, or that the question has not been well-formulated or the situation has not crystallized enough to provide more specific advice. It can also be due to the fact that during the time defined for the answer there will be no change as yet.

Once Hexagram 49 has been read with lines 2 and 5, these mutate to obtain a second hexagram that will determine what can be achieved following the advice or the manifestations indicated by the situations of the lines, in their corresponding times.

In order to accomplish those mutations and obtain the second hexagram referring to the change that can be obtained, we must follow the following rules: the great Yin mutates into the small Yang and the great Yang mutates into the small Yin, that is:

6 —x— becomes   7 ——
9 —⊖— becomes   8 — —

and the rest of the lines stay the same.

In the example of Hexagram 49:

8 = — — becomes 8 — —
9 = —⊖— becomes 8 — —
7 = —— becomes 7 ——
7 = —— becomes 7 ——
6 = —x— becomes 7 ——
7 = —— becomes 7 ——
      49   34

Looking in the chart of trigrams (figure 19, page 89) we see that it corresponds to Thunder above and the Creative below: Hexagram 34, The Power of Greatness.

In this second resulting hexagram we only read the text, without lines, since there are no 6 or 9. It shows us the result of mutating the first hexagram. The change of the 2nd and 5th lines of 49—the Revolution—results in 34—the Power of Greatness. The clues are contained in the text for lines 2 and 5 of Hexagram 49. The image and the judgment of this resulting Hexagram 34 indicate what we can obtain at the end of that period of time, in this case after 12 days, the time in which we needed the answer.

The relationship between these two hexagrams contains the whole image, if we are capable of understanding in synthesis what they mean.

We will probably not understand the advice the lines give us or we will interpret it differently when it is still very far off from the moment being referred to. That is why it's important to keep the answer and to remember the time the lines referred to, so we can read them again at the given time.

Readers might already be familiar with this use of the I-Ching, but I am going to present other formulas to enrich what can be obtained from its consultation. They will often clarify many things and add expertise to its interpretation.

The next essential move is to obtain the seed of the first hexagram. All hexagrams can be reduced to 4 basic hexagrams as a result of mutating them once or twice: to 1: The Creative, referring to creativity of spirit; to 2: The Receptive, referring to acceptance and material fulfillment; to 63: Perfection or culmination of something; and to 64: Transition and the beginning of a new situation.

The two first ones are immutable, 1 remains 1 and 2 remains 2 no matter how many times we mutate them. Nevertheless, 63 and 64 keep mutating with each other as if there were no end, just continuity. When you reach the perfection of 63, any little error makes you start again and leads to the 64 transition. We only need a few changes in the nuclear trigrams to obtain one of these 4 hexagrams that decipher the root of the hexagram, that is, whether the answer refers to 1) the spiritual or to 2) the material. With root 63 or 64, the importance is on the first root obtained, referring to something that culminates (63) or to something transitory (64).

These mutations are a result of repeating the two central lines and leaving out the two outer lines of the hexagram, what is called nuclear trigrams. For instance:

$$49 \quad \rightarrow \quad 44 \quad \rightarrow \quad 1$$

The seed of Hexagram 49, The Revolution, is The Creative of Hexagram 1, with two mutations. It indicates a creative and spiritual situation. If it were one sole mutation, it would be a hexagram in itself closer to its root. In this case, The Revolution is a root of the creative spirit going through confrontation. Another example:

$$22 \rightarrow 40 \rightarrow 63$$

The seed of Hexagram 22—Grace—is the perfection and culmination of Hexagram 63. If we continue to mutate it, the result would be a continuous change from 63 to 64 and back.

$$63 \rightarrow 64 \rightarrow 63 \rightarrow 64 \rightarrow 63$$

This depends primarily on the two central lines; if they are two Yin lines, we will end up in Hexagram 2; if they are two Yang lines, in Hexagram 1. If the central lines are one Yin and one Yang, we will end up in 63 or 64. Depending on the number of nuclear mutations, the root is closer or farther away, one single mutation or two.

The two central lines refer to the way the trigram of Heaven contacts the trigram of Earth through the human being. Other examples:

$$61 \rightarrow 27 \rightarrow 2$$

The root of Hexagram 61, Inner Truth, is the 2—The Receptive, material achievement—with an intermediate 27—Nourishment. It emphasizes paying attention
to one's words, and moderation in food and drink to attain the inner truth.

It is very interesting to study the root of each hexagram and even the hexagram that connects it to its root in the case of there being two mutations.

The root of Hexagram 28—The Preponderance of Greatness—is the creative spirit of Hexagram 1, with one single nuclear mutation.

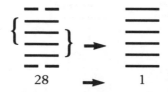

Another valuable piece of knowledge is to see what thought has produced the situation of any given hexagram. For that purpose, we will use the geomantic compass of figure 15, looking for the first hexagram referring to the circumstance
received as a reply to the consultation, in the outer circle related to the world of
senses. In the inside circle we will obtain the hexagram pertaining to the world of
thoughts. The hexagram we obtain when we consult refers to a situation in the
external, material world in the world of senses, and when we know by what
thought it has been generated, it makes it easier for us to understand how we have
arrived at that circumstance.

Using figure 15 and looking at the example of Hexagram 49—The
Revolution—we see inside it Hexagram 5—Waiting—that explains the thought
within the action of revolution. Obviously, it belongs to Hexagram 5—the
Calculated Wait—referring to the thought that everyone expects a change at the
right time.

For the more expert, we have another two formulas that give us a greater
depth in the I-Ching answers. One of them has taken me longer to verify, since it
came up as a result of conversations and intuitions shared with a friend and companion. It is undoubtedly valid when the consultation refers to the actions of several persons and their relationship with the consultant. Through it we can get to
know the actions and reactions of all those involved in a particular situation, giving a much richer overall knowledge. This method is: reading the rest of the lines
of the first hexagram. Lines 6 and 9 refer to the consultant's action and to the specific advice as to how to change the circumstance. The rest of lines 7 and 8 refer
to other persons involved in that whole situation. The 8 refers to feminine energy
in general, or to people of the feminine sex; and the 7 refers to people of the mas-

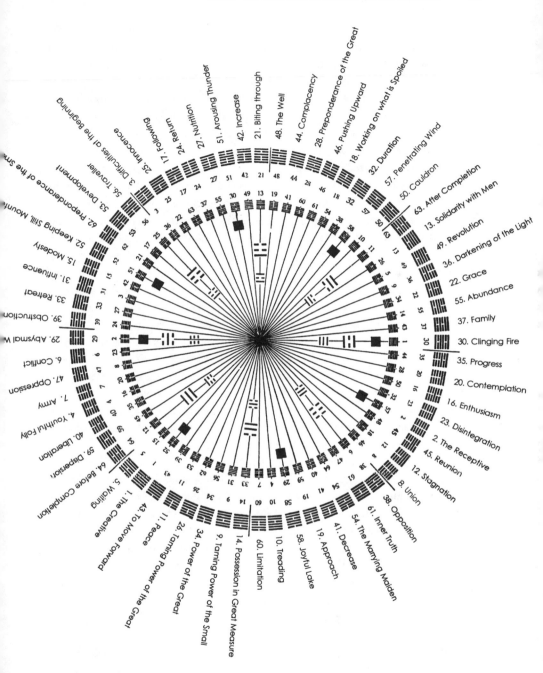

Figure 15. Definitions of the hexagrams.

culine sex, or to the masculine energy in general, that which surrounds the circumstance. In order to know the actions and reactions of those persons, we read it in the lines of the first hexagram we obtain, although the book mentions a line with 6 instead of 8 for woman, or 9 instead of 7.

For instance, in Hexagram 49, the 2nd and 5th lines that came up when we threw the stones or coins—a 6 and a 9—refer to the action or guidance of the consultant on those people or situations he or she is consulting about. The 1st, 2nd, 4th and 6th lines, with the 7th and 8th synchronizing with the whole situation, refer to the people related to or akin to this circumstance and experience. The 7th refers to the masculine gender, and the 8th to the feminine gender. Generally the closest or lowest line will refer to the person closest to the question or to the consultant. The top lines refer to other people farther from the situation or the consultant. In fact, lines 7 and 8 never referred to those people or circumstances already contained in the question, but to everything but the question, even though it is related to it.

All lines make up the totality of situations needed for the circumstance expressed in the hexagram to happen. The top lines can also refer to the same person as the lower lines, to the person's reaction and action later in time. The same is true about the timespan into which we divide the complete hexagram: in this case, the 12 days into which we had divided the example of Hexagram 49. The 1st, 3rd and 4th lines, all with a 7, can refer to the same masculine person at different times, to how that person relates to the consultant throughout time, or it can also refer to two or three different masculine persons. The 8 of the 6th line can refer to a woman farther from the situation and to how she relates to the consultant, or to what was consulted, in general.

The reference in the text of the I-Ching to the noble superior or inferior human being refers to our behavior, either superior or inferior. In this case, since it is the consultant who makes the revolution of lines 2 and 5 and the changes, the other lines (1st, 3rd, 4th and 6th) are the people around who act with, toward, or to the consultant's decisions.

In this case we have the 1st line that refers to a very close and more involved person; lines 3 and 4 refer to other masculine persons or to that same man at other more distant times or corresponding to the days into which the time of the whole hexagram has been divided; and the 6th line, to a woman. Sometimes this can also refer to an institution, company, or organization, if the question was about something of the sort.

The best way to interpret who lines 7 and 8 of the first hexagram refer to is to use your intuition. One must trust visual intuition and let imagination run free to present us with the mental image of the person—man or woman— the line refers to when we read it. This is hard to do if one has no experience with intuition or visualization. In fact, if one knows how to use the original I-Ching text, this method will present no problems.

The I-Ching helps us connect with our subconscious inner being—who already has the answers to the past, the present, and the future. It is our Self who will give it to us, or find it with its guidance.

The next and last method we can use to heighten our understanding is based on the fact that a hexagram mutates six times and at the seventh, it becomes its opposite polarity. We have to find that path and the steps we have to ascend or descend to find the hexagram of compensatory polarity of Heaven. These 7 hexagrams and the ascending lines tell us how a situation progresses and becomes its polarity, and the steps that have to be taken to get there. Mutating the hexagrams with descending lines or downward steps tells us how the situation has been created or the seed that has given rise to the present circumstance.

We read the hexagram and the corresponding line in the progression of ascending or descending steps to mutate into another. For example:

This is the ascending path that deciphers the progress of the situation until it reaches its opposite polarity.

This is the descending path that deciphers how a situation has come to be. Its seed is the opposite polarity, which is the same in both cases.

In the first example of progressive ascendant grading we read Hexagram 49, The Revolution, with the 1st line; then Hexagram 31, The Influence, with the 2nd line; Hexagram 28, The Preponderance of Greatness, with the 3rd line; Hexagram 47, Oppression, with the 4th line; Hexagram 29, Abyss, danger, with the 5th line; Hexagram 7, Group Action, with the 6th line, and finally, Hexagram 4, Difficulty at the start, which indicates that a change has already taken place and that one must be alert to the beginning of something new.

In the second example of regressive downward grading other hexagrams appear. The Revolution 49, with the 6th line; Hexagram 13, The Community, companionship, with the 5th line; Hexagram 30, Fire or adherent light, with the 4th line; Hexagram 22, Art and grace, with the 3rd line; Hexagram 27, Nourishment, careful eating and careful speech, with the 2nd line; Hexagram 41, the Decrease or loss, and finally Hexagram 4, Hard beginnings. This progression of hexagrams indicates how one has arrived at the need of a collective revolution.

If we join both ladders into one, we obtain a chart of hexagrams related to the necessary steps to proceed from a situation to its fulfillment or culmination. We discover the seed, the cause and path of all the situations expressed by the hexagrams. In order to facilitate this study, you will find the code for all the hexagrams and their evolution, with the central column as the unifying and the compensatory polarity of Heaven, the clarity of thought in the Here and Now, 7th (figure 16, pages 70–71).

When we unite 13 hexagrams to arrive, through mutations, to their 7th or opposite polarity, and then back again to the same hexagram, José Argüelles sees here the connection between the biopsychic resonance in human beings with the electromagnetic one of Heaven, by connecting the I-Ching with the Maya Calendar and its magic number 13, being the 7th central column the polarity corresponding to being in the Here and Now. He calls it the mystic column.

So, Argüelles elaborates a map of codes to find out how certain situations synchronize in the history of humanity; in fact, the path outlined by these 13 hexagrams pertaining to Hexagram 49, is the path humanity is treading in this time of revolutionary change and return to cosmic order.

It was this map from the book *Earth Ascending* by José Argüelles, that made me see enormous synchronic relationships and that started me on my true research of the I-Ching. The codes found in Map 37 of *Earth Ascending* indicate the different ages in the prehistory, history, and post-history of present humanity by means of the 64 hexagrams. The complete map of the 64 hexagrams in 13 columns reveals human movements in Heaven and on Earth; a horizontal reading refers to time and a vertical reading refers to space.

The exterior vertical columns have their numeric progression consecutive to the path of the resonance, from Hexagram 1 to 16—prehistory—from 17 to 48—history—and from 49 to 63—posthistory (figure 16).

In playing with colors and consecutive or polar relationships in numerology, I found a wealth of synchronistic relations that led me to this research and to decipher how this information can be applied.

When studying this graded path and arriving at the point where humanity finds itself right now—Hexagram 49—we find interesting clues for all of us. This process can be carried out with each of the hexagrams to understand the cause and the process of each circumstance expressed in that hexagram. When reading the whole column from right to left, we can decipher the seed that has caused those circumstances; and when reading from left to right we see how a situation will develop within its cycle.

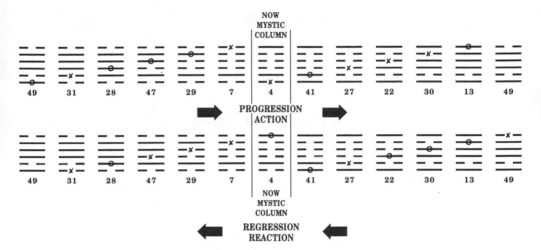

This same formula for grading and reading the lines —X— 6 and —⊖— 9 can be applied to each one of the hexagrams.

These codes for polarity action and reaction, awareness and liberation from karma, can be applied to the present destiny of human beings according to the work of José Argüelles as well as to the full understanding of the circumstance of an individual hexagram obtained upon consultation of the oracle. This method is so complete and complex that few of us have ventured taking advantage of such enormous knowledge.

I hope that this explanation will help readers understand the work and the codes of *Earth Ascending*. It can also be applied to a greater awareness of the Now as well as to gain knowledge of both inner and outer phenomena, transpersonal as well as personal. At first, while playing at coloring Map 37 of *Earth Ascending*, I discovered that the drawings had perfect synchrony. Not understanding their interpretation, I sent them to José Argüelles, marking the start of our interaction and common work that has inspired me to carry out this research by uniting these codes with the laws I already knew through "karmic psychological astrology and transpersonal psychology."

The correlation of codes on the vertical axis referring to space are more enigmatic and harder to interpret (figure 17, page 73). The spatial clues are found in

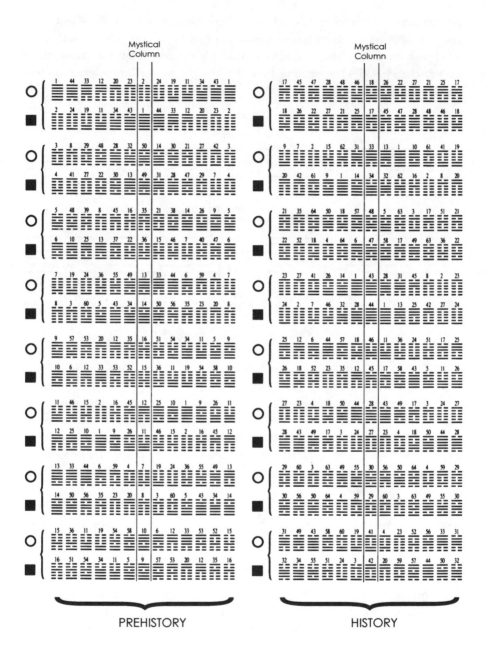

Figure 16. The hexagrams in prehistory, history, and posthistory.

Mystical Column

Mystical Column

HISTORY

33	13	1	10	61	41	19	7	2	15	62	31	33
34	32	62	16	2	8	20	42	61	9	1	14	34
35	21	38	14	26	9	5	48	39	8	45	16	35
36	15	46	7	40	47	6	10	25	13	37	22	36
37	53	57	59	6	64	40	54	51	55	36	63	37
38	6400	35	56	52	53	39	63	5	60	58	54	38
39	63	5	60	58	54	38	64	35	56	52	53	39
40	54	51	55	36	63	37	53	57	59	6	64	40
41	4	23	52	56	33	31	49	43	58	60	19	41
42	20	59	57	44	50	32	34	55	51	24	3	42
43	28	31	45	8	2	23	27	41	26	14	1	43
44	1	13	25	42	27	24	2	7	46	32	28	44
45	17	58	43	5	11	26	18	52	23	35	12	45
46	11	36	24	51	17	25	12	6	44	57	18	46
47	58	17	49	63	36	22	52	18	4	64	6	47
48	5	63	3	17	51	21	35	64	50	18	57	48

POST-HISTORY

49	31	28	47	29	7	4	41	27	22	30	13	49
50	14	30	21	27	42	3	8	29	48	28	32	50
51	16	40	32	46	48	57	9	37	42	25	21	51
52	22	26	41	38	10	58	47	45	31	39	15	52
53	37	9	61	10	38	54	40	16	62	15	39	53
54	40	16	62	15	39	53	37	9	61	10	38	54
55	62	32	40	7	29	59	61	42	37	13	30	55
56	30	14	38	41	61	60	29	8	39	31	62	56
57	9	37	42	25	21	51	16	40	32	46	48	57
58	47	45	31	39	15	52	22	26	41	38	10	58
59	61	42	37	13	30	55	62	32	40	7	29	59
60	29	8	39	31	62	56	30	14	38	41	61	60
61	59	20	53	33	56	62	55	34	54	19	60	61
62	55	34	54	19	60	61	59	20	53	33	56	62
63	39	48	29	47	40	64	38	21	30	22	37	63
64	38	21	30	22	37	63	39	48	29	47	40	64

the spread of the two horizontal lines pertaining to each pair of hexagrams, since they refer to the changes within a specific space due to the reversibility of the numeric consecutivity of the hexagrams. In space, or in the materialization of things, the sequence is such that the odd and even numbers form a unit either reversible or irreversible. It is the same figure, seen from different angles—from above or from below, from Heaven or from Earth.

In the top part of figure 17 we see how this pairing occurs, leaving irreversible hexagrams, which are those pertaining to peak moments in the history of humanity that refer to circumstances where supernatural forces have intervened. The 8 irreversible hexagrams belong to the creative from Heaven 1, and to the receptive from Earth 2, made up by duplicating the trigrams of inner change, just as Fire and Water repeated in themselves, giving us Hexagram 29—the Abyss, danger—and Hexagram 30—the Luminous, adherent. It also happens that when we combine two of the exterior trigrams among themselves, turning them around to compose the hexagram with the trigrams of the Mountain and Thunder— which act together in Nature—we get Hexagram 27—the right nourishment and care with words—or Hexagram 62—the preponderance of the small and being conscious. Also the Wind can be combined with the Lake, since they act indivisibly in Nature, forming the Hexagrams 28—the critical mass; the Preponderance of Greatness, and 61—inner truth.

Now, looking once more at the verticality of space of the columns in figure 16 (pages 70–71) and pairing them, the lower line of the hexagram refers to Earth and the upper one refers to Heaven; the lower one to the senses, and the upper one to thoughts.

We can investigate another much more complex study about what happens in the space between Heaven and Earth throughout the consecutivity of karma, and how thoughts become tangible reality.

This study is very complex and very hard to express in a practical way, but it undoubtedly deciphers the clues of being in the Here and Now where the negative karma dissolves and a positive one is created, since the reversible or irreversible consecutive relation occurs in connecting and crossing with the mystic column of the center and the Now.

When studying a couple of paired columns, we observe two ways of crossing the central mystic column: downward, from Heaven to Earth, all the pairing of Hexagrams 47 and 48. This demonstrates the synchronistic union of Heaven and Earth through the Here and Now. At other sequences there is no connection between Heaven and Earth as shown in some pairing of Hexagrams 49 and 50. This happens in some of the consecutive numbers of irreversible karma. It usually occurs when it refers to the progression or regression to the seed of the nonreversible Hexagrams 1, 2, 27, 28, 29, 30, 61 and 62, since in pairing, they con-

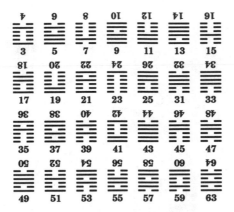

28 Reversible Pairings of Hexagrams

8 Non-Reversible Hexagrams

CONSECUTIVE SEQUENCE OF THE HEXAGRAMS

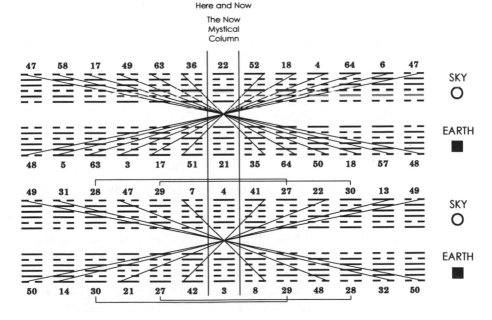

Figure 17. The special relationships between Heaven and Earth and the here and now.

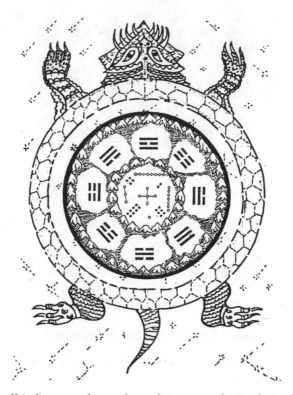

Figure 18. For all indigenous cultures, the turtle represents the Earth. In the marks of the shell of a turtle, the world of senses was first deciphered.

tain in themselves the consecutive polarity in the world of thoughts as well as the irreversible karma, so their movement is through the senses of Earth or the thoughts of Heaven, missing the Here and Now reality. It represents two parallel worlds with heavy karmic consequences. Their complementary and consecutive opposite hexagram is also found in the central column. See figure 16 (pages 70–71).

This consecutive transfer where Heaven moves independently from Earth, or vice versa, also occurs in other hexagrams that are reversible polarity: 11 and 12—Peace and Stagnation; 17 and 18—Adaptation, Following the Track and Repairing Decadence; 53 and 54—The Advancement of what is developed and the Commitment of the Subordinate; 63 and 64—Culmination and Transition. These decipher the consequences of karma still reversible.

In the spatial reality between Heaven and Earth, when thoughts and senses refer to the pairing of the consecutive polarity, as well as reversible Hexagrams 11-12, 17-18, 53-54, 63-64, they refer to moments in which their partners are in the center, in the mystic column, which are periods of time and circumstances of supernatural power in the human being. However, in order to transcend karmic conditions, Heaven moves without contacting Earth for many consecutive numbers, letting the matter of circumstances of Earth act separately in its consecutive sequence with no relation to the center, to the mystic column of the Here and Now where no karma exists.

Relating this circumstance to historical moments, it refers to times in which human beings have had the power to create or destroy their world with no heed to the plan of Heaven: the creation of the great empires of present civilization. (See figure 18, page 74.)

The study of these maps offers us incalculable wisdom about humanity, the universe, and how the forces of Heaven and of Earth act upon the actions of human beings.

Interpretation of the Book of Changes, the I-Ching

Interpretation is the art of discovering the cosmos through oneself. It depends on how well we know ourselves and this knowledge will grow with the practice and use of the I-Ching. As life, it grows and is unique for each person, as well as universal. One taps into the wisdom that weaves the threads in a fabric of infinite colors and endless variables. Thus, one responds to oneself when one can obtain perspective from the present, the Here and Now, with the assurance of knowing all the twists and turns of the past in order to disentangle all that produces an imperfection in the outline of the future.

When one consults the I-Ching, it responds according to the amount of inner synchrony, to the clarity in formulating the question and to the concentration and attention of the consultant, deciphering the threads of its own nerve tissue.

The I-Ching helps sail the Here and Now through the tangled tides of nerve connections, clarifying interferences and aiding in the understanding of each circumstance and experience of life itself, in the Way of the Tao. It gives the knowledge of how to untangle the knot that has led us to a particular circumstance.

Little by little, a feeling of synchrony in the Here and Now develops, and we can flow without judging through every experience life brings us. If at that moment the whole text cannot be understood, it can be because we have still not received all the information, and because it can only be understood when we experience it in its presence. That's why it is very important to be able to go over the text again at the precise time that the lines of the hexagram are obtained and indicated.

The first hexagram always refers to the circumstance, its development in the wisdom of its behavior, so it is easy to understand its totality. One can decipher the wisdom of what is happening at the moment and of its experience, although perhaps only a few sentences refer to the specific circumstances. Nevertheless, the overall interpretation of the hexagram involves a total knowledge of that situation if one is capable of overlooking the details and concentrating on the content and how it is expressed in the words.

The wisdom implied in the opposite hexagram and the study of the meaning of the polarity can be of great help in making the mind more flexible to understand the associations without getting lost in the particulars, attaining thus a transpersonal mentality that helps carry reason in union with intuition.

The different lines correspond to specific circumstances that act or can be acted upon at a particular moment to achieve a transformation, a change, a reaction, represented in another second resulting hexagram.

If we take into account that for each hexagram there are so many multiple combinations of 1, 2, 3, 4, 5 and 6 mutable lines, great Yin or great Yang (6 or 9), it gets to be so immense that we realize that such an amount of possibilities is related to the genetic code and to life itself. That is to say that each of the hexagrams can mutate into 63 other hexagrams, starting to mutate into its polar opposite if all the lines have great Yin or great Yang: 6 —x— 9 —θ—. Meaning that each hexagram can turn into all the other circumstances expressed by the other hexagrams. The law of probability becomes synchronicity.

If it has only one mutable line, it could turn into another 6 possibilities; if it has 2 mutable lines, 15 possibilities; with 3 mutable lines, 20 possibilities; with 4 mutable lines, 15 possibilities; and with 5 mutable lines, 6 possibilities. Total:

$$1 + 6 + 15 + 20 + 15 + 6 = 64.$$

In other words, every hexagram can mutate into all the other hexagrams. Likewise, each hexagram is divided into 3 duplets: the two upper lines refer to the action of Heaven, the two middle lines to the action of the human being and the two lower ones to the action of the Earth. In the original text, attention is given to what lines occupy the 5th place, since it is the regent of the hexagram, the line that contacts the human being from Heaven, being also the central line of the upper trigram.

Being the line that descends from Heaven, it makes a great difference whether it is Yin or Yang, since being Yang it is an active line, where one can act; but if it is Yin, it is a weak line, with passive action coming from outside as an inalterable command from Heaven in response to the previous action of the human being. One accepts the command and feels impotent to change it.

In the second book of the original text by Wilhelm and Baynes, they also consider the nuclear trigrams of each hexagram, as if they contained the inner clue to get to their root.

The image of the text arises from the union of both trigrams forming a hexagram, and the next image from superposing one on the other. Trigrams have an ascending or descending movement. The image depends on the basic tendency of each trigram as they join when the lower one rises and the top one descends. They relate to each other when both tend to rise or descend; when the lower one goes down, the upper one rises up. The movements of the trigrams are: Heaven rises, Earth descends, Fire rises, Water descends, Thunder rises, Wind descends, the Lake rises and the Mountain descends. Thus, the image contains a sense of harmony, balance, compensation, union, separation, elevation or danger.

The upper trigram represents the sublime, the things hard to attain; the lower one represents the inferior things, the closest ones. So, the reality of the human being can either join the plan of Heaven or not.

The text of the opinion or judgment is due to the historical archetype to which it belongs and it indicates how the main characteristics of the whole are going to evolve, its warnings, resolutions, challenges and dangers.

When consulting the I-Ching, if one has concentrated adequately and formulated the question correctly, the reply one gives oneself contains the accuracy with which one has approached one's own inner guide.

If specific things are asked, specific answers are provided; if abstract generalities, abstract responses will be given. Actually, its excellence in responding tells us to what extent we know what we are asking about or the mental clarity with which we have formulated the question.

As José Argüelles mentions in his article "Main Currents in Modern Thought" (January 1969): "The I-Ching acts like a computer, and its function depends on its being programmed in conformity with truth. The truth (or correctness in terms of the facts) of the programming depends on how the person consulting the book reacts to the utterances of the Book of Changes."[2]

The "I" of the Book of Changes means variability and "Ching" means book, ode or legend. From the beginning of all that exists, thought arises in the world of dreams, becoming incarnate in matter to live out its possible reality and, in turn, inspire the world of dreams once more about what is true and real. It is all a circle; the beginning is the end, although not the same; the only reality in the universe is change.

---

2. Quoted in Martin Schönberger, *The I Ching & the Genetic Code* (Santa Fe: NM: Aurora Press, 1992), p. 20. *Main Currents* was published in New York by the Center for Integrative Education.

In referring to the King or Sovereign, it indicates a person who takes command to carry out a mandate, a cultural hero who surrenders himself in sacrifice to what is necessary for the community. The Great Man is the sage, a saintly and virtuous man who knows the plan of Heaven and the destiny of human beings. One must decide who this refers to in the circumstance one finds oneself at the moment. The second book of Wilhelm's translation expresses the responsibility and hierarchies of the titles of Prince, Great Man, or Sovereign.

When it refers to the Great Water, it means that on one side is the confusion and suffering and on the other serenity, and one must cross to the other bank by wading through the turbulent waters of emotions and get to know one's instinctive impulses and desires. The term "no blame or guilt" refers to the way of correcting errors and returning to the right path.

What is favorable is the courage to be aware; what is unfavorable is self-indulgence, letting go of oneself unaware of where one will end up. However, humiliation refers to not being able to correct the small or big deviations. This is, undoubtedly, very different from being humble, which is explained in Hexagram 15, Modesty, when its opposite polarity is sincere: Conduct, Hexagram 10. Peace—Hexagram 11—is Activity and Prosperity, which is the polarity of Hexagram 12—Stagnation; and the contradiction of Hexagram 18—the Decay, working on what is deteriorated in the world of senses.

The advice of using stones marked with Yin and Yang is a way of contacting the depths of the collective unconscious, since the stones are containers for the divine power according to many aboriginal cultures, such as the Australian, the Brazilian and the Native American.

In choosing certain stones, we come in contact with the archetype of our being, as they represent our ancestors who continue to exist in the stones with their powers and virtues. In rubbing them, they are charged with electricity, attracting the spirits of our ancestors for the benefit of all, both living and dead. So, having chosen them, when we use them, we come in contact with the essence of our all-knowing being, and also with the cosmic interpretative relation.

In some cases, people find it hard to interpret anything clearly from the I-Ching text. Others tend to interpret it mistakenly because they look for specific references, or lack understanding of the basic models of the advice implicit in Taoist philosophy—where there is only change and fixed situations which would mean stagnation or death don't exist.

I will try and clarify the issues necessary to understand how the Book of Changes explains, interprets, and guides us explicitly in any situation or experience.

Hellmut Wilhelm assists us in this respect referring to Hexagram 43—the Resolution—and he says that the general is related to the specific in The Book of

Changes. The question, itself, determines the situation in time. Once that specific moment in time is determined, it is placed, just as for any other oracle consultation, in the configuration of the contradictions that define the field of action of that specific moment in time. So it is made clear in what segment of the world (and in affinity or contrast with that world) can the energy of the specific moment become effective and fertile.[3] Meaning that one must be self-aware and conscious of one's own contradictions, personal and external, so as to understand the advice of the text.

Wilhelm also said that the texts indicate how human action is responsible for the conformation of that moment. The creation or conformation is not always determined by the action of the individual. Creation can take place through an intervention of The Divine, it can be the result of a purely "natural" becoming, it can rest on the conjugation of several of the forces of the great trinity. In our case, when the breakthrough takes place, conscious human action is recommended to give shape to the new formation. The manner and the degree of individual participation is also not the same in all cases.[4]

As always, the emphasis is up to each person and to their awareness of what amount of freedom or autonomy they have in the situation consulted about. Also it is a matter of to what extent that situation depends on the action of external agents, being other people, or the karma, itself, that the consultant has acquired or provoked. It is advisable to be aware of all this to obtain the maximum benefit from the text.

The strange tension between the consciously channeled energy, and the awaiting of the echo of the invocation from the depths of the self, makes the situation exciting and extraordinary. Letting oneself be guided by the will of Divinity, giving in to the natural process of becoming, are not unfamiliar attitudes for the human being. But, what strong people, conscious of their goals, will be willing to let themselves be guided as lambs by the preformed configuration that rests within? The paradox is that it is precisely those who are aware of their goals who depend in that situation on the impulses of their own subconscious, which they, themselves, literally provoked.

In the first place, it is clear, from all we have said in this book, that the I-Ching is a means of getting in contact with our subconscious, where all the answers lie, for it takes into account what the impulses themselves have previously caused in relation to any situation consulted on, and the fact that the text helps us get in contact with our subconscious; so it is we who give ourselves the answer.

---

3. From Hellmut Wilhelm, *Sinn des I Ging* (Munich, Germany: Eugen Diederichs Verlag, 1972), pp. 111-112. Translation mine.
4. See *Sinn des I Ging* by Hellmut Wilhelm, pp. 111-112.

For those of us lacking mental vision, awareness, and the will to make our own decisions, the interpretation we tend to choose is the one that puts blame outside ourselves. We may see conflicts or difficulties as closed obstacles due to external circumstances, instead of understanding that the conflicts and difficulties rest inside ourselves, and can therefore be vanquished through awareness and responsibility.

The I-Ching puts us in contact with our inner being who knows all the answers and warns us of situations or difficulties we have already created. It guides us to know the way of action of the superior and of the inferior human being—our inferior mind—whose behavior sometimes manages to hide or carry out that situation, even without awareness and knowledge of its cause.

In the second place, when using the I-Ching as an oracle, the first hexagram deciphers the present situation and how it manifests itself. The lines 6 or 9 within that hexagram are advice or warnings of moments and forms of action which, in spite of their negative tone, are advice on how to manage these circumstances or complications and switch to the second hexagram.

A situation is only negative, closed, or blocked if the second hexagram, when changing lines 6 or 9, is a hexagram that expresses in its totality that change toward something negative or destructive. Anyway, we learn by flowing with the circumstances and following the advice of the lines of the first hexagram. Even if we know that we don't want to be involved in that situation, if we are already in it, we can learn from it, if we let ourselves flow with the circumstances and are aware of how they have been created inside ourselves. This indicates clearly how everything can be enriching.

In the third place, the text of the I-Ching usually gives indications on whether or not to act, on waiting for the right moment or even on the lack of clear vision on the part of the consultant and how they have formulated the question.

It usually gives directions: north, south, east, northwest, etc., which sometimes are very significant and sometimes not. It talks about months referring to the Chinese months that begin in February, and are therefore one month behind the Western calendar. Perhaps that month indicates the previous moment when the inner seed was planted that led to the present circumstance, or if that month is within the timespan in which we have placed the whole answer of the hexagram.

Seldom does it indicate seeing the Great Man; what it indicates is seeing someone who can help us resolve the situation and put us in contact with the manifestation of Heaven, since our inner self cannot manage to see the totality.

Sometimes, the hexagram explains a situation where destiny or karma plays a complete and absolute role, where little or nothing can be done, consciously or not, to flow with or change that situation.

Usually, the image already contains the chromatism of the answer if one has an open, unprejudiced mind, and is familiar with, and practices symbolic interpretation. The judgment refers more to the awareness the individual or the consultants should have regarding that particular circumstance. Often it is enough to read the text of the first book, but sometimes one can get an even greater clarity upon reading the text of the second book with the sequences and commentaries, the interpretation of which appears when taking into consideration the inner nuclear trigrams, that is, the first mutation that takes us to the root of the hexagram, as we have already explained.

In the fourth place, it is essential to write down the question and the answer and keep it, because often we don't understand what is being said about a circumstance we are not very familiar with, or that doesn't depend wholly on us, or that has still not become totally manifest for us to understand what it means. Therefore, instead of consulting again after some time, when that circumstance has become more manifest, we will better understand what the text tells us when we arrive at that crucial moment. The lines 6 or 9 may refer to a still distant time. Keeping this in mind and reading it again at the indicated time will be much more convincing than consulting over and over again on the same subject. Very often I've seen how the same hexagram appears even when the question is formulated differently or by another person involved in the situation; other times, after repeated consultation, Hexagram 4 appears—Inexperience—indicating one's incapacity to interpret the I-Ching adequately and use it correctly.

In the fifth place, the I-Ching, being as it is the Book of Changes, presents us with the possibility of changing any circumstance no matter how hard it may seem, and teaches us to flow better with the present circumstances and the changes. This can be achieved with conscious action and mental clarity on our part. For the Tao, all is change, all is mutation for better or worse; what is impossible is static permanence, since it is contrary to life. Even institutions mean permanence and stagnation, so it always indicates the path of individual creative will, which is born of the superior human being and of being at one's center.

The I-Ching is the instrument of synchrony, and just as it gives us a reply due to its capacity to synchronize with our true self, the destiny we ourselves have created or the karmic destiny created by divine conditions, it also helps us synchronize with the circumstances and to know how to recognize the right moment, the right place and the right people. It helps us flow with everything and allows our superior mind to flower so as to collect knowledge inaccessible to the inferior human being.

It teaches us how to pay attention to our inner self and maintain the presence of the Here and Now where the only karma created for the future is a positive one and where the negative past karma is dissolved.

Therefore, the I-Ching is the necessary instrument to contact with our center and learn how to navigate in the Now of a particular circumstance, being flexible, attentive, and flowing with what is happening.

In the sixth place, the only thing truly permanent in the universe is change. Each hexagram outlines a path that joins metaphysical or transcendental experience with the regulated, everyday world. Thus, it indicates a path, an ethical course, as it were, to stay in contact with Heaven and Earth in the midst of all the changing flow, and being able to find a meaning for all that occurs. The lines indicate the gradual evolution of the situations within that complete experience, starting by the lower line.

One must disregard the appearances of the physical, sensorial world, for we attract the contradictions of the world of senses or the difficulty of complementarity and compensation, which even occurs often when we develop one sense more than another. One must be open to comprehend the simultaneous harmony of all that occurs, and to the dynamics of existence, in order to discern in the images the regularity of the continuous. Understanding will be open to the dynamic consequence of existence which is immediately experiential, instead of the continuous and regular consequence, which is intelligible through theoretic speculation.

It is hard for most of us to let ourselves flow with the dynamic course of events of the Now through intuitive and synthetic understanding. That's why we have the tendency to trust our rational, linear interpretation that traps us in our own game of misunderstanding totality by channeling us toward individual interests which are the same mistakes that have caused the blocking and the conflicts we run into in any experience. Undoubtedly, this limits completely the understanding that the guidance of the Book of Changes offers us.

From this perspective, the world of change is experienced as chaotic, unstable, and insecure. All the contrary to what the Tao teaches us in its ancestral wisdom. If this preparation to see the synthesis and the wholeness of the new becomes dominant and, most of all, past karma, the tension that arises in the relationship with that world of disorderly change does not create myths but rather creative images that act as points of reference to put order in chaos. Through the I-Ching, change is no longer the unknown enemy since we understand its origin and its harmonic tendency.

Although the images and the interpretation of the hexagrams refer to archetypes of antiquity and to already existing situations, forming a coherent whole, that creation of images represents values and certain situations putting order in chaos. They are given a duration that can refer to any similar situation in any moment in time. However, these images do not refer to repeated archetypes, but to the permanent repetition of the archetype of change itself. That's why it adapts better to present time, helping to make the archetypal psychological understanding more flexible. It refers to the dynamics of the cosmos of human experience. Therefore, it can adapt to human experiences as well as to any kind of scientific genetic values of all that exists.

Original images express thoughts and confirm the weakness and creative strength of the human being to transform his life and his environment, without straying away from the laws of the nature of Heaven and of Earth.

Superior human beings are able to draw strength from themselves and maintain their creative will, which is precisely the connection of the inspiration from Heaven and its accomplishment on Earth. This only happens when one synchronizes with the totality of a situation and doesn't act untimely. Acting at the wrong moment would attract a series of complications, contradictions, consequences and compensations, in order to return to the start, to create anew what we could have achieved previously. But we are not the same as before and complications absorb creative will, draining the pure energy and the transparence in creative action, if one has not understood the process and the seed within oneself which has created the lack of synchronicity. In this case, one will have been able to grow by going through all those complications and difficulties, and there is almost always a second, third and fourth chance.

The hands are the sensory organs: what one does, the other undoes.

The important contribution the Book of Changes makes to our lives is to allow us to recognize the essence and the effect of the forces that operate in all that happens. It deciphers possibilities in time, it helps us center our emotions, clarify thoughts and guide actions. This is the essential for living in the Now.

The revelation is contained in the sense of the line in a hexagram which makes it change into the other hexagram. Through its observation and full participation in it, the mystery of life is unveiled, although the mystery still seems unknown until we feel it, because it cannot be expressed in words and can only be transmitted to others through subliminal, intangible, and metaphysical contacts.

So, when the I-Ching is understood, we can live in wisdom; it is the revelation we receive when we experience the synchronicity there is between our daily reality and the text we read. This really deciphers the vibration we have already created in our previous impulses and which are transmitted through the electromagnetism of thoughts and emotions. The I-Ching is the chosen instrument for the reading of the return and turn, which is obvious since it is present in our subconscious. For this reason, the I-Ching is a magic and sacred instrument that reveals, through harmonic and synchronic vibration, before it happens, all that we are sowing in our subconscious for the future.

If we approach it with the reverence and respect it deserves, we will always find, in the inner and infinite world of the subconscious, the clues we need to flow along the whirlpools of infinite possibilities our lives invite us to experience. We will always be able to live with a sense of permanence of the meaning of our lives, which is attained by the simple fact of being connected to our real transpersonal self.

For Blake the physical body's sensory organs, separated from the soul's imaginative powers, are limited and flawed. If, as Blake assumes, at its center the universe has an eternal, infinite, and immortal reality, then how can a limited, finite, and mortal observer who refuses to acknowledge that center, know the state of true existence? When an individual's sensory organs are "folded within themselves," how can he behold "the great light"? Using the eye as representative of all organs of sensation, and sight as the emblem of all sensation, Blake admonishes us to see through *the eye,* not *with* the eye: to see as if "Body is a portion of Soul discern'd by the five Senses," not with the body exclusively, as if it were separate from the soul. In other words, we must see with the soul observing reality as if it were the body, since the body by itself alone sees a lie, the human delusion. Blake clearly seems to have thought that sensation or feeling proceeds inward from the sense organs to the functioning brain, where the sensory information is received and interpreted by the agency of the soul in conjunction with the vegetable memory. Once this sensory experience is received by the vegetable memory, which contains the individual's learned experience, including the assumptions he has been taught to make about the world, an interpretative reality is projected outward upon the world, according to the individual's powers of perception. "As a man is, So he Sees", says Blake. If the senses perceive only the literal "Vegetable Ratio," then there is nothing beyond the brain but a sensory tumult, a horrible chaos in which nothing is permanent and nothing lasts. Paradoxically, this chaos seems rational and orderly, but as Blake says, this is a "delusion of Ulro." According to such a viewpoint, the individual who "sees the Ratio only, sees himself only"; he projects his rational selfhood onto the physical world. But if an individual sees with the soul, his senses discover "the Infinite in all things" and the wondrous regions of eternity.*

—Milton: A Poem by William Blake
Kay Parkhurst Easson and Roger R. Easson, eds.,
page 141.

The Sequence of Hexagrams in Human Destiny

The numbering sequence of hexagrams relating to the human biopsychic resonance can influence each one of us at some point. We shall now look at a simple method that can be used to acquire a synthesis of the karmic steps all human beings are destined to take during their lives. We have studied the hexagrams that influence the Heaven electromagnetic resonance in the world of thoughts by locating the Former Heaven trigrams of Fu-Shi, and the influence of the Earth gravitational resonance in the world of the senses by locating the Earth and Later Heaven trigrams of King Wan. Now we need to study the influence of the human biopsychic resonance through the numbering sequence of the hexagrams.

The world of thoughts shows us the compensating polarity, the cancellation of karma, because karma is related to causal material distortion and the misunderstanding of suffering. In the spirit of Heaven, suffering does not exist. It is only a distortion of material misunderstanding.

The world of the senses shows us the irreconcilable contradictions that generate movement and growth of life, the imperfection and temporality that allows matter to be, to evolve and survive the cause and effect of any material movement. The world of human destiny shows us reversible and irreversible consequences, the Karma and also the Dharma. It shows the path followed by every human being, and the steps taken to leave the Wheel of Karma on Earth—the distortion of the temporal and material world—in order to find polarity in Heaven.

It also helps us to synthesize a way of orientation, a guide, to help us advise people by establishing the steps or stages where they find themselves at the present moment and guide their superior selves in overcoming the inferior self, because the superior self connects them with the Heaven, where karma does not exist, contrary to the inferior self, whose actions make the karma of life on Earth more difficult.

In order to know the hexagram related to the Dharma or human path, we refer to the date of birth of the querent. The calendar we use is different than the Chinese, because our calendar is based on an irregular cycle of the Sun and Moon. The Chinese use the cycles of the Moon, or thirteen lunar cycles in a solar year. The solar year is divided into twelve months in the Gregorian calendar, so instead of having thirteen months of 28 days, they are twelve irregular months of 30 or 31 days. It is preferable to use (as reference) the day inside each lunar period and start counting from there. We identify psychically with the number that corresponds to the number of days after the last New Moon on the date of birth, and this itself contains, through the consecutive numbering of gradual I-Ching hexagrams, the rules of the game to be played within the Dharma.

That is, the first twenty-nine hexagrams coincide with the numbering inside the month of the date of birth, and afterward this hexagram progresses gradually upward in order to reach its karmically compensated polarity of Heaven.

For example, a person born 12 days after the New Moon of that month, will begin his or her route in Hexagram 12, and someone born 28 days after the New Moon will start on Hexagram 28. To obtain this information, we need a lunar calendar of the year of birth (or an astrological ephemeris).

This means we only use the first 29 hexagrams, but when their lines mutate in an ascending pattern, all other remaining hexagrams will be crossed. The day of the New Moon would be the first lunar day of Hexagram 1.

The method used in this mutation is the same indicated at the end of I-Ching used as Oracle, Phase 3.

For example, for a person born on May 19, 1981, we begin on Hexagram 16, because the New Moon appeared 16 days before, on May 4, and we take the following route:

16	51	54	34	11	5	9
ENTHUSIASM	SURPRISE	MARRIAGE	INITIATIVE	PEACE	PATIENCE	LIMITED PERSUASION

Reading the hexagrams and the progressing ascending lines we can interpret the destiny of that person born on the 16th day of each lunar period.

TRIGRAM / SUPERIOR ▶ / INFERIOR ▼	Ch'ien Sky	Chên Thunder	K'an Water	Kên Mountain	K'un Earth	Sun Wind	Li Fire	Tui Lake
Ch'en — Sky	1	34	5	26	11	9	14	43
Chên — Thunder	25	51	3	27	24	42	21	17
K'an — Water	6	40	29	4	7	59	64	47
Kên — Mountain	33	62	39	52	15	53	56	31
K'un — Earth	12	16	8	23	2	20	35	45
Sun — Wind	44	32	48	18	46	57	50	28
Li — Fire	13	55	63	22	36	37	30	49
Tui — Lake	10	54	60	41	19	61	38	58

Figure 19. The superior and inferior trigrams.

We could say that these ascending hexagrams interpret the process of individuation; how light turns to shadow and shadow to light, through the six mutations, until the opposite polarity is reached on the seventh. The feminine aspects of personality become masculine, and the masculine become feminine, Yin becomes Yang and Yang becomes Yin.

The destiny of complete integration is accomplished, where there is no longer light or shadow, but only internal and external evolutionary growth exists.

Certain hexagrams of the world of thought and the senses may be synchronized with one of the destined steps in one of the hexagrams of Dharma. In synchronization with the world of thoughts, our superior self tends to overcome our inferior self; whereas in synchronization with the world of the senses, the tendency is to be absorbed by the actions of the inferior self. This struggle with the light and shadow within the unconscious mind of each person takes place all the time.

It is very useful to understand human psychological development in order to comprehend the different levels in which certain aspects of the gradual progression of destiny may be experienced or repeated. Destiny and karma are not predetermined, but are open and dependent upon our personal ability to choose— and understand the consequences—which is determined by our consciousness.

We usually meet someone along our path who helps us overcome these patterns. Sometimes the people we meet are similar to us, and are not able to help us overcome such patterns, and we can't see clearly what lies ahead. Those patterns must be experienced, but our conscience and intelligence can help us prepare and freely choose the people with whom to repeat our karmic patterns.

When we understand the various cycles of life, also we comprehend that everything happens at the right time, and, although it does not seem like it, we have enough time.

It is important to know the two trigrams that make up a hexagram, and to interpret them from the union and separation of both, according to the upward or downward tendency of the trigrams. It would be helpful to have a more extensive list of definitions and explanations of hexagrams, other than the known classic names for each hexagram (see figure 19, page 89).

Key to Numbering Hexagrams

The superior trigram of Heaven moves vertically, and the inferior of Earth moves horizontally. If you remember this, you will find the union of the corresponding superior and inferior trigrams. Example: with Earth above and Water below we get Hexagram 7.

These stages of the gradual progression of hexagrams are a macro-cycle, equally occurring in micro-cycles. For this reason, the time it takes to climb from one step to the other, or to another phase, depends on the individual and how mature the consciousness is. In the macro-cycle, the final steps are not reached until after age 50, even for a conscious and highly evolved person. For others, it may seem to us that the person is on a high plane, being a magician who transforms things; however, the individual's powers may still further develop when reaching maturity. The right stage of evolution is entering or being on the fifth step after age 50.

It may also seem to us that we understand the logic of such stages and that we have experienced them before through successive micro-cycles. When we manage to be in the Here and Now, we obtain the benefits of the polarity symbolized by the last hexagram, where the human being has successively walked such stages in micro-cycles, understanding how karmic destiny changes to the polarity of Heaven.

Therefore, we only start our way with the first 29 hexagrams, relating to the initial consecutive steps; half way, historically, between civilization and the great empires. Those 29 hexagrams will mutate along the way into all the remaining ones.

The different stages of the ascending progression of hexagrams lean toward certain learning processes that we must endure. Because of that the value assigned to each line is very important, as well as whether or not the line is Yin or Yang. A Yin line is passive. Yin means that the challenge, change, or period of personal evolution of karma in life comes from outside, and must be accepted. It is a passive line within the circumstances indicated by the full hexagram with that line.

If it is a Yang line, one is active, accomplishes and practices what is indicated on that line, and on the complete hexagram. The images on each line indicate how resonances, new transformations, points of reference, or karmic steps are presented.

We now need an adequate reference for the evolution that each line indicates and how that lesson is carried out, depending on whether it is an active Yang line, which radiates upward, or Yin, which is passive, and absorbs and receives.

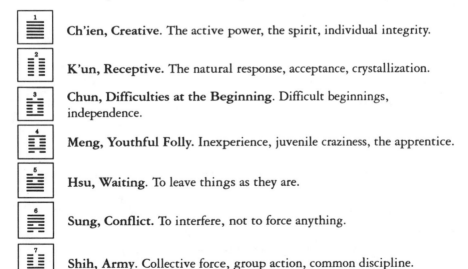

Ch'ien, Creative. The active power, the spirit, individual integrity.

K'un, Receptive. The natural response, acceptance, crystallization.

Chun, Difficulties at the Beginning. Difficult beginnings, independence.

Meng, Youthful Folly. Inexperience, juvenile craziness, the apprentice.

Hsu, Waiting. To leave things as they are.

Sung, Conflict. To interfere, not to force anything.

Shih, Army. Collective force, group action, common discipline.

Pi, Union. Staying together, harmony, association.

9 Hsiao ch'u, Taming Power of the Small. To restrain, dominate, minor limitation.

10 Lü, Treading. Conduct, to be careful, mistrust.

11 T'ai, Peace. To prosper, progress, one meeting the other, movement.

12 P'i, Stagnation. To come to a stop, oppression, obstruction.

13 T'ung Jen, Solidarity with Men. Community, friendship, companionship.

14 Ta Yu, Possession in Great Measure. Sovereign, abundance, to retain matter.

15 Ch'ien, Modesty. Moderation, humility, acceptance.

16 Yü, Enthusiasm. To harmonize, impulse, audacity, trust.

17 Sui, Following. To adapt, succession, to get followers.

18 Ku, Working on What is Corrupted. To repair, decadence, to regenerate.

19 Lin, Approach. Promotion, to teach, to influence.

20 Kuan, Contemplation. Intuition, observation, to consider, comprehension.

21 Shih Ho, Biting Through. To reform, to judge, to force, to punish.

22 Pi, Grace. Elegance, the ornamental, art.

23 Po, Disintegration. Deterioration, to put aside, to separate, dispersion.

24 Fu, Return. To repeat, the return, revision, to recover, to improve.

25 Wu Wang, Innocence. Spontaneous action, sincerity, the unexpected.

26 Ta Ch'u, Taming Power of the Great. Potential energy, limited by the strong.

27 I, Nutrition. The corners of the mouth, feeding, to give, to deliver, to provide nourishment.

Ta Kuo, Preponderance of the Great. Critical mass, excess, preference.

K'an, Abysmal Water. Danger, absorption, darkness.

Li, Clinging Fire. Synergy, cohesion, luminosity, to shoot.

Hsien, Influence. Attraction, courting, magnetize, mutual influence.

Heng, Duration. Continuing, steadiness, loyalty, perseverance.

Tun, Retreat. To refuse, repel, hide, flee.

Ta Chuang, Power of the Great. To direct, to straighten, to stop.

Chin, Progress. To conquer, overcome, advance, clarify, to dawn.

Ming I, Darkening of the Light. To grow dark, withdrawal of light, limitation, to hide.

Chia Jen, Family. The clan, roots, relationships, to belong, attachment.

K'uei, Opposition. Contradiction, to defend oneself, discord, disunity.

Chien, Obstruction. Barriers, to trip, mistakes, problems.

Hsieh, Liberation. Relief, salvation, to become independent, remove.

Sun, Decrease. To decline, reduce, diminish, loss.

I, Increase. Benefit, expansion, gain, to add, the help of destiny.

Kuai, To Move Forward. Resolution, to agree, to correspond, assembly.

Kou, Complacency. Temptation, confrontation, compromise, to give in.

Ts'ui, Reunion. To assemble, to come near, compromise, common union.

Sheng, To Push Upward. To advance, ambition, to grow, to raise up.

K'un, Oppression. Adversity, dishonor, exhaustion, repression.

Ching, Well. The fountain, to alter everything, organize, investigate.

Ko, Revolution. To change, to move, to transcend.

Ting, Kettle. Small cauldron, the transformation, to remove, to mix, alchemy.

Chen, Arousing Thunder. Surprising, to awaken, liberation, to provoke.

K'en, Keeping Still, Mountain. Meditation, to hold back, stability.

Chien, Development. Gradual advance, constancy, consequence.

Kuei Mei, Young Marriageable Woman. Agreement, proposition, compromise, subordinate.

Feng, Abundance. Zenith, to preserve, affluence, satisfaction, provisions.

Lü, Traveler. Traveling, the pilgrim, to wander, foreigner, to get lost, the stranger.

Sun, Penetrating Wind. Influence, to persuade, gracefulness, rest.

Tui, Joyful Lake. Social gathering, to enjoy, letting go, interchange.

Huan, Dispersion. Getting together, to forget, to abandon, to expand, dissolution.

Chieh, Limitation. To repress, rules, to organize, lack of recognition, chastity.

Chung Fu, The Inner Truth. Vision, inner confidence, sincerity, charisma.

Hsiao Kuo, Predominance of "Smallness." Excessive details, to be aware, to value insignificance.

Chi Chi, After Completion. Perfection, culmination, to realize oneself.

Wei Chi, Before Completion. Transition, to begin, before the end.

LINE	EVOLUTIONARY STAGE	YANG LINE	YIN LINE
6th	Magician	I transform	I am transformed
5th	Hierarch	I guide	I am guided
4th	Minister	I carry orders	I take orders
3rd	Master	I teach	I am instructed
2nd	Traveler	I perform	I assist
1st	Apprentice	I learn	I am taught

In those evolutionary stages the first hexagram already includes whether lines are Yang or Yin, but the line of the hexagram to which that stage refers, is the one that determines under which circumstances one is active or passive.

The seventh stage is reached at full maturity, when we succeed in changing the karma with which we were born, thereby overcoming the conflicts and difficulties, indicated at the time of birth, between our parents. Logically, this is only achieved by very few people.

Also, it cannot be said how long we may stay between stages, and often we remain between two stages for quite some time. The majority only reach the fifth stage, while only the more evolved reach the sixth stage—that of the Magician.

The age cycles are evolutionary stages that occur based on activity in the astral chart. The resonances are due to (more or less) high interferences. They are dependent on free will, but the people around each individual activate another set of circumstances. In these ascending steps of hexagrams, each one has an unlimited timeframe. Personal evolution, how each person handles external circumstances with internal knowledge, all this affects ascending the various steps.

The important element is to distinguish between the two sources of knowledge—to recognize and experiment. The unique human faculty is self-conscience, which raises us above the rest of Nature, through experience, but simultaneously we also alienate ourselves from the Cosmos. Only through an earthly experience with Nature, our own personal sphere entrusted us by the Cosmos, can we take part anew in the process of creation and restore our relationship with the cosmos.

Now we have to define how the superior and inferior being manifest themselves, in order to know the psychological abilities of both. It is not important, in a sphere of growth and influence, whether we act as followers on a Yin line, or take the lead on a Yang line. In both cases, it is important to define the difference between the superior and inferior being in each of us.

Superior beings are capable of assuming responsibility for their own lives, as well as being able to be themselves under all circumstances without hurting anyone. These people are guided by personal conscience and integrity, and do not judge the weaknesses of others in order to justify theirs. These people want to help others and know that personal priorities and limitations must relate to the benefit of everyone.

Superior beings know that our mental and emotional attitudes shape our destiny, and can admit humbly to personal mistakes, thankful for the opportunity to correct them. They may be influenced by any circumstances without fear of losing their own individuality, with a goal to grow and work toward inner spiritual evolution, as well as contribute to improve the world through their calling. Capable of challenging their own inner monsters and able to change without fear, keeping clear minds, being aware of negative thoughts, being able to correct them, superior beings help everyone on the planet.

Inferior beings are the ones who don't know themselves and are influenced by others; they are self-important, but seldom take responsibility for their lives and their destiny. Justifying mistakes and weaknesses, unable to admit being wrong, constantly passing problems on to others makes them hard to live around. They are unable to solve many problems or keep relationships, and, due to a sense of futility and dissatisfaction, are increasingly drawn to a life based on material things. They repress emotions considered morally reprehensible and increase the "shadow" side of themselves. The shadow is like a bag where they store everything they do not like about themselves, or anything from past experiences or relationships that they were unable to understand or deal with. Rather than defend the own ideals and principles, they find it easier to follow public opinion and blame others afterward for their own frustration and incompetence.

They are afraid of life and death, and neither suffering nor satisfaction end up making sense to them. They always need someone to show them the way, yielding their creative power. Unable to evaluate things on their own, they either allow the circumstances or other people to make decisions for them, and this inertia or lack of purpose leads to a life of resentment and resignation. Living in constant disharmony with their conscience can create a state of ill health that will further justify their lacks or incompetence, and they remain trapped in a psychic process of individuation, unable to discover who they really are.

Weighed down by relationships and solitude, life becomes a contradiction between joy and sadness, suffering and pleasure, boredom and amusement. This may lead to a kind of schizophrenia, or lack of balance. Without mental clarity or emotional appeasement, and increasingly detaching the mind from the body means the inferior types do not fulfill their destiny in the unification of Heaven and Earth.

In order to see these stages of growth, of integration or disintegration, or psychic stagnation, we can refer again to the I-Ching trigrams, to interpret the logical progression of light and darkness, the conscious and unconscious, which also become the shadow, or whatever we repress and refuse to admit about ourselves.

We have seen before, the process of human life through the world of the senses: starting with the receptive Earth ☷, the parental background, conception in Fire ☲, embryonic life in Water ☵, birth in Thunder ☳, youth in the Lake ☱, adult life in the Wind ☴, maturity in the Mountain ☶, and death in the Creative Spirit ☰.

This refers to both spiritual and physical strength in the personal growth and logical evolution of every individual. We always come into direct contact with the line below and, conscious of the middle line, we try to reach or develop the line above, which is also what we see or project outside.

On Birth, everything aims to materialize, to become or take shape physically in all Yin lines. In the conception, the spirit of Fire is conscious of its materialization and evolution toward a spiritual conscience with the Yang line above and below. In the embryonic life of Water, the material body is conscious of its material growth in the Yin line above and below. In the birth with Thunder, the spirit below causes the complete consciousness Yang line below and the material realization in the two Yin lines above.

In the youth of the Lake, it is the spirit that grants the joy and willingness to live, trying to expand into the material world and its Yin line of growth above.

In the adult life of the Wind, it is the body and the material world that is established with a consciousness of the spirit, searching for further expansion in the Yang line above.

In the maturity of the Mountain, consciousness of the conditions of the material world and the body try to transcend spiritually in the Yang line above. In Death, everything depends on spiritual consciousness.

However, in order to see psychic development, we must go to the world of thought, where we find the keys to the progression of light and shadow at a psychological level.

Previously we explored the reasons why the rhythmic pattern of the electromagnetic resonance of Heaven is axial to the compensating polarity, where there would be no need of material existence. We also have to understand the apparent backward movement of Heaven and the Sun, due to the changing horizon and the rotation of the Earth on its own axis. (See figures 3 and 4, pages 12, 15.) We choose this movement backward, but instead of starting in the creative spirit ☰, we begin in receptive matter ☷, thus joining the previous process of spiritual growth and the material world of the senses, with an understanding of the evolution of the conscious Yang and unconscious Yin in the world of thought.

In the world of thought we start in the receptive trigram and end in the creative trigram; the beginning and the end is the same in the world of the senses as it is in the world of thought. We jump also from Wind-Thunder to form the Tai-Chi symbol that belongs to the biopsychic resonance with which the union of both directions is accomplished. This includes the union of Heaven and Earth through human consciousness, except that in this case the process is reversed, and instead of progressing from the spirit of light to the materialization of darkness in the "process of individuation," we start at the psychic level with the knowledge that we have already materialized and are trying to reach spiritual consciousness. The process is as follows:

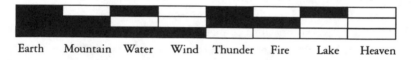

Earth   Mountain   Water   Wind   Thunder   Fire   Lake   Heaven

From the darkness or receptive dependence of the psyche during early infancy, we go to the Mountain, where in infancy and early youth the darkness and the shadow guide us and live with us, but we aim toward the light and clarity that we see coming from our external conscious world.

In youth, we manage to incorporate the clarity of consciousness into our character. The unconscious interior becomes a reflection of the water below and above.

When we reach the early maturity of the Wind, we are conscious of ourselves and repress the shadow and the unconscious within ourselves. We are surrounded by everything we consciously wish in the Yang line above.

This is the adult period, also represented by the Wind in the world of the senses where both processes coincide. In adult life, between age 30 to 40, we have become fully aware of the conscious self, the Yang line below in Thunder, but the unconscious starts to manifest itself, spilling over and projecting uncontrollably, as danger still threatens from outside and others.

When this process starts to mature, it may last for varying periods of time for different people. Some may never get to the next stage. We see this in the Fire trigram, where we start to understand that the conscience is formed by experiences that we attract from the outside world. We will recognize our shadow and dark-

Concave and convex realities: the conscious and unconscious in unison bring a revelation.

ness in the Yin line at the middle. This is the right time to accomplish a great deal in the process of individuation, otherwise it may come to a halt.

The Fire stage means we have mastered our external world, but must face the monster inside us like a warrior, by conquering ourselves and our shadow, making it a friend.

The seventh stage is only reached by people who have crossed the dark night of the soul and manage to conquer their own monsters, befriending and making this monster a part of their natures. In the Lake, the dark Yin line is discarded, not like an unconscious reflex state, but because we are still influenced by people or obscure circumstances from the external world. These external circumstances can test everything we have achieved in the learning process of personal trial. We also learn by educating others. I do not think this stage is reached, even in the case of a rapid process and developed consciousness, until after age 50.

Lastly, the stage of light, complete creativity, individual fulfillment, and the end of the individuation process is reached when we are capable of feeling and expressing the spirituality of electromagnetic polarity. This is represented by the inner joy experienced in the Lake. It is the beauty of old age and the highest readiness to face death.

Many times, we may find ourselves between two stages, and die also at a crucial stage or crucial transition between Thunder and Fire. Consciousness and illumination acquired through the experience of death is represented by Fire, where we realize that we were our only enemy. This is precisely the most difficult step to take for most people, beginning in our 40s and lasting till death; once we have passed that stage between 30 and 50, we have already entered into the complete process of personal individuation.

Now it remains for us to understand more deeply "the process of individuation" and the "shadow," and how we project this outside ourselves. In the subsequent phases of this book, we will study this concept from the Jungian perspective and then study it again with the trigrams—the unconscious interior line below, the middle line of our consciousness or the line above (representing our external reality, what we attract into our lives)—and the movement and direction of each trigram in order to gain a real understanding so we can deal with the difficult situations we have to face.

For Blake the physical body's sensory organs, separated from the soul's imaginative powers, are limited and flawed.

Blake complicates our attempts to understand his vision of physical reality by his assertion that the earth is concave and not convex.

Similarly Blake describes the sky as an "immortal Tent"; man "standing on his own roof, or in his garden" sees such concave space as his universe; he sees from within to without.

Thus, Blake pictures not a world suspended within a void, but a world centered in creativity. . . . located. . . within the crystalline domes of the multi-layered lens of the eye. The lens, while small, is an egg-shaped world unto itself within the eye, a microcosm of the Mundane Egg; it is a microcosm of vision, since it brings all the light rays impinging upon the eye into focus and sends forth rays as the lines of perception. Similarly, Golgonooza is the microcosm for Blake's world of art, bringing perception into focus through art and sending forth visionary communication as does a work of art. Further, we can see that the light rays impinging on the lens and the rays of perception emanating from it correspond to the "intellectual spears, & long winged arrows of thought". . . which are Blake's emblems for the mutual interchange between art and its audience.

Perception both flows inward to the eye as a stream of sensory data entering the brain, and outward from the eye, as a projection of reality upon the sensory tumult beyond the body.

For his description of perception, Blake employs five major images, all of which specify the characteristics of a spiritual journey. . . . And, like the perceptual process, a spiritual journey can proceed from eternity . . . or to eternity . . . both journeys can converge in a work of art.

—MILTON: A POEM BY WILLIAM BLAKE
Kay Parkhurst Easson & Roger R. Easson, eds.,
pages 142, 149, 150.

The Individuation Process: Light and Shadow

When we refer to the "individuation process" we are referring to C.G. Jung's concept of the journey of the psyche in search of individuality. It is a journey of growth and integrity where we fully live the unity of the feminine and masculine aspects, the conscious and the unconscious. It is living out on Earth the creative and unique power granted by Heaven through synchronicity. According to our present understanding of the receptive feminine Yin and the masculine creative Yang, we attain pure transformation by experiencing universal androgyny.

Many people go through the individuation process in different ways and at different levels of consciousness, but everyone is forced to integrate part of their other, unconscious side into their lives. In fact, the unconscious hounds us until it catches up with us at the moment of death.

Jung expresses it as the unification or separation of the soul at death, when the feminine form and realization sinks into the Earth and the manifestation and the will of the masculine form rises up to Heaven. If people die with integrity in the masculine-feminine soul or animus-anima, the manifestation of Heaven gathers the realization of the Earth, elevating both as a single entity of evolved consciousness.

All life teaches us how to be the fully unique and creative being our material and cosmic nature has granted us. Therefore, by birthright and by living in synchronicity, we are able to become a revelation of the total universe through a tiny act of growth of light within darkness. We participate in the reverberation of the transmission of light all around the universe. In ourselves we are nothing, but we are very important if our failures and successes have a subconscious influence on other human beings of future generations synchronized to us. These future generations can live out and continue similar experiences to ours—what we usually call "other lives."

Jung was the first non-Oriental scientific psychiatrist who had a deep knowledge of the I-Ching. It inspired him to become familiar with the conscious and unconscious universe of the human being and the transformation potential of the psyche, which he called "the individuation process," as well as the transference of leadership from conscious to unconscious factors. This he called "enenthidromy," inspired by the pendular effect of the Yin and Yang in the Book of Changes, the I-Ching, by the interplay of the pairs of opposites, not only of their four functions, but also of those two opposing attitudes of psychic energy called introversion and extroversion.

Jung's psychological concept is that, in order to attain the maximum development of individual creativity, the other side—the unconscious—must in no way be suppressed or repressed, but rather must become familiar to us. Thus people will be able to enjoy and control the total scope of their skills by getting to know themselves and attaining a transcendental function.

The psychic lives of modern, civilized human beings are plagued with problems. Our psychic processes are made up, mainly, of reflections, doubts, experiments, and all that is almost totally foreign to the subconscious. The intuitive mind of primitive human beings leads the way to the growth of consciousness; we can even learn to be grateful that problems exist; it is simply the retreat of instincts that creates consciousness. Instinct is nature and it strives to perpetuate nature, while the conscious mind strives for culture or for transforming instinctive desires.

The secret lies in opening up to another way of responding to problems by making conscious decisions instead of relying on natural instincts. Whenever we have to deal with problems, we instinctively resist, provoking the forms that lead us to darkness and obstruction. The only way of penetrating darkness is to enter inside it and, at the same time, invoke the powers of light that consciousness offers us.

Problems arise when there is a lack of consciousness. Therefore, the priority is finding out how consciousness can emerge for the general mass of humanity, and this, no one is sure about!

It is very revealing to be aware of how children develop consciousness from the moment of birth up to age 7, when they become more aware of the visible reality of things. Especially when we can observe our own children, in which each father and mother can recognize this and recognize themselves if they pay close attention. We see when the child recognizes someone or something and we feel he or she has consciousness. Recognition is knowledge; it is perceiving the connection between psychic contents and messages.

This process is vitally important, but today parents take very little responsibility for their children, which makes the children feel insecure in their capacity for making conscious decisions. This hampers the development of individuality and causes a constant return to the past, to the known and secure world, by which the inherited karma is increased and recharged with energy.

In the childhood level of consciousness there are still no personal problems; nothing depends on the subject, for the child depends totally on the parents. It is as if he or she were still not completely born, but is still enclosed in the psychic atmosphere of the parents. This is the first receptive stage. Psychic birth usually occurs during puberty with the eruption of sexuality. Physiological change is aided by a psychological revolution. Up until this period, the child's life is governed by instinct. Even when there are external limitations opposing subjective impulses, these restrictions do not alter the relationship the subject has with him- or herself. The child submits to them or avoids them, maintaining an inner integrity. The child still does not know the state of inner tension induced by a problem. This state arises when an external limitation becomes interiorized, when one impulse clashes with another, leading to inner division, contradiction, and internal strife.

Here begins the second stage, where problems are not outside and are not solved by challenges or running away from parental circumstances, but where problems lie inside. This is the beginning of adulthood.

We are all aware of the source of the problems arising during youth and we can still cast responsibility outside of ourselves. When we pass on to the next stage, we cannot avoid assuming certain things that are often false, trapped in the conditions we have unnoticingly created. We can choose a whole set of negative attitudes and take on contradictions that give birth to the first conscious problems.

This next stage lasts from age 30 to 40. If the individuals are well-prepared and self-confident, the transition to a profession occurs smoothly and is often also linked to the vocation. Nevertheless, for most people, life's demands put a cruel end to the dream of youth. We cannot cling to illusions, but must face reality, and surely problems are going to arise. We cannot enter our individuation with false assumptions: low self-esteem, expectations, unjustified optimism, or exaggerations become very obvious and provocative from the Saturn return (age 29-30) to the Uranus opposition (age 40-42). These are astrological cycles that can be timed if we have a natal horoscope prepared and read.

The sense of ego, feelings of inferiority and superiority, problems arising from our temperament can all turn into neurosis. Illnesses and imbalances breed on a reluctance to see our problems. We may also have a difficult personality—

one that provokes conscious problems—although these "problems" would not be called mental illness.

We may desire to remain like an unconscious child or we may be conscious only of our own ego, rejecting all that is foreign and being subject only to our own will: for doing nothing, for desire, for pleasure, or for power. Because of a reluctance to grow, our subconscious remains immature and estranged, as if not belonging to our own life.

Some of the most serious problems in life are never entirely solved; when they are, we feel as if something had been lost or left behind. The sense, the meaning, and the purpose of a problem does not lie in eliminating it, but in the continuous effort to resolve it. That is what prevents it from solidifying and crystallizing into illness. We also suffer from an unconscious inner struggle in which one part of the self wants to get rid of the problem and another part feels that without the problem, we would lose our individuality. We all experience this feeling at some point in life.

One important evolution within the psyche is the preparation to integrate the deep secrets that lie in the subconscious. This takes place around age 35 to 49. The explosion of the recognition of the individuality and peculiarity of the subconscious, of the monster, of our own enemy and shadow, takes place in the lives of brave individuals. If we are fearful and mistrust our own nature, this is repressed and distorts our conscious reality.

We become aware, at this stage, of the difficulty involved in accepting our own inner monster. An enormous transformation and evolution will come about by facing up to our shadow, to the darkness within ourselves. It is important to experience this stage. If we do not, come old age, we will sink into unconsciousness and dependence on others, just as in childhood.

The structure of the psyche as a reflection of the world and of the human being is so complex that it can only be studied from the angle of multiplicity. We each create our own segment of the world and build our own principle and value system, which, if not false, will resist the transformations caused by confronting the unconscious shadow.

On the other hand, consciousness seems to come upon us from outside in the form of perceptions and sensations, of conscious things that bring about the union of Heaven and Earth. Not only perception is needed, but also appreciation, which is a much more complex process. It comes from the same mental process of considering and recognizing things as they are in the Now. In recognizing, we think; in evaluating, we feel the tonalities; and the intuitive process pertains to another basic function of the psyche that is indispensable for consciousness.

In the capacity for vision and intuitive synthesis, we perceive the possibilities and alternatives inherent in a situation and we develop the capacity to interpret the synchronistic messages. These help us flow correctly, moment to moment, by trusting our connection with ourselves and the path we have set out on in the outer world. It is a constant provocation to illuminate our own blind zone, the dark blindness of the soul. We can say that blindness stems from perceiving, feeling, thinking, remembering, deciding, and acting out unconsciously what others do consciously. This process is registered by conscience, either through dreams or through conscious self-attention. Psychic life obviously remains the same, since unconscious activity still persists in the waking state.

Conscious intentions and actions are often frustrated by unconscious processes, surprising us continuously with their mere existence and manifestation. We betray ourselves when we speak, write, or act, revealing any unconscious aspect we would like to repress. When this is aggravated, it turns into physical or mental illness, into pathological behaviors of hysteria, compulsion, neurosis. It cannot be directly observed as due to specific motivations, that's why it belongs to the unconscious part of the psyche and to darkness, which takes on specific forms not recognized as our own. It is often projected outward onto specific people who become the projection of our shadow.

Dreams are the contents of consciousness which bring in previously unconscious material, if we manage to remember the content of the dream. Dreams are a direct contact with the unconscious, revealing the archetypes. These are forms of awareness—either regular and recurring or astonishing—belonging to deep images of the psyche, whether their mythological character and their ancestral cause is acknowledged or not.

Furthermore, the psyche is also made up of the collective unconscious, which is the sum of instincts and their correlation with archetypal images. Proof of this is that in the schizophrenic state, images of the collective unconscious appear, along with archaic impulses together with images unquestionably mythological. The collective unconscious is the part of the psyche not belonging to a personal experience. It is more related to the archetypes (shared by the different social and cultural groups) which are forms defined in the psyche that are present always and everywhere. The personal unconscious is made up, essentially, of the contents which at one time were conscious but are now forgotten or repressed. The contents of the collective unconscious have never been in the conscious mind and have not been individually acquired, but inherited. The personal unconscious is made up for the most part of complexes, while the collective unconscious is essentially made up of the archetypes. The individuation process is a result of integrating all the unconscious totality one goes through, bringing to light the capacity of awareness, to become conscious.

This is the most difficult process a human being must go through, much greater than the difficulties encountered in the world of matter. The forces that burst from the collective psyche have a confusing and blinding effect. The person can dissolve in an illusory fantasy and an involuntary activity, whose contents one did not even suspect before, with both negative and destructive overtones as well as positive and regenerating ones. While the conscious mind loses its power, the unconscious mind increases. When conscious control is lost, one is driven by impersonal, involuntary and unconscious processes. Aware or not, personality is pushed as in a mortal game, by an invisible player in the magical chess board of the fabric of life. It is this invisible player who decides the destiny of life, not the conscious mind nor the planets, nor karma, although all these are ways of deciphering what he or she is up to.

Penetration in the process is inevitable; the only alternative we have is to make great efforts to maintain a contact of cohesion and coherence with some parts of ourselves, maintaining a certain conscious attention and mental awareness within the realm of the unconscious psyche.

Once we are immersed in the individuation process, in the effort of freeing the individual self from the collective psyche, we discover potentials, knowledge, and values that we can incorporate consciously in the personality, enriching our lives and our particular and unique contribution. This helps us achieve a regressive restoration of the person, a self-healing and self-purification, allowing us to rise from our ashes like a Phoenix by transforming our complexes. This gives us an irresistible power and charisma, a brilliant light of peace and integrity in maturity and old age.

In the archetypes of the collective unconscious lie the images of individual destruction or transformation; thus, the balance between our inner and outer world is a delicate matter. The provocation of unconscious complexes becomes linked to unconscious archetypal images, making the process successful for only a relative minority of human beings. However, at this time there is an increase of the will to take conscious power to aid in the collective process that the macrocosmic entity of humanity, planet Earth, is going through.

In any case, it is as if the process of all human beings went through great stages, similar to the four basic combination possibilities of the Yin and Yang, or that of the four basic amino acids. More obvious even is the link with the generic cycle of the planets and the moon: from conjunction to first quarter, opposition and last quarter.

The first quarter (or stage) pertains to instinct, to instinctive growth where intuition makes all the decisions.

The second stage (after the first quarter) is the emotional one, putting feelings inside or outside, depending on the level of awareness and responsibility.

The third stage, after opposition or full moon—in general after the opposition of Uranus to natal Uranus (40 years)—is reflection, thinking upon the results one sees and knowing the reason for things.

Finally, the fourth stage is either giving up because of dissatisfaction or a lack of personal fulfillment, or feeling satisfaction and personal achievement. The triumph over the shadow should always be considered with humility and compassion toward others and oneself, in case one has not been able to go through the individuation process.

Individuation means "becoming oneself," an individuality with maximum singularity, meaning that one can achieve fulfillment and express one's unique potential without selfishness and individualism.

The goal of the individuation process is to bare the self of false personal concepts, to let go of all that is not true of the person but has been acquired through family or society, and also to disentangle from the suggestive power of primeval images.

Many things that we consider insignificant are part of the individuation process: forgetting something, bad moods, misunderstood reactions, repressions, fears, mistrust, etc. These become visible in dreams—if we remember them—but are consistent symptoms of unconscious activity. We can say that unconscious processes are there in a compensatory relationship between the conscious mind and the ego; that is, they contain all the elements necessary for the self-regulation of the psyche. This explains the relationship between the world of the senses and the world of thought in the I-Ching.

On a personal scale, these are the motives not consciously recognized which appear in dreams or in the meaning of daily situations we don't usually pay attention to. They also appear in the conclusions we can't manage to draw, in the effects we have not permitted or in the self-critique we don't want to go through. The more conscious we become of ourselves through self-knowledge and the more we act in accordance with it, the more the layer of the personal unconscious superimposed on the collective unconscious will diminish. Thus emerges a consciousness no longer imprisoned by the world of the personal ego full of susceptibility and pettiness.

This enlarged consciousness no longer carries the load of egotistical personal desires, fears, hopes, and ambitions which must always be compensated or corrected by the opposite tendencies in the unconscious. It becomes a function of relationships to things of the world, leading the individual toward an absolute and uniting the individual to the world in general. So it evolves into the transcendental psyche, for by transcending the ego, we reach all that is beyond it. The ego, subject to all personal acts of consciousness, becomes the criterion for consciousness, often pertaining to the narrow principles and mentality promoting selfishness. Therefore, in order to transcend the ego, we must recognize its role in the world and its own individual contribution, transcending physical and mental barriers and developing the skill of seeing beyond matter. Such a strong link with the unconscious psyche allows us to manifest paranormal phenomena and ESP without losing our individual essence and losing ourselves. It is a permanent openness both to our own selves and to others, giving of ourselves with no fear, and trusting ourselves completely. This transcendental vision recognizes the androgynous in all and is capable of expressing the masculine-feminine qualities inherent in all human beings.

In order to examine this psychological phenomenon in more detail, I want to discuss the dualistic concept of the psyche. In the first place, the psyche is divided into two parts—feminine and masculine—which Jung calls "anima" and "animus." Man expresses his masculine side, animus, while repressing in his unconscious his archetypal feminine side, the anima. On the other hand, in a woman, the feminine qualities of the anima are easily expressed, and she represses her masculine archetype, the animus, in the unconscious.

In astrological terms, this other unconscious side is represented in the qualities of the sign opposed to the Sun. That's why couples who have the Sun in opposition (for example, a Leo and an Aquarian) have a lot to learn from each other by mutual compensation and enrichment.

Just like this division we have contemplated, which usually tends to dualistic distortion, we see two brain hemispheres: the right being intuitive and synthetic, and the left, rational and lineal. Each one of these parts tends to subdivide again, so we have in the psyche two forms of feminine expression and two masculine ones. Thus it becomes that fourfold relationship we have also seen in all relations between the Yin and the Yang and in the methods presented here.

Afterward, when we subdivide them again, they become eight transformation stages in the whole process of individuation, represented, as we said, by the eight trigrams of the I-Ching.

Going back to this fourfold relationship, as the four stages of the generic evolution cycle, there always arises a fifth one. That fifth one in the generic cycle is the central crossing, or the attitude of being constantly centered, compensating and utilizing all the positive things from the previous stages, letting pairs cross and living a life of evolution. Likewise, the perfect combination of the four elements—Water-Earth and Fire-Air—leads to life in the Ether element, or as we would call it now, the Plasma or Wood in the Chinese culture.

When we study this subdivision in the human psyche, the anima and the animus, and looking at that fifth element appearing in the center, we identify it with what Jung calls "the shadow," what appears when a person has not yet wholly expressed conscious and unconscious capacities. In the transpersonal Self that has achieved the expression of its individuality, being totally "him- or herself," that fifth element also transcends all personal and physical limits. The shadow or Self is that invisible player who rules our existence or individuality from the unconscious.

Returning to the anima and animus and dividing each into two parts, we have the four possibilities of Yin and Yang, as well as the four basic amino acids of the DNA. In the I-Ching they appear as ▰▰ the great Yin, the small Yin ▰▬, the great Yang ▬▬ and the small Yang ▬▰.

The greater the capacity one has to express one of the two sides, the more one represses the other. The individuation process tries to consciously compensate and balance both, integrating their expressive capacities. This means that if a woman has a great conscious feminine intuitive capacity, when she integrates fully the unconscious masculine side of her psyche, she will have the same intellectual capacity in her masculine conscious expression. Likewise, if a man expresses his masculine aggressiveness and independence, he represses his equal feminine dependency and capacity to surrender. So, the capacities on one side equal those of the other, and the distortions strive at repressing or suppressing the other side, maintaining them in the unconscious until they become personified in the qualities of the shadow. They may also be personified in a specific person that provokes us and who is always of our same sex. This is called "projection."

Usually a man has both sides of his animus integrated and is capable of expressing them consciously at the expense of totally repressing the two sides of the anima. This refers also to the woman, but the other way around. However, nowadays it's not easy to find the full archetype of man or woman, since humankind has evolved toward the androgynous through the ample sexual experimentation of these last generations and has therefore already integrated one quality of the animus and one of the anima. Nevertheless, the other two are still repressed and projected unto the shadow.

Let us now look at the two qualities of the anima and those of the animus.

The anima, or feminine soul of the human being, is made up, on one side, of feminine receptivity that follows the other and surrenders completely to him; it accepts dependency and lets herself be carried away, molded and penetrated. When this quality is not integrated, it becomes seduction, vindictiveness, manipulation, infantile dependency and wild passions. On the other side is the maternal, protecting quality that gives all for nothing, that senses where abundance lies; when repressed and misintegrated, it becomes possessiveness, dominant protection, attachment, resentment, and selfishness.

The animus, or masculine soul of the human being, is made up of daring, courage, decision, and self-confidence, which in the negative aspect becomes aggressiveness, violence, selfishness, and hate. The other side is the intellectual one that wants to understand everything, act logically and find common solutions. When repressed and misintegrated, it turns into intellectual manipulation, coldness, skepticism, mistrust, cruelty, and egocentricity.

Whenever one of these sides is out of balance, suffering occurs and the compensatory polarity from Heaven is prevented from acting.

We search in our partner for the qualities we have to develop in ourselves and although, in this case, we belong to a generation that has already in some way integrated part of the other side, be it masculine or feminine (it can also happen within a couple of the same sex). However, relationships with the same sex are more difficult, not only because of social rejection, but because the shadow turns out to be always of the same sex. Thus the same person can go from being the compensatory lover to being the provoking shadow, without that compensatory sexual polarity with which one learns to integrate those repressed or unknown qualities within the personality as a whole. This calms down some of the irrational emotional expression in heterosexual partners.

The shadow always manages to disclose the irrational or negative side of all we are unable to integrate into our transcendent personality. The shadow is made up of the contents of the personal unconscious, which are mostly negative, but can also be repressed positive qualities.

The shadow is a moral problem that defies the ego-personality, and we all have to make a huge moral effort to be aware of our shadow, since this means acknowledging the dark aspects of our inner monster, which we often reject, but which are as real as the personality we identify with. This recognition is an essential condition for any kind of self-knowledge. We all generally resist it since it involves a lot of pain, effort, and time.

The shadow is made up of emotional inferiorities and has its own autonomy. Because we repress the emotional characteristics we rejected in our parents, they become stronger, to the point of possessing and obsessing us. In the same way as earthquakes, where the continuous movement of the Earth's crust builds up at a certain point until it splits the Earth causing the earthquake, so it is with the shadow. It belongs to the dark Yin part of the human psyche and refers to weaknesses and to the degree of inferiority and passiveness, being of a primitive, uncontrolled nature.

With vision, courage, and willpower, it is possible to incorporate these qualities into the personality, turning them into fortitude and activity. Some facets of the shadow maintain an obstinate resistance, moral control, and are almost impossible to assimilate. These resistances are generally experienced as unacknowledged projections of ourselves onto the external world. Being able to acknowledge it in ourselves, instead of seeing it in others, is an enormous and inordinate moral success.

Some aspects of the shadow can be recognized easily in ourselves, while others are veiled to us, though we identify them easily in other people. No matter how obvious it is for an outsider, there is little hope that the individual will acknowledge it in himself. It is very hard and requires a revelation of conscience to realize that the shadow is a projection of oneself.

If people have the inclination to recognize their projections, they are free to draw upon another situation that characterizes their power. In projecting that quality outward, they lose the power they grant, and become something dark and negative that we are afraid of. It is the unconscious that makes the projections, and that's why it's hard to recognize that it comes from ourselves. The effect of projections is to isolate us from our environment and turn our relationship to it into an illusion.

Projections change the world into a replica of our "unknown face." It is like an artistic condition in which we dream an impossible world, with an enormous sense of incompletion. Moreover, it becomes a vicious circle that intensifies more and more the isolation and lack of recognition of why we have attracted certain things to our life.

The ego and the shadow, although different, are inevitably joined, in the same way that thought and feeling are related to each other.

The shadow usually contains values that are necessary for consciousness, but which exist in a way that make it difficult to integrate them into life. For most people, the dark, negative part of the personality remains unconscious. Enlightened people, on the contrary, must realize that the shadow exists and acquire and extract power from it. They reach an agreement with their destructive potential; they vanquish the dragon, the inner monster. Before the ego can triumph, they must tame and assimilate the shadow. Just as the ego has also destructive and unfavorable attitudes, so the shadow has good qualities, instincts, and creative impulses.

The shadow represents all that we fear, what we are; it is painful to admit and therefore we repress it. We get involved in others' lives without realizing how much everything that happens affects us and relates to us and to our unconscious, giving a new sense to everything in order to learn from it. Our unconscious constantly reinforces that situation and maintains it. So it is with the deep characteristics of karmic patterns, while unconsciously we blame the world for all incapacities and mishaps. Little by little, an armor is formed around us so hard that it is impossible to dissolve, and it belongs to the negative side of the psyche.

The shadow is always of the same sex, and during the period of greater activity in the individuation process, it is projected on one or several persons that provoke us irrationally, either expressed openly or only by thought.

Usually, when our partner feels attracted to and becomes intimate with someone else, it is more dangerous than our freewheeling generation can imagine, for that person will represent exteriorly those qualities of the shadow we repress, and that our partner unconsciously looks for or is attracted to. That's why many people nowadays experience their individuation process with a much greater intensity simply because of sexual freedom. All that we thought we could put up with becomes unbearable and irrational; we even do, say, and think things we don't recognize in ourselves. Often it is only projected on the other, not being aware that the difficulty stems from living out freedom in love and we only see it as someone else's fault. The other person represents everything we despise and punish morally.

This happens in the fourth stage of the individuation process, and undoubt-edly after the first return of Saturn, from age 30 on.

When the psyche matures it begins to lose the distinction between mascu-line and feminine, active and passive, and it is then that we can encounter the pro-jections of the shadow upon the opposite sex, becoming part of the qualities of the negative animus and anima, making it more difficult to integrate and assimilate the qualities of the shadow. Being unable to acknowledge that those negative traits are our own, it is even harder to acknowledge the psychological projection we make upon another. When we become aware of it, consciousness grows enor-mously.

The shadow deciphers the personal as well as the collective unconscious. It represents the other side of the ego which has been active while we are in the process of developing individually. The shadow, in any case, is easier to recognize because it belongs to the personal unconscious, while the archetypal depths of the anima-animus are farther from awareness, for the simple reason of making a clear distinction of our sex and being unable to see the androgyny of the universe. However, in many cases, the shadow also belongs to the archetypal collective unconscious, either genetically familiar or social and cultural, becoming a task of unsuspected depth.

At times, with good criteria, with a capacity for looking at ourselves for self-evaluation, we can see the effects of the shadow if they refer to qualities of the per-sonal unconscious. However, being as it is an archetype of the collective uncon-scious, it seems to be out of our reach to acknowledge the evil in our own nature, and it is a devastating experience to look at our own evil face in the mirror. That is the reason why this type of deep individuation can only be achieved by a few individuals, brave warriors with a special talent or skill.

The anima and animus begin to be deciphered through the relationship of a son with his mother or of a daughter with her father. Here we can see the more obvious aspects related to the personal unconscious, while many of these qualities can be found in archetypes of the collective unconscious. They can also be recog-nized by certain aspects of the social and cultural mentality that we belong to, which provokes the conflicts in man-woman relationships, and the difficulty in integrating the rational masculine and the intuitive feminine, as well as in developing both brain hemispheres and a good communication between them. As it is, the process of the human being has already reached psychological maturity and has developed parts of both feminine and masculine qualities. Therefore it can be unveiled and integrated much more easily if we strive for a total development of consciousness through self-knowledge.

However, because we are living the end of history, and the civilization created by the masculine ideal, the growth and transformation of the material that lets itself be molded by the mental, this also makes the task of recognizing our shadow more difficult, since many people have completely lost contact with their inner selves where their greatest personal wealth lies. Another impediment stems from the fact that people think they are incapable of solving their problems by themselves.

At the present time, while we have achieved a psychological development in the integration of sexes, we have a deficiency of maturity due to a lack of personal power and a dependency on social and cultural movements.

Also, undoubtedly, now that we are returning to the feminine side of humanity, to intuition, synthesis, abundance, and globality, the struggle between the masculine and the feminine in every human being, regardless of their sex, is becoming more obvious, violent, and crude. Humanity felt compelled to achieve and change nature, to dominate and conquer it—an essentially masculine quality—while the feminine is passive, letting things be. Material and technological development were a result of going from a matriarcate to a patriarcate. Now we find ourselves again at the painful transition point of having to return to the feminine, to caring for the Earth, to trusting and nurturing the ecosystem that has been severely and dangerously deteriorated by the nerve cells of the planet: the human beings.

The archetype of the animus makes us cling to doing things as we used to, selfishly, and to close our eyes to the consequences of such development, without compensating it with the qualities of the anima that doesn't look for immediate output, but for the effect on the whole, beyond personal life, caring and preparing the way for future generations.

Just as man is compensated by an element of femininity represented basically in the qualities of the sign opposed to the Sun, woman is also compensated by masculine elements that belong to the unconscious and to the qualities of the sign opposed to the Sun in the astrological chart.

Often, contradictions that seem irreconcilable become obvious in our consciousness and lead to huge misinterpretations within ourselves or are projected on other people. This happens when we are opinionated, or because we are eager to believe certain things to be true when we don't know the other person. That's why the "other side" is so tremendously irritating and incompatible. We may make ourselves victims of the unconscious side and we use its negative traits— the anima in the case of a man and the animus in the case of a woman.

When animus and anima meet, animus grabs his sword of power and logic, while anima expels her poison of illusion and seduction. This is not necessarily negative, for both can fall in love and there is the desire to conquer and possess the other for the sake of completion. In both cases, in animus-anima relationships we find a lot of emotional antagonism, full of resentment and misunderstood sentimentality on the part of the man, and of faulty reasoning and opinionation on the part of woman. It is interesting to see the reflection of one on the other, and to know that couples merge where the projection of the anima or animus fits in with what is unconscious in either one. Thus, in this unconscious way, we attract our own karma and the patterns we might want to avoid or get rid of. We cannot rid ourselves of the patterns until we have an understanding or awareness of how these patterns have actually enriched our inner life.

The effect of the animus and the anima on the ego is the same in principle and is very hard to eliminate by resorting to rigor and morals. The cause and the effect is projected outward on to the person or persons who make up the characteristics of the archetype. Consciousness feels inexplicably fascinated and trapped by these aspects, producing in the ego a sense of moral defeat, which increases the vicious circle, and produces a feeling of incapacity and inferiority. In fact, in the individuation process, it is common for men to have irrational mood changes while women have "too" rational opinions.

It is harder to become aware of the anima-animus projections than to recognize the dark aspect of oneself—the shadow. It can be done, however, by overcoming certain morals or immoralities, or what has been perceived as moral or immoral. In many cases, people doubt whether it was really worthwhile to probe into the unconscious, for everything seems to get so complicated. People sometimes feel betrayed and they lose self-confidence in the process of probing the depths of their unique and personal beings.

Not all aspects of the anima-animus are projected and reflected on other people. They can reveal themselves spontaneously through active imagination and artistic creation, which helps tap feelings and thoughts we may not imagine we have.

The anima can be defined as an image or an archetype, or as the result of all the experiences of a man with a woman. Therefore it is projected and personified in other women. Likewise, the animus is represented in the relationships with men that a woman has experienced.

The animus and the anima have positive archetypes which are identified with the image of the father or the mother, with spirit, philosophical ideas or their resulting activity. The animus is a mediator between the conscious and the unconscious, reasoning and assimilating unconscious stimuli. It corresponds more to the left, logical brain hemisphere that Western civilization has promoted and accentuated to the detriment of the right, intuitive and feminine hemisphere. The East, however, has accentuated this left side of the brain, more related to the anima of integration, synthesis, emotional experience, and sense of spiritual belonging. Likewise, men relate to the animus, developing it to such an extent in our Western society that they have forsaken their feminine aspects, or distorted them in such a way, that they project an unconscious anima onto women. This enormously complicates their relationship with women in all aspects, especially sexual relationships. However, in our culture, women have been driven to increase logic and the search for the animus archetype, especially nowadays, in order to incorporate and participate in professional and independent life. Nevertheless, the feminine integrating side is still more developed.

In the East, due to its more holistic and passive tendencies, men have maintained contact with the unconscious anima while women have repressed further their masculine, material logic animus, remaining still very dominated by men. Women have, moreover, developed their feminine, holistic, unifying capacity even more, through contact with nature and survival. It will be interesting to observe the change and integration of the animus logic in modern Oriental women and the development of their society in view of the greater contact people have with the feminine side of nature.

In mythological archetypes, Eros represents the anima and deals with mingling and associating. Logos represents the animus that knows how to differentiate knowledge, discrimination and detached attitude.

Anima gives men the realization of relating through feelings and letting go, while animus gives women the capacity of reflection, deliberation, self-knowledge and self-control.

The effect animus and anima have on the ego is, in principle, the same, and is extremely hard to eliminate since, on the one hand, it is very intense and full of rights and principles, and on the other, because the cause of the effect is projected outward toward other people, it seems to lie in objective situations or things. Both characteristics can be processed backward to the peculiarities of the archetype by analyzing the mixture of experiences and genetic behavior patterns of the ancestors of both parents. This often explains the peculiarities of various types of humor or the existence of irrational opinions. We are referring to the specific aspects of the psyche of each individual that are extremely difficult to influence due to the suggestive effect emanating from the archetype, and because fascinated consciousness feels trapped even against its will. Consciousness is blocked even in trying to be conscious, for it sometimes seems to be hypnotized into repeating the same patterns and echoes of emotions and feelings.

Many women complain that their husbands don't communicate with them. This is one of the more common problems arising from the difference between animus and anima. Women are not concerned about not being reasonable when they speak, and they need to communicate their emotional problems, as it is the only way of making the problems conscious so they can solve them. That is the principle on which psychology is based; no matter how slow and burdensome the treatment may be, when we consciously choose to talk about all that is bothering and causing pain, even if we do not understand why, it becomes clarified in the process of talking about it.

Men do not like to talk about emotions and rationalize them, saying that it's not good to dig up the past. However, in their thoughts they are digging it up constantly and unconsciously. They also dislike not making sense when talking about emotional matters, although logical reasoning plays no role here. In fact, that is what men reproach women about: all the senseless opinions their animus tries to communicate. Also, there is an even more dangerous factor: when talking about it with close people, men may react irrationally, lose control and even feel ridiculous, which would make the problem even worse. But everything must get worse before it gets better, before we can consciously recognize traumatic motivation that causes blockage in order to transform it, thus enriching personality.

It is always difficult to talk about certain things with partners, because the partner is part of the problem and the partner's reaction causes a counterreaction and so on. That's why we prefer to talk to a third person, one who has a detached attitude toward the issue. Even friends get blindly involved and identify with the problem, which is more hindrance than help. Although hard and sometimes dangerous, the only way women can contact the animus and men the anima is precisely by communicating through all means available, especially speech. Talking makes unconscious thoughts conscious and makes the unconscious deal with things it tries to bury or forget, which would only aggravate our shadow and increase the load we carry of unfinished business and relationships. Sooner or later, this load reaches its limit and starts to explode and, to make room for more, we start to spread its contents, projecting these "contents" on others at the slightest behavior that reminds us of the unfinished business we ourselves carry around.

All this must be discussed with our partners, but we must also be able to detect when it gets too dangerous and we can lose control, although sometimes we must lose what we claim to have but lack, in order to realize the error of matter and how dense permanent things seem when they are not. Obviously, intense, emotional love relationships increase psychological development, the individuation process, and the process of maturing psychologically and emotionally.

Another conflictive relationship caused by projections of the negative shadow animus or anima is with in-laws, mother and father. When one person becomes emotionally committed to another, two types of psychological marriages occur. For example, when a woman finally finds someone who fits her best, the partner is actually personifying her positive and negative animus; both seem to fit into the psychological emotional pattern. Sometimes this loved one represents more the positive animus than the negative one, but it is with that person that the woman can elaborate better the psychological residues she may project on her parents.

A person unites with another consciously, but unconsciously, this person also unites with all the unfinished relationships that the person has; so somehow, she or he is also marrying the in-laws, be they far or near, dead or alive.

At the same time the marriage ceremony is taking place, either in the traditional way (or by a verbal or emotional commitment to live together), other encounters take place at a psychic level that may be expressed in dreams: the woman's father encounters the spouse and grants him the power to continue the projection of his daughter's negative animus; or the man's mother encounters the bride in dreams and grants her the power to continue the projection of her son's negative anima. That's why parents often feel great psychological relief when their children fall in love and begin serious relationships. Moreover, the person who marries their son or daughter usually represents the shadow of the other. That accounts for unconscious complications or irrational reactions on the part of both mother and father in-law and son and daughter in-law, depending on their age or stage of their individuation process.

These archetypal projections are all inevitable and, moreover, necessary for the psychological maturing process. If a person avoids having relationships or commitments, the process will be hindered, resulting in emotional immaturity.

At times, although a relationship fits well into the psychological pattern, it must break up in order to be resolved or repeated. This happens when one of the partners represents more the negative animus/anima of the other, and considers the other as embodying the positive animus or anima. This pattern applies even when it seems one has chosen the exact opposite to father or mother, but while one is elaborating negative patterns, the other believes to have found the positive one. Although it is not advisable to break up or divorce—because what we don't solve with one person we repeat even more strongly with the next—these cases reach a point where one partner blocks the other partner's growth process. The partner experiencing the negative projection is the most conscious of the process and wants to break it, while the other is taking advantage of his luck and refuses to face his negative side. This leads to a blow up, or a dangerous explosion caused by the error in psychological perceptions.

Since we have four psychological divisions within our being but are only one sex, in order to express ourselves adequately, we must identify with only one of these aspects of the psyche, leaving the other three buried in our unconscious. The two aspects of the opposite represent the anima or animus, the positive and the negative; the anima in the case of the male and the animus in the case of the female. The third element is of the same sex as the person and pertains to the elements we refuse to develop, turning into what we call the shadow. These three aspects of ourselves, when openly expressed—though not consciously realized—are experienced through projection onto other people in our surroundings. These aspects form the totality of our psyche, although it gets harder and harder for us to understand how various aspects of ourselves and our projections spring from our own inner world. The experiences that shape our lives originate in the unconscious personal psyche.

All events and people we attract to our lives have to do with ourselves and have been created by our unconscious. Later, we attract and add our own definitions of experiences and personal loads, but we often hide behind them to avoid acknowledging how they have all sprouted from within ourselves.

When we want to learn to recognize the shadow, we gain an advantage when we admit we are not completely perfect and good. When I use the term shadow, I am also referring to inferiority feelings and complexes.

However, when we want to learn about the anima and animus, it is more complicated because we are not taught much about the archetype. We have a tendency to recognize the behaviors belonging to our own sex, and accept more easily the imbalances of the opposite sex. We are content to verify ourselves through what we see in the outside world, instead of recognizing that we are capable of projection.

A person's collective unconscious can be accepted, understood and processed through understanding the family heritage, as well as the cultural and educational heritage, and the social mentality of the time. The autonomy of the collective unconscious also expresses itself in the form of the animus and anima, which can only be integrated into personality through self-knowledge. The individual can personify those contents that can be integrated by consciousness when the content ceases to be projected outward, greatly enriching the ego and personality, concentrating on expressing the unique individuality and creativity.

Both anima and animus filter the contents of the collective unconscious through the conscious mind. When tension arises, the functions of the animus and anima—which were previously not harmful—confront the conscious mind and represent bothersome attributes.

The contents of the animus-anima can be integrated, but they themselves cannot be integrated into personality, being as they are archetypes. As such, they are the basic foundation of psychic structure, exceeding the limits of consciousness and never becoming the direct object of knowledge. Although the effects of the animus-anima can be recognized consciously, they are, in themselves, factors that transcend consciousness of perception and will. They remain autonomous even though their contents might be integrated, therefore they must be tolerated and need to get along with each other. This is extremely important from the therapeutic point of view. As we know it, the unconscious can never be eliminated; either known or finished, it is as unlimited as are the stars in our galaxy. We must pay continuous attention to the symptoms of the contents of the unconscious and to their processes, because the conscious mind is always in danger of becoming unilateral, repeating patterns, getting blocked and blinded. Contact with one's unconscious world, its observation and the assimilation of the contents of the animus-anima archetype, maintains multidimensionality, and a complementary function that helps us avoid the dangers of neurosis.

The only danger is in what seems the ideal circumstances, where life is still simple and unconscious enough to let itself be lead by instinct, without doubts or regrets. This kind of compensation is successful in artistic expression, where feminine imagination merges with productive masculine accomplishment. The more "civilized" human beings are, the more unconscious they may be, for they are less able to follow their instincts. Living conditions and the influence of the environment may be so strong that people become attached to their opinions, beliefs, theories, and collective tendencies. As intensely as men are rational, they are also intuitive through the anima, if they allow themselves to assimilate its contents. Likewise, the more intuitive women are, the more rational and structured the animus, when its contents are assimilated.

The fleeting images and constant ghostly sensations the archetypes present us are at times premonitory, occasionally leading to tragic results, especially in love relationships. They are images belonging to the deep unconscious and to other ages of human knowledge, picked up through the power of resonance. The unconscious shows itself as a secret reflection through which consciousness can recognize itself and join its forces in maturing and entering the higher stages of the individuation process. This stage is only attained by fulfilled people who are happy with themselves, upon reaching a rather mature age.

The archetypes, in fact, are the cause, they are father and mother of the disastrous knots of destiny and karma. When we illuminate the dark depths of the psyche and explore the strange and tortuous paths of human destiny we discover a minimal part of this destiny and karma.

I must emphasize integration of the shadow, or the awareness of the personal unconscious, that marks the first stage of the analytical process, without which the recognition of the anima-animus would be impossible. The shadow becomes visible through the relationship with another person of the same sex, while the anima-animus is usually carried out with a person of the opposite sex, although this is now changing due to the new forms of homosexual relationships. By "psychological relationship" I mean a conscious relationship between two people, because unconscious ones cannot be included under that heading.

In children, consciousness emerges from the depths of the unconscious psychic life, at first in the form of separate islands that gradually join to form a continent, a continuous mass of consciousness in progressive state of growth. When, and not before, the growth of consciousness continues, psychological relationships can arise with another person. The first thing we are aware of is the ego, for we must first tell ourselves apart from the others before we can relate without losing ourselves or thinking that we are the other.

When we do not know ourselves, relationships become more and more complicated, especially after age 30, when the individuation process reaches its peak. Young people have only an incomplete understanding of themselves. The greater the unconscious areas, the less freedom we actually have when choosing our partners. Relationships will happen compulsively and we feel it acutely when in love.

Unconscious motivation is influenced by the parents and through determinant factors in the father-daughter or mother-son relationship. This unconscious link influences choosing one partner or another; and even karmic patterns relate to unconscious patterns and influences belonging to the other person and his or her heritage.

Children, in fact, are often unconsciously driven in a direction intended to compensate the mishaps in their parents' life. That's why exceedingly moralistic parents sometimes have amoral children, or why irresponsible parents sometimes have highly ambitious children. But even if the children have managed to compensate for these behaviors, when they grow up they realize that they haven't been able to correct many of the parents' faults that remained unconscious. They find themselves repeating many of the parents' karmic patterns. The worst results come from parents who have remained unconscious and don't even show their faults to their children. The children don't know where the patterns come from.

When the time comes to choose a partner, if natural instincts have been mitigated or buried, young adults may believe that they are out of their influence, but sooner or later they will show up again, interfering with a satisfying relationship with the other person. When only instinct is involved in the choice, individual happiness is destined to suffer.

If a relationship is to be based on preservation of the species, on sex or procreation, then instinct is the best way, but since the basis of that choice is unconscious, only an impersonal, non-possessive alliance is achieved. This works perfectly in more primitive societies, with no rules for marriage.

The forms that lead to conscious choice appear after the first return of Saturn (about age 29), making it more difficult to find someone to our liking. When the union takes place before age 30, most people do not know themselves, nor their desires, drives, egoism, their desire to conquer, or the difficulties of the outer world that are at their peak. That explains why the couples formed before that age find it hard to survive in a modern world that allows divorce. In order for a relationship to continue enriching one another, both must work very hard at correcting conscious patterns and at being aware of the obstacles arising from lack of integration of unconscious faults and virtues. In a critical atmosphere, weaknesses and complexes can be put into the open so that both partners can recognize them.

In many relationships, only pale reflections of oneself are seen, and we blame the other person, instead of taking responsibility for unconscious aspects or failings, and integrating them. Adaptation and daily life may become difficult and complicated for many aspects of life cannot be shared unless we accept the reflection of ourselves that we have chosen in the other person.

When one achieves true union with an authentic partner, either based on love or on necessity, one will be prepared to integrate and face the deepest parts of one's unconscious. The beginning of a wholesome relationship with another person, with all the effort it entails, allows one to get ready for a more authentic relationship with oneself, and therefore, enriches one's life with more impersonal relationships.

We each have the image of the man or woman within, and this image represents the archetype of the anima-animus. We cannot integrate this image without an honest self-examination of all that we repress and thus project on another person. The image is unconscious and so we project it on the other person. This is one of the reasons for personal attraction: we want to attract into ourselves what is reflected on the other person.

No matter how a relationship is, whether it is conventional or unconventional, everyone goes through most of the stages of the individuation process through one or several relationships. What is not solved with one partner is repeated or complicated with the next. We can even look at astrological patterns to see how the natal charts coincide and discover that all the unsolved unconscious reflections and projections placed on our previous partner will appear again in the astral code of the next partner we choose.

The strife within our true self is the cause of what we call suffering; however, when we achieve union with another person, it helps us attain union within ourselves.

Once this union has been attained and we assimilate the depths of our being, we achieve that unique individual being and that union within the psyche, within the spirit, where suffering due to material distortion or to the sense of void and incompletion no longer exists.

Through a real relationship with yourself, a sense of peace starts to appear and a sense of self-belonging in which everything also belongs to you. This is the return to a non-dualistic mystic state. As in all psychic phenomena, you don't understand anything psychologically until you have experienced it previously in yourself.

The image of God coincides with the unconscious as that special archetypal content of our own image of God, which has little to do, in most cases, with the images presented by religion. Instead it arises spontaneously from the depths of our psychic nature. Although archetypes are autonomous entities and factors, they can only be reached through the intervention of transcendental dynamics, leading to the deepest psychological transformations which cannot occur without the introspection of observation of consciousness.

Whether this happens induced by the archetype or initiated by consciousness is impossible to know, but the best is to let the archetype have a certain measure of independence and let consciousness have a certain degree of creative freedom so that the reciprocal action of both can take place. In it we find our individual creative strength through our own image of God. Otherwise, the inner archetype could split in two: a relationship inspired by God and a sinful human being induced by the devil, which would produce even more complications in integrating the archetypes psychologically. This happens often in minds strongly influenced by religious dogma which, although consciously rejected by the person, keeps on acting in the collective unconscious, creating strong moral conflicts in the process of individuation.

So it is necessary to have an idea of our religious archetypes and some kind of religious education, without fanatic and strict morals that create internal strife and hide the archetype of our own image of God. Union, then, is with the inner light, with the subtle body and the union of the astral and mental bodies, that we could call Christ-consciousness. It is the illumination of the crystal at the top center of the skull, and the development of the diamond body, or the elixir of the Golden Flower, mentioned in ancient Taoist texts. However, it is in the Tibetan Buddhist tradition that we find a highly valid explanation:

> What we call a Demon is very, very huge, and colored all black. Whoever sees one is truly terrified and trembles from head to foot— but Demons don't really exist!
>
> The truth of the matter is this: Anything whatsoever that obstructs the attainment of liberation is a Demon. Even loving and affectionate relatives can become Demons if they hinder your practice. But the greatest Demon of all is belief in a self as an independent and lasting principle. If you don't destroy this clinging to a self, Demons will just keep lifting you up and letting you down.[1]

Liberation is being oneself, a unique being integrated in the whole, with a unique wisdom to interrelate with one's anima and to discriminate with one's animus. One feels, then, the integrated center of the All, with an individual integrity that flows, expressing the All through itself every moment of its life.

If the unconscious can be acknowledged as a codetermined quantity and a cooperative quality with the conscious, we live in such a way that both the conscious and the unconscious coexist inside a person with no conflict, and our instinctive demands are acknowledged and integrated in our mind, then the center of our personality changes into the Self, which is the true center. It is no longer in the ego—which is merely the center of personality—and starts to relate to consciousness, which lies at the hypothetical point between the conscious and the subconscious: "the Self."

The individual Self is a mystical experience with the whole world and all surrounding circumstances; it is detached from bodily suffering and the emotional impacts of life. It is an indestructible attitude which, psychologically and symbolically, refers to an attitude not attained through an intensely emotional commitment. Thus, one experiences the tremor and fright of being detached from the world, and at the same time, the enriching intensity of living sensations with the freshness and flowing quality of a newborn. Every human being has an opportunity to attain this state at middle age, as a natural and beautiful preparation for death and birth into another dimension of consciousness.

---

1. Ma-Chig-La, a 12th-century yogini, quoted in Clifford, *Tibetan Buddhist Medicine and Psychiatry: The Diamond Healing* (York Beach, ME: Samuel Weiser, 1984), p. 149.

Both the philosophy and practice of Taoist meditation are based on the goal of death and preparing for it as a preparation for a spiritual existence, giving birth to the psychological spiritual body that guarantees the continuity of consciousness.

This has been the common search of all cultures and religions, for most religions are more similar in practice than we may think. The basic tenet of Western mystical experience is that Jesus Christ is considered a redeemer and hero who helps us accept suffering so we can find our own personal form of redemption. In the East, it is the Golden Flower that blooms at the violet entrance of the Jade city; it is the "Jewel" as central theme for each individual, who is believed to have no beginning, no end, no past and no future, in contrast to the Western divine-human incarnation. Eastern philosophy considers that redemption depends on the work and effort the individual undertakes, not in following the divine example of one man who embodied the most profound meanings of life. So, in imitating Western divinity, we may forget to realize our own deep meaning: self-realization. It is easier to renounce our own meaning on behalf of the conscious image of the crucifixion, but we transcend suffering with pathos instead of with joy and revelation.

That's why the forms and images of the East offer the West a freedom we can only accept and assimilate with difficulty for we only know of redemption through suffering. Although the goal is the same, it breaks the illusion of the conscious belief of the "I live" to arrive at the conscious experience of "He lives in me," as the apostle Paul said: "Not I, but Christ lives in me." So it becomes a duty to give full expression and reality to the deepest conviction of the Christ within oneself, and this is the beginning of a self-acceptance that allows us to accept other people and circumstances as they are.

To expose morality is just one step beyond in the same direction, where humans confess to themselves—as would correspond to Oriental "illumination"— that God is within each one, that He is real, as a reality containing all possibilities, and He is therefore alive!

"When God or the Tao is termed an impulse of the soul, or a state of the soul, something has been said about the knowable only, but nothing about the unknowable, about which nothing can be determined."[2] Therefore we are always based on physically defined knowledge, since metaphysically knowledge is unlimited.

Humanity's individuation process unites both external and internal processes, joining East and West through a deep search for individual creativity

---

2. Richard Wilhelm, trans., *The Secret of the Golden Flower: A Chinese Book of Life*, with foreword and commentary by C.G. Jung (New York: Harcourt, Brace & World, 1931), p. 135.

and spirit. Afterward, the fusion of spirit and science will come about, eliminating one of the main factors of humanity's present schizophrenia: the fact that scientific explanations about our universe no longer coincide with our religious beliefs.

Inside, there is a spiritual need that cannot be a product of the beliefs and contradictory experiences scientists offer as explanation. Today we begin to glimpse how this fusion can happen in the near future. This doesn't mean that the borders of metaphysics will be defined, but rather that it will give humans good clues about what awaits at the other side of death—and about unlimited metaphysical experiences.

C.G. Jung was very interested in spiritual life and in the union of the three most important disciplines—science, art, and spirit. He investigated the symbolism of artistic expression as a means of beginning to understand metaphysics and to develop unitive methods to help human beings find a deep metaphysical meaning for their existence. Through his studies of dreams and mandala drawings, we arrive today at body language and psychodance. He also considered personal experience as crucial and non-transferable. People cannot read their path in a book, nor their own method or way of realization, and no specific master or discipline contains the whole reality that can make individuals function. Examples only help people find their own reality.

Each one of us is an infinitesimal point in the Great Universe, and we each embody a specific array of psychological experiences. Living intensely will help science to become sufficiently flexible to probe individual minds, and to research them with clarity.

In order to achieve a fusion of science and spirit, we cannot interpret anything in a physical-material way, nor can we grab onto anything metaphysically; but we can do it psychologically. Therefore, we unwrap the metaphysical concepts to make them objects of psychology. Then we can obtain something intelligible and have the opportunity to have a revelation of the universe, liberating us from the terrible duality of our civilization. Since the material world has priority over the spiritual world, instead of working at securing an eternal life in another dimension, more lasting than material life, our priorities have us seeing the world upside down.

The process used to achieve unity between matter and spirit—or science and religion—without deviating from our own individuation process is an involvement with artistic activity and research, both solitary and shared with many other people. Our continuous enrichment comes from harmonizing our own well being in life with doing something useful and valid for others. So we can say that art achieves true union between science and spirit. Very few artists are aware of this psychological connection. Physics and psychology are a reality that mystical artists—who were also often scientists and inventors—have penetrated.

The mandala has been present in all religious traditions as a symbol of the universe, and it is also a symbol for physics. It is a process of identification, of centering, of unification and disintegration into the universe by the artist or individual who creates it. It has a dynamic quality implied in the creation process, which is also the process of attaining wholeness.

Franz Marc, a turn of the century painter said: "The new Art will give formal expression to our scientific conviction."[3] He knew that the element linking science and spirit was art. He knew the connection between quantum physics and modern abstract art. Aniela Jaffé has said:

> To put it in simple, non-scientific terms, nuclear physics has robbed the basic units of matter of their absolute concreteness. It has made matter mysterious. Paradoxically, mass and energy, wave and particle, have proved to be interchangeable. The laws of cause and effect have become valid only up to a certain point. It does not matter at all that these relativities, discontinuities, and paradoxes hold good only on the margins of our world—only for the infinitely small (the atom) and the infinitely great (the cosmos). They have caused a revolutionary change in the concept of reality, for a new, totally different, and irrational reality has dawned behind the reality of our "natural" world, which is ruled by the laws of classical physics.
>
> Corresponding relativities and paradoxes were discovered in the domain of the psyche. Here, too, another world dawned on the margin of the world of consciousness, governed by new and hitherto unknown laws that are strangely akin to the laws of nuclear physics. The parallelism between nuclear physics and the psychology of the collective unconscious was often a subject of discussion between Jung and Wolfgang Pauli, the Nobel prizewinner in physics. The space-time continuum of physics and the collective unconscious can be seen, so to speak, as the outer and inner aspects of one and the same reality behind appearances.[4]

The concepts Jung introduced are mere tools or hypothesis to help us explore the enormous reality that is disclosed by the discovery of the collective unconscious. The vision of our "selves" and of the world around us expands and

---

3. Quoted in C.G. Jung, *Man and his Symbols* (New York: Doubleday, 1964; London: Aldus Books, 1964), p. 261.

4. Aniela Jaffé in *Man and his Symbols*, p. 261.

introduces us to the knowledge of the next dimension, where we will live after death.

We can always question whether a mental phenomenon is conscious or unconscious, and whether what we perceive as "real" in ourselves and in the external world is perceived by conscious or unconscious means. The power of the forces of the unconscious world is constantly with us, asleep and awake. The lack of acknowledgment of its coexistence with us makes us rigid and unbalanced, and this disequilibrium can crystallize into illness.

All emotional and mental behavior patterns are common and inherited, either by family or race; they are symbolic fantasies and archetypes with which we are reexperimenting and developing planet Earth together.

Space voyages and the vision of planet Earth as a living being—Gaia—has allowed us to see such things as biology and genetics differently. The whole bio-psychological growth of planet Earth has happened much faster than it would have due to mere chance. This has happened through the law of synchronicity that explains how exceptional phenomena can happen rapidly when an archetype is activated, and synchronically, the simultaneous events take on a meaning, projecting a path of synchronicity through "significant coincidences." So, contacting an animus-anima archetype in the collective unconscious provokes a continuous creation process, where consciousness evolves at an accelerated rate of growth. In this growth, it makes sense for conscious and unconscious to be united at first, then separate—as in the present development of matter and spirit. They will finally let themselves enter into total synchronicity and union so as to take the great evolutionary quantum leap of the human being—also considered as the change in biopsychic frequency.

We are at the threshold of this union, after the enormous gap between the accelerated growth of matter at the expense of spirit, of science and religion, of the human being and of nature. Disharmony is at its peak, and we are the generation that will touch bottom and do a somersault, letting ourselves go, giving in to "simultaneity," to a boundless synchronicity, to "acts of creation at the precise time."

This phenomenon, this quantum leap, happens with species when there is a vital collective need. Then, a lot of information is revealed by extrasensory means, and very rapid changes and mutations in the physical, mental, and emotional structures can occur, in order to adapt to the new milieu.

There is also a close link between microphysics and psychology, since the basic concepts are archetypes from the Greek or Chinese philosophers—space, time, matter, energy, continuity, field, particle, etc. In the wave or the particle of the manifestation of light (photon), if one of the two sides is detected, the other must be lost. The observer must choose, or else there is always the chance of an

All the people we attract into our world are different aspects of ourselves: understanding our relationships, we understand ourselves.

uncontrollable influence coming from lab instruments or from research personnel. The same is true for any psychological research. Every moment and every individual is unique amid the complexity of surrounding influences, and, whenever necessary, the multiplicity of "significant coincidences" accelerates the evolution of a regeneration or degeneration process.

All is related to all in the huge complexity of psychological influences; we cannot be absolutely sure about anything but our own minds, if and when we have become centered on the experience of the moment, of the now, and recognize here and now, the path of synchronicity.

Quantum physics has reached the conclusion that we shall never know what something is in itself, since there is always the influence of the observer. Any participant in the reaction of any phenomenon (observer and observed) is the same thing, there is only participation.

The idea of the unconscious can be compared to the concept of "field" in physics. We can call it a magnetic field of particles that seem to have an order (or certain psychological contents), that seem to be structured in the subconscious. If something seems to be "significant" or "coincidental," we accept it consciously because it fits into the harmony of a preconscious constellation of the contents of the collective unconscious, contacting with the forces of an archetype of the animus (or the anima) that grants us paranormal powers to carry out its constructive or destructive mission. This depends almost completely on the recognition and attention granted the unconscious. If it has maintained contact with us, it is very likely that we have established contact with its creative, regenerating Source. But if we have repressed it, not exercising contact with the unconscious either through art, dreams or spiritual practices, the unconscious archetype can surprise us with its destructive and degenerating potential.

We can also say that our conscious imagery has a pattern, even before it has become conscious. When we become aware, just as when we discover something and it becomes human consciousness, not only does it change the effect on the observed (planet, atom...) but also the understanding and consciousness of the observer.

The parallel phenomena now occurring between microphysics and Jung's idea of synchronicity is the search for purpose through the connections, in nature or in the psyche, helping us escape the laws of determinism and karma.

Through the therapeutic sciences we begin to discover the psychophysical unity of all phenomena of life. Even what we call inorganic life, a still-life structure with no apparent life or consciousness, refers to karmic patterns, psychosomatic problems, or what might be called chronic pathologies.

When contacting a deep archetype in our psyche, synchronic events increase. That means that there is a significant arrangement between the inner psyche and external factors. A creative interrelationship comes about if people are adept in some way; the knowledge acquired by that existence springs up spontaneously and finds a way of expression that can be observed and analyzed to bring to consciousness what has occurred unconsciously.

Blake believes that "Opposition is true Friendship."

Like Milton in Blake's poem, the loving reader of Blake journeys into recognition of his selfhood, that error in perception which limits imaginative and spiritual growth. . . . One of the basic tasks of Blake's poem is to expose the false reality of the so-called "natural world" and its assertion that it is the only reality. This false reality is a result of the selfhood of each reader; it is that world we naturally perceive as "without," the world we externalize and desire to control and which in turn controls us. Consequently, Blakes's vision of the world is so dissonant with our usual understanding that we must "unlearn"; we must give up our preconceptions about the world and about ourselves within that world.

Some of us are surprised to learn that the world beyond the body is uncertain, yet one of the basic tenets of Einstein and scientific methods after him is the impossibility of separating the observer from his observations. That is to say, our perception of events beyond the body is the result of our views about the nature of reality. Blake thought that we become what we behold. For this reason, he sets out to transform the relationships between the perceiver and perceived by guiding his reader into a journey of spiritual discovery. . . . Modern psychologists have catalogued . . . the assumptions of orthodox Western psychology: . . . a person is his body and nothing more; each person is isolated from all others, locked in his nervous system; . . . death is the termination of human consciousness; a person perceives the physical world and obtains sensations from the internal operations of his body and nervous system; a person can trust his senses to inform him accurately about the nature of the physical world.

According to Blake, the individual living by such "truths" equates his identity with his physical body; he trusts his senses to inform him accurately about the objective world and is, thus, "shut in narrow, doleful form." Such people are isolated: "folded within themselves," they see only the "Vegetable Ratio" and deny the eternal perspectives of the spirit. Blake would say that because we have hardened our optic nerves into opaque bones, we perceive the world without as a "black pebble." This reciprocity of perception is a "dull round," it is death, the termination of what Blake would have called consciousness, the human and, therefore, eternal perception. Instead, Blake urges a person to see himself "like the diamond, which, tho' cloth'd / In rugged covering in the mine, is open all within, / And in his hallow'd center holds the heavens of bright eternity." This reciprocity of perception is imagination, the world of body and spirit, the world where "God is within and without."

—MILTON: A POEM BY WILLIAM BLAKE
Kay Parkhurst Easson and Roger R. Easson, eds.,
pages 138-139.

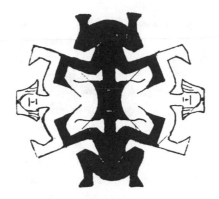

The Tension Between Life and Death

Entrance into the mysterious chamber of death is a solitary matter, and in this path of solitary understanding, the unity with all things is revealed. Even involuntarily, there is a deep feeling of self-belonging and intense vibration with ourselves and with-all-at-once. It is something only we ourselves can interpret and fully understand if we have the courage to strip our souls and see ourselves just as we are.

Therapeutically, it is known that the most regenerating bodily activities are totally involuntary—a yawn, a smile, laughter, weeping, sleep, etc. So it is also with the contact with the archetype and the assimilation of its information; the extasis and the heartbeat are all involuntary, but belong to the sensory field where the conscious contacts the nonconscious.

The individuation process is a particular and unique psychological development pattern for each person, by which we accomplish our "self," the Greek "diamond," the individual genius for the Romans, the "soul" for the Egyptians and the protecting spirit for primitive societies. For us it is identified with the inner center, "the crystal of the Self."

In dreams, our lives are changing patterns where our tendencies appear, then disappear, and return again. By observing this winding woven line during a certain period of time, we can see a hidden regulating tendency which, when activated, creates a process of psychic growth. This growth process cannot be provoked by conscious effort, or by willpower, but it is an involuntary process that grows with a specific form in a natural and involuntary way, like a tree.

Dreams are the process by which human beings experience their most inborn nature. But the individualization process is "real" only when individuals are conscious and connect intensely and vividly, through their attention, with their creative process.

The individuation process is much more than being on good terms with our inborn seed of plenitude and the outer factors of destiny. Its subjective experience entails a feeling of supernatural strength that is constantly interfering in a creative way, be it in joy or in suffering. We can participate consciously in our own development—in the weaving of our patterns. We are able to alter our psycho-physical patterns during certain yearly cycles. With mental clarity and impeccable will, karmic patterns are repeated every seven to nine years, and these are definitely altered every fourteen to nineteen years. These cycles correspond to the cycles of Saturn and the lunar Nodes, to the Metonic Cycle, the cycle of each turn in the DNA spiral. It is as if, from time to time, we feel that we can choose freely and consciously, cooperate actively with our own "individualization process." We can shape our own tree of destiny, our cabalistic tree, and our future genealogical tree.

A tree can represent the symbol of satisfaction in individual destiny; it is an altar of the Earth where we perform our ritual, where a pattern becomes impregnated or transcended and a body crystallizes in another dimension. It is the communicative contact and the voice of the heart with the crystal of the cranial vault that produces the feeling of transcending the ego and contemplating ourselves honestly, impartially, and in a detached way.

The psychic core takes on a "synchronistic-magic-maya" role when the ego has freed itself from all the purposeful and desired intentions and has made an effort to probe into the meaning of its existence. The ego is willing to surrender and listen attentively, with no ulterior motives or plans, to that urge and inner demand for growth that flows from the self.

We give in to a conscious attitude of control to promote the inner growth of personality and develop maturity. We simply listen to that secret design and discover what the inner, fulfilled self wants us to do in a particular situation in the Here and Now. When we trust that inner self completely, we discover the pattern—and the meaning of the pattern—in the huge tapestry of the human, planetary, and galactic universe.

Emotions are more passionate and intense than we can imagine. Life is lived intensely, we follow each impulse and respond to the most subtle motivation, desire, or passion. There is the risk, however, of becoming obsessed and hindering our journey toward creative self-realization, not knowing clearly whether we are advancing or sliding back in our search for the self. It is a process that we choose involuntarily, with more or less awareness, in cyclic periods. We constantly search for our own purpose in life and strive to follow the impulses and clues laid out, not by the ego, but by the fullness and totality of the psyche, of the "self." We each have a unique task to fulfill in our self-realization process.

We cannot forget that emotions, the irrational component, play a major role in the psyche. It is impossible to analyze or rationalize from any preconceived limit, order, or definition, the fact that we become absorbed by the ever-changing response or emotions in our surroundings. I can only outline some traits of the different stages of growth we go through as we progress. However, it is possible to be in one stage without having totally abandoned the previous one, and having thoughts revealing the next stage, since in the quantum physics of the psyche, present, past, and future have no borders and exist simultaneously. We can see the impact on the future of certain decisions we have made, and the karma or pattern of the past. Thus, we can see any psychic event from as many angles as necessary to achieve a hologram, an inner and outer reality.

Each one of us is a replica of the entire universe, as a small and diffuse piece of the entire hologram that progressively loses its precision and blurs its galactic meaning. In the Neuropsychology Department of Stanford University, research has proven that the mind can generate electromagnetic force fields of a similar nature to the holographic projections of a tridimensional picture.

In order to create a hologram, we must film the action of the movement from at least eight different points around the subject or object in action: from the top, the bottom, sideways and diagonally. It can then be reproduced on the plates with holographic lineal slits, giving a sense of movement due to the change of position of the observer. It is all a matter of the diffraction of light, like the consciousness that reaches us from the galactic ray, the umbilical cord, or the magnetic cords recently discovered by astrophysics, which unite us to the center of the creation of our galaxy.

When we fix our attention on the dark material opacity instead of fixing it on the inner light, the resulting state is a sense of emptiness, of giving up, that is projected on parents and partners. Some people can't understand the reason for their feeling, since there are no circumstances or specific people to blame, which complicates even more the psychological unrest this feeling produces. Others exaggerate petty explanations they find in their relationships with their parents or peers. This great emptiness comes from having abandoned the spiritual self and our body of light, since giving up means we must abandon something. In fact, instead of letting go of our material comfort, or feeling secure in it, we abandon the truly permanent reality, our spiritual integrity. (The stages of the resulting darkness are represented in Mountain and Water; the information about these sensations and traumas explodes in the stage of Thunder.)

Figure 20. The shadow, the animus and anima.

This feeling of emptiness comes directly from having abandoned the responsibility of our mother Earth and from not responding adequately to our own nature, distorting the reality of the material vehicle, and separating the material body more and more from the spirit. That emptiness or void is the receptive hollow of the dark matter Yin that awaits its fulfillment by the light of the Yang spirit or inner self of each individual.

Contact with the inner individual self implies responding to our lives and maintaining our own creative power, since we don't want to share the responsibility for our suffering and growth with another person. This means, also, not putting the blame outside nor feeling guilt or shame for being who we are.

When all paths join in a particular unit, we accomplish the wonderful mission assigned to each being at the moment of birth: being who we are! and, at the same time, contributing to the growth of the Whole. It is essential to understand that all negative experiences with our environment spring from the center of our being, and that, therefore, our conscience is attracting that which we have not integrated and that hinders our full integration as reflection of ourselves.

Just as the tree weaves its branches, so are the roots woven also, with a parallel similarity. As in figure 20, the individuation process is a matter of bringing the roots out into the light without killing the tree, thus disclosing the images of the monsters or allies we have in other dimensions. Like masks and images of indigenous cultures, these inner monsters look frightful and terrifying, for our roots contain the supernatural powers we can acquire if we incorporate them into the conscious.

Maya is illusion, mainly the illusion that reality is the material world. Since these supernatural beings seem frightful and cannot be controlled, like the Chinese dragon and the feathered serpent, Maya is both monstrous and beautiful. These images really represent metaphysical powers that destroy the illusion of the material.

The warrior of light is the one who has dominated the outer world but who also must dominate his or her inner monster. We only fear the "inner monster" because we have no control over it. This the real fight, the conquest of our own unconscious—contacting our archetypes and incorporating them into our personality. This is the source of both metaphysical and supernatural powers—besides being a preparation for death—with which we can transform the surrounding material world. It is the alchemy of the fusion of the subtle bodies—astral, mental, and vital—with the material body. It concentrates individual power in an incomparable creative energy that can be used to carry out what lies beyond the normal limits of life.

In death there is a real liberation, with no suffering or pain. The subtle bodies unite to carry with them all they have experienced on Earth. According to accounts from people who have gone through Near Death Experiences (NDEs), people go through a long tunnel with a blinding light at the end, and they see deceased kin, friends, or other people who tell them to return, for their time has not yet come. It has been researched and proven that there is a sudden loss of weight at the moment of death. That means that even invisible bodies have a minimum weight. Perhaps that was what the Egyptian god Thoth weighed, symbolizing the weight of the soul or karmic load.

The latest discoveries speak about four bodies, like the four amino acids, or the four basic combinations of light and darkness, the four doublets of the I-Ching. These four coexisting bodies or vehicles have a different nature, and each one has a different special function. Through each of these bodies, human beings live out certain experience in a specific space, field, or plane that is incorporated into the physical body while we are alive and aware of life: in waking state. That is, each of these bodies inhabits those other dimensions coinhabiting with what we call real. These dimensions, spaces or fields, require a body, just as in religion we hear about Hell, Purgatory and Paradise, which are spaces or dimensions where we live after death, but which are already within us while we are still alive. That is to say, human beings keep on living after physical death in more subtle planes of existence, and they live with these other bodies or vehicles.

While we live on the physical plane, we incorporate all the other subtle bodies at the same time, and it is the physical one that supports us in a dark milieu which resembles us, but which allows for experiencing that which the physical body cannot: feeling emotions coming from the astral body, or thinking from the mental body. At the moment of death, the first thing that separates is the vital body, which is the link between the astral and mental bodies, interpenetrating them and giving life to inert matter.

In this case, with the doublets of Yin and Yang, the mental body will be the two Yang lines ═══ , and the vital body is Yang within Yin ══ ; the physical body is two Yin ══ , and the astral body is Yin within Yang ══ .

Since the vital body acts as a link with the physical body, it has only that function and no other task in the other planes of existence, nor could it penetrate into them. The mental and astral bodies go on their own way and the vital one joins with Earth, remaining closer to the physical one and contributing to its regeneration or degeneration depending on the degree of integration with the mental and astral bodies.

At the moment of death, these bodies leave the physical body through what is called the silver cord coming out of the heart. According to some seers, it is from there that the deceased behold the events of their lives as if in a film that was being filmed on the spot for the other bodies to take along to the other two inter-dimensional levels of consciousness. It seems that the length of time required for "copying" this information varies according to each individual, since their disorientation, fear, or lack of habit in contacting these dimensions produces a greater confusion or repetition in the transfer of the information.

People who have contacted these dimensions through meditation or prayer will possibly be more adept, since they are used to living at the interdimensional level.

The important thing is that through an adequate individuation process and, therefore, a higher consciousness, both the mental and astral bodies (animus-anima) are trained in integration. This is similar to what Jung meant when he spoke about how the animus and the anima joined and ascended softly at death in those people who have managed to mature consciously in this life.

People who die do not suffer during the transit, and the feeling of peace is absolute. But in the case of violent or sudden death, there can be a greater difficulty in letting go of the vital and physical body. These people cling more to themselves or must review in more detail all that happened so that the consciousness can understand it and what led them to it. At that point it is consciousness that rules. When people have not prepared for death, the review takes longer at the moment of death, and is harder to assimilate. People who have prepared for death do not need such a detailed review and do not struggle against their new existence.

The silver cord is the link, and when it finally breaks, the mental and astral bodies coinhabit in that other plane with greater or lesser harmony. Since in that plane they coinhabit with the astral and mental bodies of the living, at the time of death they might not want to abandon matter, in order to understand something that happened in the physical plane they are leaving. Sometimes they are what we call ghosts, or beings, who interact with us to aid or hinder our task. The astral body gets stuck in the emotions and to the people and places where they were felt.

This theory in no way contradicts the theory of reincarnation by resonance. The psychic connections that influence us subconsciously are the experiences lived by other people's astral-mental bodies and these relate to our emotions and desires through the astral body, and through the thoughts and visions of the mental body.

It is due to a lack of purity that we cannot filter certain influences and resonances. This leads us to repeat mistakes or even make them worse. Or sometimes it keeps us from seeing clearly the reasons for an inherited karmic pattern, which makes it more and more tangled and may manifest in the form of hereditary illnesses.

The problems that have already attained a solution and a superior light consciousness become more subtle and coinhabit higher interdimensional levels. Furthermore, they can only be contacted by the astral-mental bodies of living people who have enough preparation and training to penetrate into those realms. In order to reach the more subtle things recorded in human archives, there must be an awareness of their mission, as small as it may be, and, most of all, great purity of intention, a crystal will, and spiritual beauty.

This was the task of mystics and shamans of all religions, and this is what initiations and rituals are really about. There are many methods (and multiple combinations) that must be found and developed by the individual. It is important that we trust our purity of intention and avoid the "spiritual ego" trap, or the fascination with the powers gained at that other side.

C.G. Jung introduced us to this experience through the individuation process: individualized people who are conscious of all the experiences that the Self has gone through at death understand all that has happened during their physical lives. The animus and anima unite and coinhabit in another dimension enriched by the experiences on the physical plane. When this does not occur, the mental continues to relate with the astral through the silver cord, even though the astral is stuck to physical life. These people observe what happens after death with all the unresolved business in their life, but are unable to effect any change in the physical world for lack of an adequate vehicle. Some people let themselves become imprisoned by the same astral sensations, and interactions with the physical realm can take place in some way, though its autonomy is different since it appears and disappears as in a dream. They understand that they cannot interfere in the psychological process of another psychic entity, unless the person reactivating it has lost his or her identity completely.

The loss of identity is not only dangerous for the living person, but it is also a torture for the experience of the astral body, which gets more and more lost in its mental understanding, tangling its karma with physical experience because of the interference with another living being. This happens very seldom, but it can lead the person who has allowed such contact to madness. These astral bodies can be called evil spirits or demons and they can have various effects upon living beings.

Tibetan Buddhist medicine recognizes the effect and the imbalance that evil spirits can generate in the body. Although all is elaborated in the mind, the psychological disorders that attract these demons are dualistic thought, attachment, pride, and sectarianism. They are classified in three groups—attracted by rage, attachment, or ignorance, and are the cause of pain and fear in the world. Among them are those born of doubt and those born of false hopes. They are the obstacles in our path toward illumination and they create unending vicious circles. They are the habits that must be broken so we can free ourselves from the phantoms created by our own minds or personified in extreme cases by the attraction of a real evil spirit that inhabits the astral plane.

All existence consists of radiations of energetic vibrations (or force fields) of different speeds and density that interact with our own frequencies according to the karma we either bring into or create in this life. These create more dense bodies through negative projections launched outward when they are too awful to be acknowledged as a part of ourselves.

The state of consciousness abandons each person at death, and has great effect on the potential for the more solid formation of these phantoms, especially if the dying person is full of hatred, panic, or attachment. So, whether the person dies or recovers, the important thing to consider is the sensation that may occur at the physio-psycho-cosmic level. The human being experiences a "psycho-moral continuum," or what we call past-life karma. An accumulated experience of karmic reaction takes years to disappear, dissolve, or get solved. These karmic forces are called external demons of other people, ghosts, or simply mental projections or attractions.

Mental habits can gain momentum until they take shape in a ghost created by mental distortions. In certain serious cases, this energy merges with some astral form that coincides with the projections created by the mind of the unbalanced person, who doesn't want to realize that the problem springs from within, that it is not outside but inside. Contact with one of those astral spirits makes the projection "real" outside, in an uncontrollable dimension.

Actually, demons do not exist; they are only a result of the duality of the mind and they become real when we believe they are. They can only be vanquished by the light of truth and by a pure vision on the part of people who begin to acknowledge their own disorders.

We can identify with our demons all that we don't clearly understand when it arises from our psychic depths, and that is not only bothersome, but it can also dominate us. If we persist in putting responsibility outside, there is the danger that one of those astral entities might, in fact, take possession of our own ghost, to confirm our belief that we are powerless against it and can neither liberate ourselves nor take responsibility for it.

According to Tibetan medical psychiatry, there are 360 types of ghosts that can be related to the frequencies of the 360 degrees of the Zodiac and with the different qualities of the planetary entities. They usually remain 9.5 years in the astral plane after being disembodied; that is, they take 9.5 years to understand and resolve their unfinished business at the moment of death. This coincides with the 9.5 years that is a half cycle of the Lunar Node and half a cycle of the Greek Methonic cycle.

If one is conscious, the astral unites with the mental, one lives on the mental plane and goes to another dimension in a short time. If, on the contrary, the process of acquiring consciousness takes longer than 9.5 years, and the astral remains on this plane, there is a rupture between the mental and astral planes.

Once the 9.5 transition years have elapsed, when there is the interconnection of the astral and the mental planes of a deceased person, and after the astral has assimilated the process of experiencing on the physical plane, one enters the "Great Silence," where the astral travels toward the mental plane, to reencounter its true origin. It then attains full understanding of its essence and the reason for its pilgrimage in the realm of matter. People with a superior consciousness enter death already in a mental-astral state.

The existence of the mental world and the assimilation of the astral world is an encounter of happiness and Cosmic Divinity, where all takes form in the mind, in the body of dreams, and where all things have their origin. From there, it is possible to understand individual experience as merging and woven into collective and cosmic experience. From there it is possible to understand the need for reincarnation and the decision is made to relive in a human experience in order to continue certain unresolved connections that hinder the evolution of the planet and of humanity.

Tibetans believe that many mental illnesses are the irreparable result of the karma of humanity, the idea of cruel and violent thoughts, negative words and actions that have caused a disharmony in the general alchemy of the human body.

They use an astrological procedure to recognize the effects and attractions of these demons and ghosts, in people as well as in their homes.

From Tibetan Buddhist wisdom we learn the techniques to expel demons: mantras, visualizing protecting circles, returning to a deity, and several types of exorcisms. They are, ultimately, an expression of the medicine of compassion and emptiness. These are the two great powers, two great meditations that calm all illnesses and evil spirits. The ghosts, the forms of negative thought, the demons, the evil energies and harmful spirits, etc., are the names and forms the Tibetan system has given those dark forces that influence, take hold of and possess us to prevent us from acting and thinking in a harmonious way. In other words, we become insane, self-destructive, and not really ourselves. Such forces range in a great variety, from the purely psychological—our own demons—to the cosmic forces that attack us according to the major laws of karma. These are, in a very developed form, "the numerous types and qualities of mental illnesses expressed in the Tibetan classification system.

> These "ghosts" and "demons" are a shared symbolic language which is rich in meaning to the members of the community and something that the Tibetan people relate to very vividly.
>
> The variety of negative forces and demons causing various kinds of madness and mental disease mirror the variety of distinct psychopathology expressed in the Tibetan system. As such they offer rich material for psychological interpretation and for ways of viewing psychosis.[1]

From the union with the Cosmic Divinity, one awaits the moment and the right circumstances for repeating all that was left unsolved in the physical world. One follows intently all that happens from the time of sexual union of a man and a woman who possess the right vibrations for the repetition of the said circumstances. We could say that it is then that certain circumstances experienced by that soul will reincarnate in the physical world through another human being. This leads to the conception of another person who, in turn, is influenced by previous experiences and vibrations. However, that person also has complete autonomy to change them through his or her own decisions, free will, and the choice of how and with whom he or she chooses to relive those unsolved experiences. That's why the planetary positions at the moment of birth express the different archetypes of the incarnate soul, and, in the course of the years, planetary cycles acti-

---

1. Terry Clifford, *Tibetan Buddhist Medicine and Psychiatry: The Diamond Healing* (York Beach, ME: Samuel Weiser, 1984), p. 170.

vate these archetypes and their potential recollection of psychic influences prere-corded in those specific frequencies.

We die, but information does not, for all that springs from the psychic depths of the human being subsists. Everything we do in the material world counts for centuries and many generations.

What is common to all doctrines is that emotions are the most dense vibra-tions and are closely linked to the material physical world. That's why the astral body survives, since it keeps on vibrating, still connecting with the gravitational force of the Earth when it has not been able to disintegrate more rapidly because of a lack of understanding of the emotions.

Passion and emotion are attachments to the body and form the connecting tissue of the larger body of humanity. All human beings influence one another through "feelings," and it is there that the ties, knots, and the traumatic cysts of all human experience are formed. Love is the transcendent expression of this inter-action, of which art is another sublime and creative expression. On the other hand, possessive passions and wars are the destructive knots and cysts of this vibrational field. The sexual act contains such an intensity of connection with all bodies—physical, vital, astral and mental—that it causes the cosmic vibrational explosion that conceives life through the alchemy of the union of all the energetic vibra-tional fields. This happens with the whole range of possibilities the human being has created by tangling and braiding the emotional body throughout countless existences. Many unresolved experiences in the psychic bank of the human being are repeated and allow for the possibility of another human being to relive and perhaps resolve that knot. Then, union with the mental field would be recovered, allowing many other human beings to tap into that unconscious understanding and wisdom that the "self" can make conscious.

We can compare the descent from the more subtle to the more dense in the four fields, to the I-Ching doublets. Its vibrational field expands and densifies with the action of the gravitational force. The mental field and body ══ corre-sponds to the widest part of the spiral. The most subtle subatomic particles are the least affected by the gravitational pull; they are the lightest and most volatile, and lead to a greater expansion shared by many people.

The astral field and body ══ is at the end of the spiral where gravitation-al force exerts its power. It is also shared by many human beings, but here are the greatest distortions, produced by complicated knots, cysts, and tangles. This cre-ates a mesh of unbelievable color. Within the human body, this is reflected in the connective tissue, where the alchemy of water and fire takes place, along with that of the liquids, membranes, and nerve endings.

These cysts and wrinkles affect the cranio-sacral pulse, the constant pump-ing of cerebrospinal fluid from the sacrum to the cranium, which can even be influenced by the magnetism of hand contact with another person, causing the mobility of cysts through the magnet produced by the gravitational force of the bone of one person to another's hand-bone surrounded by water and fire, tissues and nerves.

The vital field and body ☰ exists while there is a connection of the other two bodies with the physical one. It is the one activating creativity and movement, temporarily dominating the weight of the gravity pull. It gives the feeling of freedom and individuality to be active, putting aside or untying the knots, or making them even tighter when they are chronic. It pertains to the lineal perception of things and the mental stimulus to do something, which can lead to a greater tangle when there is not enough awareness. Within the body, it relates to vitality, the heart pulse and the nervous system.

The physical field and body ☰ is the most dense and dark. It concentrates at the base of the spiral, the most compact cyst or knot, the inner beginning of the vortex of the centrifugal spiral that produces its own gravitational force together with the planetary body. It produces a greater molecular speed that maintains a cohesion of stagnation in its own material density. This separates the different individualities into different and unique entities from the moment of their birth in a particular time and space. Although a similarity is maintained in the other fields or bodies of gravitational density, each entity or individual being has a separate destiny in walking a unique cyclic path to tangle or untangle the connection with the mental field. Each person has a similar destiny in being a macrocosm: each person is born and dies, a lineal reality in this field and in the vital one, a circular reality in the mental and astral fields.

We can create a comparison between the vibrational ascent from the most dense to the most subtle and the influence of the electromagnetic force and the spiral that concentrates in a centripetal form, through research of the four brain rhythms. Then we can make a coherent comparison of life through the molecules and particles, and a study of the union of spirit and human matter, the mind and the body when Heaven and Earth fuse.

These four brain rhythms represent four levels of consciousness, from the sleep state to the waking state, divided into rhythms. The Delta rhythm ranges from 0.4 to 4 cycles per second ☰. It is comparable to the wider and more subtle mental field, that is also slower in terms of the rhythm of perception. It pertains to the sleep state, to the loss of consciousness, or coma states, to deep sleep and deep hypnosis.

The sleep of a newborn has this rhythm where there is no separation between one and others, between all and nothing, where nothing and all exists, because the compensatory polarity is perfect, and there are no limits in space or time. Thus, there are no minor memories, since nothing is crystallized. These are the deep dreams our conscious cannot recover or remember. Nevertheless, it can be compared to the transformed consciousness that a magician or an individual with a superior consciousness can acquire at certain moments.

The Theta rhythms of 5 to 8 cycles per second ▬▬ correspond to the vital field and are characterized by great stimulation and a creative capacity, imagination, and dream visions, intense dreams that are easily remembered. This might activate awareness and help resolve the knots and tangles of karmic psychological patterns. Newborns live this stage intensely, where they have access to the karmic patterns they have come to this life to relive and solve. Children live these rhythms strongly, even until ages 7 to 12. It is the rhythm for exploring and living out childhood experiences, or even for reliving the experiences of other lives, that are affecting us in this one. We can free ourselves from childhood traumas or blocks caused by the repetition of unconscious psychic phobias by elaborating, activating, and connecting them with the waking Beta state, creating a bridge between the psychological mental-astral and the somatized physical. Many things are discharged by putting them in mental action. The difference between this semi-sleep state and the Delta state is that in the latter, the experiences of the psychological conscious have no effect on the body, being as it is inert and motionless, while the Theta rhythm creates dreams in which the body has movement and sensation. Therefore it is the rhythm where the knots are either untied or tied more tightly, leading to repression and traumas.

The Alpha rhythm, 9 to 19 cycles per second ▬▬ , corresponds to the astral and emotional field that leads to a state of relaxation, of inner peace and harmony, where one feels all the surroundings and is aware of one's participation in them being awake with a full attention on oneself and all else, without losing individual consciousness. In deep meditation one passes from the Alpha to the Theta rhythm, and from there to the Delta only when one achieves a deep relaxation without revealing the vision that belonged to the Theta rhythm.

The Alpha rhythm is the same as the planet Earth's, bringing into consciousness an awareness created by the slowness of perception and the extension of time. In regard to the emotional field, all is felt and solutions are sensed in the Here and Now. However, due to a lack of preparation, most humans do not utilize this rhythm. They are more apt to stay in the Beta rhythm waking state, and many sensations that could be experienced in the Alpha state are left unfinished and unresolved. Attention is turned to everything that moves at a faster rhythm, one more concentrated at the vortex of the cone of light and in the material density of the consciousness of the Beta rhythm. In the Alpha rhythm state, time is transcended and the Now is related to the past and the future.

The Beta rhythm—15 to 40 cycles per second—corresponds to material density ▬▬ and to the field of the physical body. It knows time as a lineal reality. If one is aware of its density, it means that one lives and also dies. It is the waking state rhythm of the objective world, fragmented into densities, objects, you and me, belongings, yours and mine. The speed of rhythm crystallizes thoughts and feelings into a tangible and concrete reality with a particular cycle of existence that is generated and degenerated. What is truly important is consciousness and having learned something about the experience and the universe in the fall into degeneration. This is only possible if one remains connected with the other three fields of consciousness, in a wider, more durable, and eternal rhythm.

The eternal return of karma is a consequence of the lack of experiential unity among all the dimensional fields and between the four rhythms of consciousness.

In each true experience of unity, some knot is untied which resolves a lot of complications for human beings—who recreate the same drama—and facilitates our access to the knowledge imprinted in the mental field, influencing the resolution of our problems. In the opposite case, it makes it more chronic and crystallizes it more and more. It forms a greater density and a deep and unrecognizable instinct for repeating the same error, like a hardened stone or the hardened optic nerve that only sees the same suffering again and again, forgetting what has created it. The knot becomes so tight that the solution can no longer be perceived, nor its connection to the other realms of existence or rhythms of consciousness.

It is the field where individuality becomes a tangible reality and, at the same time, by forming a mass, contained in itself, its own gravitational force field, attracting to itself the union of the two forces of the universe: the gravitational and the electromagnetic. Heaven and Earth are conjugated with greater or lesser intensity in each of the particular densities of existence born of the joint conjunction of the four dimensions of existence and the four rhythms of consciousness. The result is eight states of transformation that act jointly in each entity endowed with spiritual and material existence. They represent eight states of transformation that, during the short physical existence of the human being, try to recover their connection with individual experience. Brain waves can descend to a frequency of 10 cycles per second or less, and from there relate to the incredibly rapid frequencies of the subatomic level where atoms are composed and decomposed.

We exist in the field of physical experience and in the Beta rhythm only temporarily—although its density and speed make us believe it is the most real—because psychologically all the other fields and rhythms of existence and consciousness interact there. The individuation process is the path to recover awareness of this union with that which continues existence in other dimensional fields of consciousness after death.

Some people have a greater degree of free will and consciousness. Others are conditioned cosmically and astrally, reflected in their social, cultural, and family milieu, and in their choice of people who fit into their karmic pattern, making the situation even worse. Their life then becomes a repetition of the previous one, giving them the impression of having very little autonomy. Today it is possible to change the karmic pattern of external circumstances by moving to another country, which modifies the horoscope (the ascendant and the placement of the houses), and often many patterns and vibratory frequencies can be modified by speaking another language.

In my opinion, the ascendant is the only astrological point we choose from the mental realm. If there is enough clarity and autonomy, the soul is not so confused as to let the mother and the doctor decide the moment of birth. Nowadays, induced labor leads to a greater exterior conditioning.

The ascendant in the birth chart is the filter we choose to live through on the earthly plane. It is through the sign on the ascendant that we filter personal and impersonal karma. It expresses the qualities we want to develop, and it symbolizes the energy we express when we interact with others. Individual potential can be directed to whatever allows the soul the greatest evolution by means of a significant contact with its environment. One masters the energies and lessons inside, synchronizing, everything that is symbolized by the planetary positions shown in the natal chart.

An error in thought, word, or action can interrupt our experiential harmony and result in rage, fear, envy, and doubt, the main causes for the disconnection of our mental-astral body from the vital-physical body, causing illness.

The dark cave of our unconscious is the spiritual vortex of our Self.

The physical body is the world of vibrations created by the dream body to express itself so it can realize its potential to learn, mobilize and grow, in a constant genesis, with the continuum of creation. Only doubt, anger, rage, resentment, fear, vanity, envy, and guilt tie up the energy that flows from the dream realm to the physical one, forming a clot, a crystallization or blocking of understanding and the assimilation of life experiences.

The only means of purifying these crystallized condensations and disharmonies is through an open heart, by forgiving oneself and others from the depths of the soul. It is a process of balancing from the center the spirals coming from above and below, making them return to harmony. It is letting Water calm emotions to give stability and clarity to the mind, and letting Fire interact in a cosmic alchemy with Water in the elixir of life. This is the magic of the transformation of matter through spirit.

Understanding each obstacle as an opportunity for growth and learning, we can manifest compassion in our relationships without letting misunderstandings cause us suffering or resignation. When we let inner peace and truth merge with external experience, we transcend time and space and trust completely in the synchronicity that guides us by being a vehicle connecting Heaven and Earth. We can activate the dream body and feel that our hearts are one with the heart of Mother Earth and that our minds are one with the mind of the galaxy.

We have come to Earth to learn all forms of personal and impersonal LOVE, and this is the only thing that will count at the moment of death. How we have resolved the problems of love we were allotted, if we tightened the knot of the astral emotional tissue of humanity, or if we opened paths to disentangle cysts of suffering and pain resulting from the lack of human love, will be something that we deal with at death.

Hopefully we will truly be able to walk upon the Earth while living and realizing our dreams.

Blake's image of spiritual travel is the vortex . . .his poetry and designs abound with a variety of figures which invoke the vortex. When the observer is standing within the vortex looking directly upon its whirling center, it assumes a circular appearance as if it were a broad disk. . . . When the vortex is delivering the traveler into the chaos, then it is dark, and we may see only a whirling cloud. . . . If the vortex is dark, and light is seen through it only in points, then it assumes the characteristics of a constellation or a starry universe.

Blake knew that the spiritual travel actually opens the traveler to infinity, redeeming the limits of opacity and contraction the reasoning mind imposes upon existence. For Blake "there is no Limit of Expansion; there is no Limit of Translucence / In the bosom of Man for ever from eternity to eternity.". . . But if everything has its own vortex, then the thin membrane of opacity which closes off our world from eternity is an illusion, and we are open within and without to limitless translucence.

If the vortex is not perceived by the traveler, if he is not open to the "infinite plane," the vortex becomes the polypus, Blake's image for enclosure within the vegetable world. . . . Thus, in order to have living perception, the traveler must avoid the polypus which negates visionary rebirth.

Milton's trip through the perceptual vortex is the active projection of a reality upon the physical world. Consequently, it follows the path of visual projection through the eye into the void. . . .To leave Eden and to enter the void is to undertake a process of dying, of entering into death; it is progressive annihilation of error by entering the body of death. . . .Blake characterizes the process as if it were shedding life, taking off the "robe of the promise.". . . When Milton enters his own Shadow, he separates from his Edenic form and Blake describes it this way: "when he enter'd into his Shadow, Himself, / His real and immortal Self, was as appear'd to those / Who dwell in immortality, as One sleeping on a couch / Of gold," but Milton's Shadow "vegetated underneath the Couch." The second couch appears as the Rock of Ages where Albion lies "deadly pale." Here Milton bends down to "the bosom of death" . . . and Blake comments cryptically, "what was underneath soon seem'd above." The comment reminds us that death is a matter of perspective. . . . Milton's temptation, to become a "covering" for Satan, to do Satan's will, echoes the configuration of the transi tomb. The fourth couch is the Couch of Death in the physical world. . . . Thus, the four couches are stages of perceptual projection of mental reality upon the world: the retina (Eden); the lens (The Rock of Ages); the focal point (Satan's Seat); and the phenomenal world of perceived objects (Ulro). These stages are the increasing intensity of error which Milton must enter, and likewise shed, to turn his vision inward, back toward Eden.

—Milton: A Poem by William Blake
Kay Parkhurst Easson and Roger R. Easson, eds.,
pages 151, 152, 155, 156.

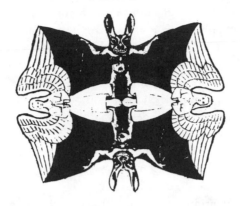

From Darkness to the Dispersion of Light

The structure of the psyche that the I-Ching offers us is made up of eight stages. These eight stages of the placement of the eight trigrams show the constant reflection of the psyche on each person and his or her surroundings. The symbol of the Tao turns in both directions so that ideas materialize. We begin with Heaven ☰ ; the Lake ☱ picks up the reflection of light; Fire realizes it ☲ ; Thunder ☳ puts it in motion and jumps to the Wind ☴, that disperses the idea throughout all the elements that need to be integrated; in Water ☵ it is carried out with the emotional intensity needed to put the idea into practice. In the Mountain ☶ it takes on a final form, until it materializes completely in the Earth ☷ . This movement expresses the idea in the process of materializing.

In order to track the "individuation process" in the psyche, we undergo the same movement, but backward: from darkness to light. As babies in a state of absolute dependency, we begin the process in the receptive darkness of Earth that absorbs the psychological surroundings, until we see the light out in the Mountain. Then we trust in matter, guided by the light and by the others and integrate fully in the external world of friends and loved ones in Water. In the Wind, we manage to overcome difficulties and take command over our own life. Then in jumping to our center, the positive light enters inside and explodes outward in Thunder, where one attracts the provocation of "the shadow" to integrate all our positive-negative being into our personality. Then we begin to understand what elements we have repressed and we begin to integrate them in Fire, to feel once more the joy of life. So we can be like a mirror that reflects in the Lake without projecting, preparing consciously to enter death and the luminosity of the Heavenly Spirit. Darkness absorbs light in its bosom, light illuminates the four corners of darkness, transforming it and giving it an unlimited meaning.

The three lines of a trigram represent the three phases from unconsciousness to consciousness. The first lower line is all that remains hidden, anything buried in the subconscious that we are capable of making conscious. The second is that which we recognize consciously about ourselves, while the third and top line represents all that comes from the outside, all that we attract into our lives or project outward, so we can recognize our whole reality. If we separate the trigrams pertaining to Heaven (O, the Circle), and Earth (■, the Square), their meanings can vary depending on the meaning of a more physical reality—the Earth—or a more spiritual one—Heaven. (See figure 21.)

The psyche is imprinted on the placement of the trigrams of the world of thoughts, with the biopsychic pulsation to materialize in the human being. It changes its backward turn, going from the darkness of matter in the direction of the magnetic resonance of Heaven and backward, jumping into the center from the Wind to the Thunder, and continuing in the forward direction of the gravitational Earth, from the direction of the world of thoughts to the world of the senses. So it is that the human psyche takes form, as well as the struggle between light and darkness, consciousness and unconsciousness.

Just as in the path of the trigrams in the world of the senses and the life of human beings (figure 12, page 28), it seems reasonable that this path should begin with the trigram of darkness—the receptive Earth—and should progress toward integration in the light. Both last stages would finish in the creative Heaven and the Lake, the metal element. The blaze of light, the metal, the mineral that enriches the water, the mirror of the soul is the last stage before turning completely into spirit at the time of death in the trigram of Heaven, the creative.

When we study the relation of lines in the trigrams, we also see that the bottom line refers to Earth, the middle one to the human being, and the top one to Heaven. Therefore, the lower line is that which is buried in our subconscious and is hard to recognize. The middle line refers to the human being, and obviously represents what we know, while the top line is what we think comes from the outside, what we project. Unknowingly, we express it, it is accepted by others, and returned to us through others' reactions. Unaware of the process, we often think the process is outside of us.

Light penetrates into darkness from the outside; it starts descending, and in the 4th or 5th stage (Wind-Thunder) it turns around, and in entering inside, it explodes, because as light enters, it pushes darkness out (figure 22, page 154).

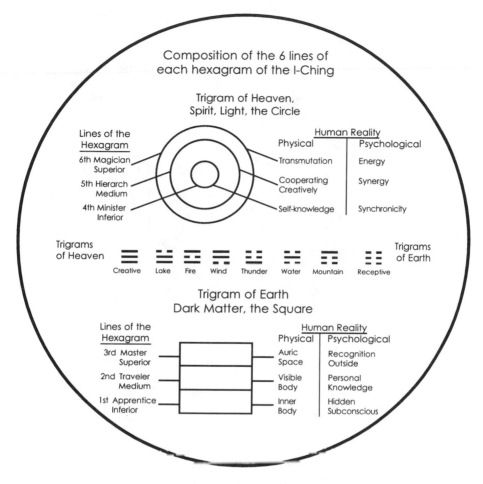

Figure 21. Six areas of the mandala. Physically, we only live outside the square of matter, and at present, we are only within the two central circles.

We can use these psychological stages practically by analyzing a person's life recollection to see the traumas of each stage and understand the effect of each one on the others. If a person has still not managed to feel united to others—which corresponds to Water—he or she will have to make up for these feelings by belonging to groups, although already placed in the stages between Wind and Thunder. If, in the Mountain stage, the person did not have any security, it will be necessary to calculate the effect caused on all stages.

Just as in the other path of physical life (Phase 2), time is different for each stage because of our consciousness and evolution. It may seem that the middle

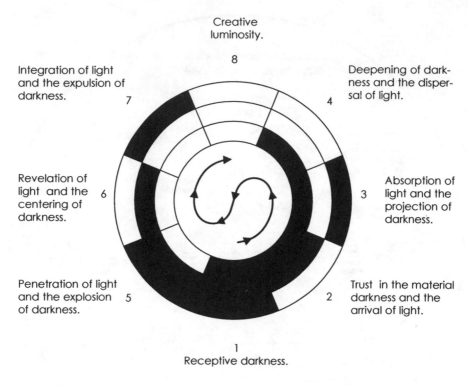

Creative
luminosity.

8

Integration of light
and the expulsion of
darkness.
7

Deepening of dark-
ness and the disper-
sal of light.
4

Revelation of
light and the
centering of
darkness.
6

Absorption of
light and the
projection of
darkness.
3

Penetration of light
and the explosion
of darkness.
5

Trust in the material
darkness and the
arrival of light.
2

1
Receptive darkness.

The rhythm of the biopsychic resonance inside the world of thought,
turned around starting at material darkness, reaching the light of the
spirit when one leaves matter at the moment of death.

1 Darkness	2 Mountain
3 Water	4 Wind
5 Thunder	6 Fire
7 Lake	8 Light

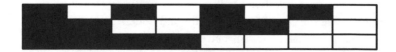

The same rhythm is in the top trigrams in both hexagrams for the world
of thought and the world of the senses, only turned around.

Figure 22. Eight stages of the individuation process with the trigrams.

stages are swapped due to psychological immaturity or, on the contrary, due to an excess maturity for the age (Phase 2) in this other path of the psyche where there is more freedom. The body is destined to go through all the stages, unless it dies by accident. In the journey of the psyche, it might happen that not all stages are lived out, even stopping at Stages 3 and 4 or trying to control or repress the unconscious for too long. Usually, the critical point is reached between the 4th and the 5th from age 30 to 45. If the explosion of the shadow of Thunder is further delayed until an older age, after age 50-60, it can lead to a serious illness and even death. The rest of the stages can be experienced during and after death, since they refer to a state of the psyche, to the world of thoughts.

If this happens, the anima-animus or astral-mental separate and Stages 6, 7, and 8 are lived out from that other dimension, in the process of assimilating and becoming aware of what one has lived in the physical experience. We could say that it is the path walked by the psyche when it integrates fully into the world of dreams and in the spiritual dimension.

Integrating this knowledge with the Methonic cycles of the lunar Nodes marked by lunar and solar eclipses, we could say that each stage equals 9.5 years in most human beings. Therefore, it is the ages of the returns of the North Node every 19 years—which is the time the sun and moon take to return to the same point where that changes with every two stages. Nevertheless, among the people who nowadays search for consciousness, the leap from Stage 4 (the Wind) to Thunder (Stage 5) takes place between age 30-37. It also happens that very evolved beings can reach Stage 8 temporarily, since they travel in spirit to pick up revelations and wisdom from other dimensions and bring them to physical awareness to illuminate the path of others.

When speaking of the electromagnetic resonance and of the subatomic particles of the microcosm, we must remember that their main trait is their freedom of speed, reaching waves at rhythms above the speed of light. By doing so, they distort the time-space continuum in such a way that all is possible, the invisible becomes visible. From all the creatures of the universe that we know at present, only the human brain can affect this source of inextinguishable visual creativity and sensory perception.

Obviously, it is impossible to determine how long a person can remain between two stages, or the length of each stage, since this has as many possibilities as individuals. Therefore, while one might remain over 14 years in a certain stage or 7 years between two stages, another person might only remain in that stage for 19 months, and 9.5 or 19 years in another. I always relate the periods of stage changes to the cycles of 9.5 or 19 years or months of the lunar Nodes and to genetic and karmic changes. But in fact, all human beings go through all stages. The first stage starts before birth and the last stage is definitely after death. So we have six remaining stages of 19 years that would total 152 years, which is never reached. Most stages are nine years and another nine in transition with the next stage, until it becomes fully present.

When one is going through a critical period, one is placed between two stages, needing to go on to the more evolved one. Sometimes, certain stages are provoked and happen very rapidly due to serious events in the external circumstances, to illness or even to death. Most times, the stage of Thunder sends the individual back to heal and to realize the problems of the previous phases.

Each individual being, in the individualization process, has freedom to incorporate into the psyche certain aspects that belong to a greater psychological maturity than that of their age. On the other hand, some are socially dependent or dependent on the family and can be infantile or immature.

The Eight Stages of the Psyche and the Trigrams: The Relativity of Time and the Eight Stages of the Psyche

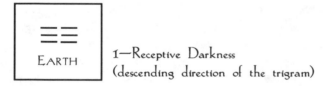

EARTH

1—Receptive Darkness
(descending direction of the trigram)

From the moment of conception, life in the womb, birth and childhood, until the moment of the coloring of the iris and being able to see, walk, and talk.

The entire psychic world is oriented toward absolute receptivity to the environment. Neurons are created from thoughts and emotions existing in the child's surroundings, mostly from the parents.

MOUNTAIN

2—Trust in Material Darkness and the Arrival of Light
(descending direction of the trigram)

Childhood and youth until the first traumas are experienced. Learning, trusting in matter and learning to trust in life and deciding for oneself. The first traumas from the outside world.

The programming of the neurons and the perceptions acquired in Stage 1 become activated, and one unconsciously decides to emphasize some experiences and concentrates on them. One recognizes darkness and many fears appear. One recognizes one's inner dependence on experiences coming from the outside world and one strives to become independent. The key age for having this stage integrated is approximately 19 years.

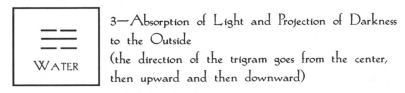

3—Absorption of Light and Projection of Darkness to the Outside
(the direction of the trigram goes from the center, then upward and then downward)

Emotionally, one gives of oneself totally to the outside world, whether to friends or to a love relationship. During youth and adult life traumas, crises and mental blocks occur that condition the emotional being. One's shadow is repressed, and it is either projected or only visible in the outside world. Darkness is both inside and outside, but one only recognizes oneself as radiant energy. If the union that takes place at this stage is painful or it never happens, the traumas are left pending and one must return to this stage to regenerate it. This reinforces the belief that life is unjust and its luminous force (Yang, center line) has neither been recognized nor accepted. The only thing one is conscious of is the center line.

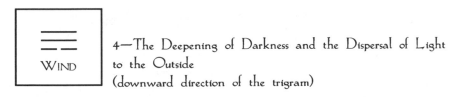

4—The Deepening of Darkness and the Dispersal of Light to the Outside
(downward direction of the trigram)

The conquest of one's surroundings and relationships. During adult life, one loses contact with one's inner being and one dedicates oneself only to that which one decides is positive in the outside world, without seeing the negative in the inside world. As one is unable to accept the unconscious shadow, one represses it. The lesson here is to dominate the outside world while controlling the darkness and instincts inside oneself. In some cases this stage lasts for the rest of one's life, if one has not been able to dominate the outside world and become emotionally and intellectually independent and construct one's own reality. When one has, to some extent, conquered the outside world, one feels sufficiently strong psychologically for the next stage, where one undoes much of what one has constructed comfortably in the unconscious. The last age for having this stage integrated is around 37 years.

THUNDER

5—The Penetration of Light and the
Explosion of Darkness
(ascending direction of the trigram)

At this stage the shadow provokes us to enable us to see the monster we have inside that we refuse to recognize. In conscious individuals, this stage starts after age 30. If one doesn't enter this stage before reaching 50, it becomes dangerous, because the explosion of the shadow could provoke physical illness. When light enters inside, it explodes all the darkness outside, attracting to oneself persons of the same gender who act out all that one judges morally to be negative and all one has repressed. To defend oneself from these persons that characterize these negative aspects of oneself, one uses these same negative aspects against them, which then go out of control, leading to an emotional and psychological crisis. Through this, one becomes aware of one's own weakness and negativities, even though one still continues to blame the outside. Whether one lets oneself be provoked into transformation or not depends upon the security acquired in the previous stage of Wind. It has the longest period of time, sometimes starting at 31 and going until 50.

FIRE

6—The Revelation of Light and the Centering of
Darkness Upon Recognizing It
(the direction of the hexagram goes from
downward to upward to the center)

Recognizing and incorporating aspects of the shadow. One does not enter this stage until reaching age 45 or more, but in the case of some individuals of low consciousness, it is impossible for them to enter this stage until reaching the threshold of death. One recognizes the darkness in oneself and is able to harmonize with the outside acquiring wisdom and even enlightenment that in many cases may attract positive situations from the outside. One integrates the positive values of the unconscious and everything one rejected before, becoming aware of how this can enrich us psychologically and learning to incorporate into our personality some of the repressed elements of the shadow. This stage represents the opening of the heart without judgment. Much depends on the love and traumas acquired during the Water stage. The key age to integrate this stage is approximately 52–58.

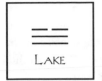

7—The Integration of Inner Light and the
Expulsion of Darkness
(ascending direction of the trigram)

One is at peace with oneself, reflecting upon what one has learned, and one can enjoy all the lessons of life. In the case of specially evolved individuals, this stage will start after age 50 and in normal conscious individuals, after age 60. One irradiates light and is able to transform the darkness of the outside, attracting to oneself people who need to be guided. One manifests a transforming personality full of the light and joy of living and having lived. One starts to handle other dimensions of psychic existence and one can help to enlighten the path of others. One acquires the sense of security and happiness which circumstances may not have allowed to occur during the Mountain stage in childhood.

8—The Creative Luminosity
(ascending direction of the trigram)

The experience of death for conscious individuals and for others. This stage may not be reached until an indefinite time after death, once one has understood what one has experienced during physical incarnation. The Great Silence. Existence in the mental-astral world can signify out-of-body experiences, traveling to other dimensions temporarily for some evolved individuals, after age 50 or 60. For the majority, this stage is reached 9 or 19 years after death.

The Trigrams and the Eight Stages of the Psyche

1st Stage:
The Receptive Darkness

It begins from the moment the spirit accepts taking on a material life, from the moment of conception, fetal life and infancy, where there is dependency on the mother and on all the elements of nature to accomplish the mission of physical existence. The spirit becomes aware of its dependency and all the senses awake to perceive the new world one is living in. The perception rhythm is slow, and can notice small details that usually escape our attention. The material density is not seen, only the electromagnetic energy emanating from it is seen. This psychic process of existence is open to receive all the emotions and thoughts from the immediate surroundings, unable to distinguish whether it happens outside or inside, since the spirit is not used to this individualized density. Even the digestion processes, physical discomfort and pain are projected outward with the hope of causing an alleviating reaction on the part of the environment and the other existing entities.

Little by little, the senses begin to tell the difference between inside and outside. Some sounds come from inside and others from the outside, the eyes start to distinguish forms, the touch can tell mother apart from the rest, as well as smells. One enjoys flavors, realizing, for the first time, the need for nourishment to keep the spirit from physical suffering. But during this whole period, there is no distinction between the thoughts and emotions of others, since the spirit has come to learn and to receive psychologically the circumstances of the environment, especially the psychological trash from both parents; also, the whole rhythm of mother's sounds, voice, gestures, and movements from the time of life in the womb. The child keeps receiving from the environment until it acquires independence to move, talk, and communicate, and becomes aware that part of the thought process is his or her own. In any case, the child perceives everything that people feel and think. A child is naturally psychic, but learns that he or she cannot communicate it with words, or at least it is not convenient at the risk of rejection from elders. A child is also aware of what grown-ups will not acknowledge.

Energy and positive light irradiate around every child like a balloon of energy emitting from all sides of the body and the psyche. Childhood is a state where the individual gradually awakes to the world and to the self. There is a sudden emphasis on the word "I" or "mine," preparing the child to enter the next stage. It is a time of huge emotional intensity, and dreams reveal the basic structure of the psyche that gives shape to the individual's destiny. These dreams relate to the inner conflicts experienced through psychological contact with both parents, present or not in the immediate surroundings, for in the first months the psyche reaches all the terrestrial and non-terrestrial spaces and maintains contact with the parents.

Practically, all is within. Sensations don't arrive, they are simply there and we feel them. To objectivize and know that something is outside, we use the sense of touch that defines and begins to make us understand what is outside and not inside. When the eye sees the shapes, we also begin to learn to objectivize what is outside.

Nevertheless, many years after seeing the density of the material, the child's psyche sees the perceptions of thoughts and feelings of other people, and must learn to distinguish between one world and the other. With this umbilical cord that unites the child to everything related to his or her individual psychological learning process, and mostly to the psyche of the parents, it seems obvious that in those conditions of subjectivity/objectivity, there is nothing external to change. The child is in contact with the collective unconscious and with the knowledge that rules the cosmos as a whole.

Each day is a series of linked events, each one being whole and full, experienced with an enormous sensory intensity. Each newborn establishes with the external world participatory relationships as if he or she had not been separated from the world and from one another. Within the flow of consciousness, relationships are a series of specific things: hunger, mother, breast, pain, smell. . . . There is no separation between the I and the It; all are one. From this perception of unity of the world, the mystical experience each person pursues lies in recovering this state of psychological receptivity, having the capacity to reason and understand what is experienced.

Children have a vivid recollection of certain incidents that retain the basic problem of the psyche, although perhaps they do not remember an unimportant event in itself, but only the feeling associated with it which is present throughout most of the life.

Sometimes children, from an early age, see the mother as a witch and the father as a tyrant, and begin to project on them their own witch and tyrant when they feel impotent in certain things, simply because they also know that there is nothing they can do to change the monstrous expression of their parents when it appears. Children are aware of these expressions because their rhythm of perception is slower and perhaps that monstrous expression has only lasted a few seconds on their parent's face.

The individuation process of the psyche begins when personality is hurt for the first time and we feel the pain of not being accepted as we are. It happens when we realize that our parents don't like some part of our radiant energy aura which may be similar to something they have carefully repressed. We show them the wild side they have tried to dominate and so they only want and accept a "good boy or girl," with good manners and an education who will not bother them. In some way, we never leave the psychological dependency on our parents typical of this stage, since we want to be accepted by them. So, we learn to repress certain parts of our personality, as they do, to get what we need from them.

In the course of a few weeks we assimilate information from our environ-ment and our sensory determinism begins, together with our rigid eating habits and convictions. Nerve cells are like small sticks, and from 2 months until 2 years, they become a complicated labyrinth of connections and programming. Every experience lived indirectly leaves a trace of intertwined and complicated neural nodes. If we hear another language, neurons are formed to facilitate learning this language. Later on, the same happens with bad habits and everything around us. Each nerve cell itself is like a computer. From this stage on, a great conscious effort must be made to unlearn or unprogram a nerve cell and leave space and flexibili-ty for new information.

MOUNTAIN

2nd Stage:
Trust in Material Darkness and the Arrival of the Light

This stage is characterized by enormous mobility, where children start to play and dance with the weight of gravity and to defy it with the positive force of the spir-it. At the same time, we need to trust our parents and our environment, and if this does not happen, we will have a scar of mistrust for the next stages.

It is at this time that the father becomes the transformer of the boy and the mother of the girl, teaching them to channel that extra energy into something useful, but the true example is what they see in the life of their parents and whether or not there is a feeling of satisfaction. That is, if the daughter perceives the mother's frustration in doing housework, she won't like it either and will rebel when told to do it. Likewise, the son who is aware of the father's frustration in his job under the command of a boss, or great institution, will begin to reject that lifestyle. The easiest way of focusing a boy's extra energy is in sports or in creative activities shared by the father. When children break something or do something that makes the parents very angry, they feel fear and begin to show an evil weak-ness, which provokes an even greater rage in the parents as an inappropriate response, instead of understanding that it is a more exaggerated reflection of their own incompetence. They excuse their exaggerated response as discipline or edu-cation of the irresponsible weaknesses the child manifests.

Some parents block children's transformation completely, and especially restrict early sexual sensations with their own morality, lack of spontaneity, or their own inhibitions.

At this stage, children become less dependent on parents, trying to avoid parental pressures. They feel close to their peers, but there is a new source of problems in the fact that children sometimes reject each other due to the different mentality of their parents. Older children continue to express spontaneously the radiant energy of the spirit, but they soon realize that this also gets them in trouble with classmates, so they learn to inhibit certain behaviors and progress slowly to the next stage.

They now achieve a more rapid waking rhythm, trusting in the material density of what they see that causes the separation of things, people, and themselves. Most of all, they block out psychological perceptions of other people's emotions and thoughts because they cause the children pain and they can't understand why there is so much distortion in physical life. Older children begin to trust what they see and touch, and begin to reason, to understand what they see, forgetting what they used to perceive through extrasensory means.

In fact, young people begin to enjoy material and physical life and want to play, prattle, and laugh, still using imagination and play activities. They have no doubts about confronting whatever hurts them nor in expressing wild aggressiveness with peers, and still have a tribal or community attitude, if not with family, with peers. They have a defensive attitude toward anything that might break the unity that transcends them and have no remorse in doing any atrocity to defend that union.

With a just sense of light and darkness, they know they receive from the outside just what they deserve; if they take more than they need, it will be taken away. But due to a lack of clarity on the part of grownups guiding young people, this part of the growth cycle is often misunderstood and distorted. Without guidance, young people may get tangled in selfish abuses and unsatisfied needs.

Young people do not reject cruelty, but see it as something natural within the law of survival. They accept the facts, their parents' life and their surroundings as something completely natural. That's why they get into trouble with other children and begin to notice the differences, giving rise to infantile traumas and inhibitions because they are unable to understand what is real and what is fiction. Furthermore, the parents may not have provided a mature foundation to build on.

In school, children learn to adapt to the external world instead of letting the ego grow, and this stage brings many painful problems. Some children feel very different from the rest, making them sad and lonely. The imperfections and evil of the world and of themselves become conscious problems or internal impulses that are not understood. They may retreat from the external world and build an inner wall, repressing much of the personality and the psyche, which then only appears in symbolic dreams. They begin to repress their own contents and to store them in a big sac.[2]

Many children search for meaning for life so they can deal with the chaos inside and outside. They may seek spiritual or religious guidance to understand all that hinders and obstructs them. Others suffer from a deadly boredom, or from a meaningless void that may express in a certain kind of defiance.

Usually, the repressed material begins to take on its own life, like an "inner friend," an imaginary character with whom they elaborate their dark side. It can be projected on their special teddy-bear or on the hero in a television series or movie, or on a sports hero. Sometimes it is their own secret, and many children experience a companion who sometimes appears to nudge them into something bad, as someone who is real and external to them. The purpose of these actions is to provoke life or be able to observe the uncontrolled response from elders and thus excuse their own bad behavior, or else let out repressed individualism. They also excuse themselves saying that their "secret friend" told them to do it and that it isn't their fault. Often they project themselves into movie heroes and cartoon characters. Here the shadow appears as a personal and imaginary entity many children live with and on which they still focus the extrasensory capacity that remains from the previous stage. This is a crucial stage of the individualization process, for now people decide how the total personality of the individual will be projected outward in the next stages, and how these contents will be recovered or integrated once more in the individual personality.

All these confrontations help young adults learn to integrate the light of the individual psyche in themselves and to fit in with their social environment. Nowadays, this process is becoming more accelerated and intensified due to the profusion of cultural mentalities that children are exposed to from an early age.

Many things that are misunderstood, or that become distorted between the reality children experience and what they believe, are projected in this last stage of the Lake. Many errors or misunderstandings of the people around us can't be just categorized as true or false, and will have to be discerned during the process of life. What is most feared and rejected will have to be experienced. This includes all the concepts that elders distort most during our childhood, such as the fear of death. Our fear of death, for example, produces an enormous conditioning impact that hinders the full experience of the preparation for death in Stage 7 of the Lake.

The Mountain and the Lake are complementary polarities, for the Lake is where we recover the joy of having lived and enjoy fully what is left to live. This

---

2. Sac is more than a bag-like receptacle. It is the ink-sac of a squid, a cavity in an animal or vegetable organism. It is like the membrane envelope of a hernia, a cyst or a tumor. The image is so strong, that the sac becomes part of the skin and of our being, and it's really hard to get rid of it. It is also a "cul de sac" in French: dead-end.

joy begins to be lost in this stage of the Mountain if we have not accepted and understood what life has granted us.

3rd Stage: The Absorption of the Light and the Projection of Darkness

WATER

Little by little, we begin to value our emotional ties to other people. We voluntarily place the parts of ourselves that we don't like (personality traits that we judge and condemn in ourselves, or that we learn other people don't like in us) in a sac that is called the shadow. The substance in this "sac" is locked up and furious; it assumes its own entity and regresses into barbarism. It has a primitive sense of humor, and, unfortunately, a sexuality of savage courage. Anger becomes a kind of controlled hostility that resembles the tyrant father and the witch mother, who both seem to have been blown up to an exaggerated dimension. We do not realize that we are controlled by this "secret inner friend" for our logic tells us that this "friend inside" does not exist. We don't admit having anything to do with the contents of this sac. This inner friend becomes an inner voice that sometimes tells us, or makes us think, the biggest atrocities. It splits in two, one outside and another inside, conscious and unconscious. This monstrous being is often projected outward, and we recognize it in certain activities of other people which we not only try to avoid, but we tend to judge morally. We create ties of friendship with people who think and feel like we do, which makes us feel sheltered in some way. We all know a lot about giving up our power and not acting in a firm way as individuals. How much we give in depends on how much we have sacrificed in this stage to feel close to other people. That's why we don't say many things we feel, or we repress instincts and aspects we identified with in the previous stage.

Sometimes adult males let their mothers carry their inner witch for them, just as many women let their fathers carry their inner tyrant for them, and this energy is projected unconsciously on a series of people who in some way represent or openly manifest all that we have been repressing in ourselves. We manage, however, to keep these people away from our lives during this time.

We perceive from our environment and from the people in it what is expected from us. The greatest emotional intensity is experienced through sexuality: belonging to and fully possessing another person, that "other half" who seems to be able to carry out all that we feel unable to. When we give up our power, we also lose our independence and individuality. During this stage, individual power is usually given up in favor of social trends, groups, and friends who seem to think like us and have a similar lifestyle, or who at least do not provoke us morally.

In our culture we believe in joining in marriage during this stage, so that, during the marriage ceremony, the man can transfer his projection of the inner witch (previously attached to his mother) to the wife he has chosen, and the bride does likewise with the projection of her inner tyrant. This happens to all people who have experienced an intense sexual and emotional relationship. That's also why some people decline serious relationships. Falling in love is part of our unconscious desire to participate in an intense psychological process that takes place when two people's karmic patterns interact. When we recognize the process, we can integrate what we need to learn. However, if we are not "awake," we blame destiny or other people when we don't understand the karmic urges.

In other stages we begin to acknowledge ourselves, making excuses for any bad behavior or unbalanced reactions. In this stage, we observe our own unconscious tendencies in other people and this is called "projection of the psyche." Making projections, oftentimes unconsciously, is part of relating. These projections blur our vision of our partners and our objectivity, hampering true relationships. Most people retain this form of behavior until they contact the true self and unite the feminine and masculine principles. Then they enter into a real synergy of cooperation and love that only few attain in the last stages of psychological maturity.

Psychological maturity indicates a complete alteration of brain frequency that corresponds to our perception of time and duality. In the previous stage, life was experienced, and in this stage we learn that life is to be interpreted intellectually. Too much stress on intellectual concepts may indicate a kind of fragmented reasoning. We forget other forms of perception and knowledge. People who have other brain frequencies open are sometimes thought to be "crazy."

The mystic state of fusion with the All can be lost and the feeling of loneliness and isolation increases when the mind is rigid. This feeling has nothing to do with individualism, for it produces not pleasure but anxiety, and people feel that they must repress more and more facets of themselves in order to be accepted by the group. We become docile and malleable, sensing what is expected of us, which increases our unconscious projections.

Here, the psychic transformer could be the study and admiration for a historical or artistic character. It might also be the grandparents, if they have reached psychological maturity and can help the youngster become more conscious. A wise person or a magical character could have some illuminating effect on people who want to become conscious of projections and premature judgments of other people. Someone will come along to inspire youong people to channel their psychological ideals into some practical and useful activity for spiritual growth. Nowadays, this role may be played by gurus and spiritual masters, through the Eastern traditions the West has adopted. In the East it is believed that people become schizophrenic because they are caught by inexplicable extrasensory perceptions which only meditation and spiritual guidance can balance.

Westerners have reached such a degree of duality that they are often living in a state of collective and chronic "schizophrenia." Unfortunately, our new Western trend of seeking the guru to establish balance does not solve the problem entirely, since modern gurus also become infected by the Western pathology of scarcity and materialism. This provokes another kind of dependency, since gurus usually don't liberate their pupils and give them responsibility and creative control over their own psychological, emotional, and spiritual evolution.

In this stage, people are forced to abandon the family home, although this is done by levels and there is a substitution of another social family group, or they create their own family, in spite of a lack of self-knowledge that forces them to relive intensely the repressed and projected behavior patterns. In some cases, the family is excessively protective and keeps young people blocked between the previous stage and this one, causing them to remain emotionally immature and psychologically involuted.

In any case, this stage is characterized by rejection of the parents and a rejection of some of the parents' restrictive procedures. Young people express their individuality by rebelling against the parents and their codes. This is the opposite of dependency, but contains the same characteristics, and is called "counter-dependence."

One of the major concerns of this stage is the channeling of sexual energy. It is a taboo for certain Western cultures and causes a lot of conflicts born of misunderstandings that become twisted inside the psyche due to a lack of knowledge on the subject. When sexual energy is repressed, it becomes an obsession.

Because of a lack of transformative examples in our culture, many women project their happiness on their relationships with the opposite sex and they are often conditioned by men and a "macho" mentality. They voluntarily give up their free and wild feminine being; they give up the capacity to deal with the world independently. Women have the gift of union and few are capable of remaining independent without guiding examples in their recent archetypes.

When the inner tyrant or the witch of the young man or woman are repressed, and they have only incomprehensible resentments or frustrations in their relationship with their parents, they cannot achieve a positive relationship with the anima and animus. At that point, the greatest inner power has become controlled and involuted. It is precisely the anima and animus that are responsible for choosing the partner with whom the drama of that misunderstood and twisted projection created with the parents will be lived out. Perhaps if we did not project there would be nothing to connect us to the outside world.

The projection of the anima or the animus in a passionate love relationship can upset the balance the young person is developing during this stage. Love is necessary to go on to the next stage for it forces the individual to develop his or her own maturity. Love helps the individual become aware of the unconscious side of the personality.

The anima takes shape through the young man's mother and the animus through the young woman's father. This archetype, in our Western culture, has been characterized by servitude and overprotection on the part of the mother, who maintains the young man in an infantile and dependent state. On the part of the father there is a lack of trust in the logical reasoning and self-sufficiency of the young woman, which is also the cause of a psychological complex; she believes herself incapable of defending herself and so remains dependent.

Sometimes, consciously, one chooses the opposite to what parents represent externally; however the tyrant or witch in the partner will coincide with that of the parents. This isn't discovered until the relationship develops.

This is the period of life in which the Water element of unconscious emotions penetrates the psyche. Traumas remain buried and are only brought to consciousness through dreams or creative imagination. Darkness surrounds light, it is inside and outside, and the individual only recognizes his or her own light, suffering, and effort. The individual is not aware that it is all a projection of the mind and a repetition of drama lived through parents and the environment in the receptivity of darkness. Both the negative and the positive things received at that stage are deepened in the Self in order to be used, known and controlled consciously and unconsciously.

The first frustrated love relationships make young people prefer the world of dual reality, devoid of fantasies and dreams. Also at this time, many unconscious fears are absorbed from the environment. We face the meaning of death and many of the sensations and fears absorbed by the unconscious mind are projected strongly upon experiences that must be lived later on. Many of the things we hold as traumas have a special urge to become conscious in the 6th stage of Fire. Alchemically, the contents repressed during the Water stage will be transformed into the psychological maturity of Fire, although at that time we may consider them unjustified fears that must be understood in the 6th stage of revelation and understanding.

WIND

4th Stage:
The Deepening of Darkness and the Dispersion of Light

This corresponds to the stage where all weaknesses seem to have been vanquished and we have moved away from all those who represented a moral risk. We have taken control over our life and know that, to a great extent, we have made our own decisions. We structure our world with our logic. We are often lost in external activities and have arguments to excuse our weaknesses and behaviors.

We may even think that we are doing good for others; we are concerned with others' well-being and think that we have gotten rid of any irrational behavior. The voice of the "inner friend" has turned into mental dialogues modeled after those we would have with other people when a conflict occurs.

We know that satisfaction is a personal matter and we see how we project ourselves outward to obtain positive response and external recognition. The darkness, which in the previous stage came from the outside, has been vanquished. We rely on our sense of inner responsibility, strength, or even luck, but in some way we are unaware of how big the sac is, and where we have buried the darkness in our subconscious. This shadow grows a lot and it is becoming more and more savage, since it has no way to express itself. It becomes a monstrous caged animal in the sac we carry with us, and it gets harder and harder to acknowledge that it is still there. The retreat of the shadow is caused by an idea that we dominate the external world, and we think there is no participation from the shadow. However, the shadow is our other negative half, and represents the lower Yin line.

This dark side has both negative elements and positive gifts that we have negated and which we only contact through dreams, through psychic existence or through the development of some artistic or creative talent.

In that sac are all the frustrations, incompetence, losses, misunderstandings, unsolved relationships, suffering, love traumas, rejections, hatreds, doubts, and physical pains that have turned into chronic illnesses, or turned into psychological karmic pathology, or into a crystallization of emotional patterns.

During this stage of life, one must feel some type of individual fulfillment, satisfaction, or achievement for overcoming difficulties. This fulfillment helps us look inward in the next stage without causing an imbalance in the psyche. If, in this 4th stage, we have not acquired good feelings about ourselves, we feel shaky and need to control the inner monster longer, delaying or prolonging the general process of individuation, or deepening the shadow dangerously. This imbalance can lead to illness.

If women, in the desire to be accepted and admired, have put their masculinity in the sac, they will later realize its hostility, and they can be cold and brutal in their self-criticism. If they find a hostile man to live with, they will put the blame on him in order to vent inner pressure. They might even feel a two-fold projection: one from the inner masculine side and one from the outer one, for every part of the personality that we dislike will become hostile toward us. All the rage that men have kept in the sac for twenty years, will be reflected, suddenly, in the expression on their wives' faces.

The more things have been put in the sac, the less energy will be available for other things. But, in any case, as we learned during childhood, we have too much energy, which would lead us to constant clashes and struggles with the external environment and with other people. Aggression pours out of the sac and attacks everyone. We tame it and control its contents for fear of rejection, which we also put in the sac when it happens. So we progressively forget what is in the sac and it gets traumatized into chronic emotions. We only get to know the contents of the shadow that we carry on our backs when we innocently lay it down and project it on a person who provokes negative feelings in us. Then it causes an effect of action-reaction, interacting with the law of karma.

There are also social and cultural prejudices that are put in the sac, in an attempt to control and judge our social interactions. We are dealing with a network of shadows that lead us to turn in our power to a reaction, to the defense of an ideal.

For instance, a man may turn his sense of pride or strength over to his wife, and lose control over it. Then, when a problem with the children arises, he lets her handle it the way he has given her power to do it. Likewise, the feeling of weakness, impotence, or even idealism can also be projected, putting her on a pedestal where she does not belong. The soft appearance of men lies, nowadays, in the absence of their witch, which they let their wives or mothers carry for them. The same could be said of the absence of independence and authority in women, who let their fathers or husbands embody their tyrant or patriarch for them.

When we project the various qualities we reject, these projected substances or forms of power that come from within, we get them back as belonging to another person. We don't understand how psychological projections can take place, for we no longer have our inner friend and we only trust what we can see with our opaque eyes.

Disappointments in love relationships is a prime cause of the imprisonment of our senses and of losing trust in the fantasy and hopes of the dream world and the fourth dimension. Love and sexuality are contacts that keep us linked to this dimension, enslaving us more and more to the material world and to finite time.

During this stage people are civilized and manage to adapt to the surrounding world. If it seems very hostile and hard to dominate, it is due to the amount of substances and powers buried and not integrated that escape from the sac, blocking the progress of self-knowledge and self-control in the outer world. If this is not achieved, we might remain indefinitely in a stage of conquest of the environment, causing a psychological immaturity and an emotional imbalance that can be dangerous at certain older ages. It then becomes the "moral intelligence" that devastates everything with its judgments, which are only self-projections or projections of that which we will not acknowledge in ourselves.

The more knowledge and awareness we have, the greater the requirement for global spiritual in all relationships with the world. In order to feel satisfied with ourselves in this psychological stage, we need spiritual integration in our external relationships.

Friends play a very important role in this psychological stage, since we choose and attract, unconsciously, people who have similar contents in their sac. We know that they will not provoke us to take any content out of our sac. Even if they see our flaws or inner monsters, they dare not tell us because they are in the same situation: this is a fear of rejection, or confusing reality with projection, etc. In fact, every time some content escapes from one of their sacs, it produces such a conflict that it places us in an obvious conflict or makes us lose a friend. Moreover, most of our friends have gotten used to us the way we are and the relationship gets complicated whenever we change significantly. If we feel compulsive anger or when a friend blames us for a certain fault, it is certain that we are facing some part of the content of the unconscious sac and of our shadow. That's why the ego is now concerned with self-education and not having to feel that silent shame for being different or being ridiculed.

Even when we decide to choose a teacher in technical or spiritual matters, we must be aware that we are granting our power to another person and that we are going to be diminished in our own power of autonomy for some time. A certain exchange can be positive if autonomy is maintained throughout the period of influence and both parties are familiar with the mechanism of this relationship. The leader must be aware of the disadvantage resulting from students giving over their power unconsciously. The teacher needs to be careful not to abuse power. This same mechanism happens in the relationship between fathers and sons. The projections include each others' weaknesses and ambiguities. These can be corrected when fathers help their sons choose their own autonomy instead of provoking more dependency, contradiction, or rebellion.

In the Western world, this stage is characterized by "moral intelligence," in which the world is redefined in compartments and we excuse the cruelty or abuse of others' psyche by educating them and teaching them the standard morality of the society they belong to, which is, in turn, interpreted as acts of love. "Moral intelligence" is the aberration of people who try to continue with the masks a certain culture or society has chosen, so that the projections continue.

In this psychological dilemma, people find support and friendship pacts to control the contents of the sac and delay the process of individuation, remaining in this stage far too long. If the situation of social reaffirmation and "moral intelligence" continues after age 50, it can become dangerous for the psychological balance of the individual. This stage will merge with the following one where all is returned to us from the outside, and unconscious provocations take form in our children, family members, associates, and friends in such an uncomfortable way that it is hard to realize that they come from inside us. The blockage can easily develop into mental or physical illness.

The need to obtain "psychic transformers" during this stage is essential, since we cannot repress our radiant energy and power without, at least, going through transformation initiations that we understand and assimilate. By doing so, we can come to good terms with our own loneliness and the evident separation between egos, as well as the relativity of all that is experienced at an emotional level. A good attitude in the face of suffering and a view of it as part of the growth process allows us to see the positive aspect of what we have experienced in the past, as well as developing a good attitude toward death. These are requirements for entering into the next stage without an excess of psychological defenses or so we don't try to blame others or project upon them.

The intuitive reason for looking inside is more or less conscious, for we choose a person who reflects our animus or our anima in the love relationship and so change or repeat the pattern that began with our parents. The Yin line at the base of the trigram establishes its relationship with the opposite sex in oneself.

In this period, we elaborate on our anchors, the social obligations, professional commitments, memories, and emotions that must be questioned in order to know whether they truly belong to us or if they have been "borrowed" from the other actors and characters of the drama of our life.

While we are alone, we seem to get along fairly well, but as soon as other people appear, we begin to do strange things, things dark or primitive. We begin to feel fear that we are not like the others, afraid if we don't "follow the crowd." So, we let ourselves be dragged down by impulses that don't belong to us.

The contents of the sac give shape to our "shadow," enhanced by the tendency to give up our power to another, or to project our personality on others and to put all that is bothersome in the sac. The shadow appears in dreams and in the psychological world, and takes its place as the "secret friend" from childhood days.

Our personality remains in the physical world through the ego, identifying that shadow with what we abhor socially, for instance: blacks, whites, reds and yellows, communists, fascists, homosexuals, or all that we condemn. However, we are not aware that by being opposed and in control, we are giving our energy to feed it and attract it. If we were aware of it being a projection, we would stop our fear and hostility and handle it with more understanding. Whether the shadow becomes our friend or our enemy depends to a large extent on us.

For many different reasons, we can all feel pushed to live out our worst side and repress the best. In this case, the shadow will be made up of those positive aspects and will reveal itself in dreams. This always represents the other side of the ego and takes shape with the qualities we dislike in other people: tyrannical reactions, negative thoughts, poisoned judgments and cold, intellectual and cruel reasoning. Instead of facing our faults, we project them on other people in order to experience them, for it is the negative traits that we notice.

All that is unknown to the ego is mixed in with the shadow, even higher and valuable forces. That's why we repress and project all that we consider pertains to the opposite sex, or else keep it in a primitive state even if it may be useful in many situations in life. Therefore, the anima of man or the animus of women is recognized as an inner power and we learn to integrate it into the personality through the reflection and response of the member of the opposite sex we have chosen as love partner.

A man's intellectual stress can be due to a negative anima that constantly presents him with unsolvable riddles that lead him more and more to cold, intellectual responses and to dualism. The anima also represents childhood erotic fantasies and pornography, which keep this man in a state of emotional and sexual immaturity. Possessiveness and extreme care of one's car, gun, or other idol, are also the projections of the anima. All this, together with the idealization of the feminine role through religion, makes a man lose contact with other aspects of himself, and he becomes a victim of his projections from the outside, becoming compulsively dependent on a woman.

Just as the character of the anima of a man is formed, originally, by his mother, the woman's is formed by the father with unquestionable convictions and truths, although they might not fit into the personal reality of her life. Sometimes this is projected upon a man who does not return her love.

The animus personifies a series of fantasies, desires, and judgments about how things should be that separate a woman from the reality of her own life. She only gets involved in obligations she projects on her husband so that he feels happy with her, and she often enslaves herself by trying to live out numerous calculated thoughts full of malice and intrigue. This can even manifest in her wish-

Seeing with the eye of the Soul (mandala by A. de Diego).

ing death on those people who are apparently tying her down, instead of realizing that her feelings come from the demands of her own animus.

In mythology and in certain cultures, the animus was represented as a figure of mystery, never to be confused with the understanding of death itself. This archetype can also be represented by authority figures, laws, prohibitions and obligations.

The animus, or inner man in a woman, leads her to complicated situations, automatically producing possessiveness in the people she lives with and on whom she projects.

Very often, a loss of balance, although not very apparent in this stage, is produced by an excess of fantasy and dream desires surrounding certain complexes.

A resistance to freeing ourselves from the thoughts and prejudices shared with others blocks contact with the true inner self. Fashions, opinions, and collective activities created during this stage represent unconscious complexes that we protect in ourselves. That's why it is essential in this stage to experience broken relationships and conflicts with friends. We should not get stuck in this stage of the individuation process for too long a time.

Religious symbols represent certain idealizations and for the people whose religious and cultural symbols satisfy them, there seems to be little space for self-doubt. These people live for a certain time in a relative state of harmony and it seems that faith sustains and nourishes them. People who have lost their faith and who have replaced it by rational opinions may investigate psychological discoveries. Still others believe partly in religious traditions, but question some of them. This means they have several sets of values, and it is harder to recognize the unconscious, for it requires courage and integrity.

Religious beliefs arose from the collective unconscious, but today, however, they are part of the collective consciousness. During a long evolution process, that original material that arose from the psyche of individuals in synergy has been adapted to the present time, and has lost its richness of inner contact with the original unconscious psyche. This crystallization process is a great handicap, for it separates more and more from the true essence that originated the need for the symbol. The rational mind begins to manipulate and theorize on that which it dangerously condemns, and separates us from essential knowledge, while our symbols become articles of blind faith. Without a psyche capable of receiving divine inspiration that can be expressed in words and in art, there would be no reality in our religious symbols.

During this stage, some kind of isolation, some solitary and self-sufficient reflection, is advisable so that we don't get stuck pursuing social standards that we use to hide what the true self really wants to express. If we obtain good support at this stage, we can dare to go deeply into the psyche, probing into ourselves in the following stages.

What we think about at this stage has an enormous force of projection into the future. Most people are not aware of the whole of their thoughts—the unconscious ones—and therefore, in the next and 5th stage of Thunder these thoughts explode into the conscious mind and awareness comes. By provocation from the outside, we see outward and are consciously provoked to also see inside. All that we fear and repress is expressed immediately in its compensatory polarity of Thunder.

❦

The residence of the soul within the brain case and the anatomy of the eye {is an} emblem of perception. Blake . . . believed this to be a visionary world, a world created by perception from within. It was therefore a world with the soul as focus of perception. . . . The sensorium, then, was the space to which all sensation was brought and from which all perception proceeded, determined, it was supposed, by the action of an observer-soul. Blake, it would seem, discovered in the anatomy of the eye and in an understanding of its optics a precise image of the processes of his visionary soul-centered world.

Blake's map of consciousness . . . contain{s} much of his understanding of the eternal nature of human experience. . . . Albion is the archetypal man, the pattern of all con-sciousnes. The Four Zoas are the four eternal and archetypal faculties of Man . . . Imagination . . . Passion . . . Reason . . . Instinct.

Finally, we may understand this egg to contain all the universe of conscious experi-ence of the individual and the spiritual existence "of a brain open to heaven & hell."

When the aqueous humor, which disperses and amplifies light rays proceeding into the eye, . . . the heart, lungs and stomach—organs which disperse, distribute, and amplify energy within the human body; or when the iris, which causes the pupil to dilate and con-tract, thus influencing the amount of light let into the eye, is compared to . . . the men-tal cultivation, open the visionary eye to eternity. . . . Golgonooza is a place of energy and cultivation . . . the setting where artistic form is given to the human body, and . . . redeems mortality to eternity.

It is especially valuable to see the eternal forms . . . as existing within Blake's under-standing of the anatomy and physiology of perception. Blake saw Beulah in terms which parallel a description of the chamber of vitreous humor within the eye. {It is} a passage-way for travelers to and from eternity {through this} vitreous humor which is a passage-way for the rays of light as they converge into foci upon the retina. Moreover, just as the vitreous humor functions to keep the surface of the retina uniformly spherical, so Beulah functions to protect and preserve "love & pity & sweet compassion." . . . The impression of light rays upon the retina produces perception . . . opening that center and expanding the ever-enduring doors of art and the creative individual. . . . Since light rays impressing upon the retina produce inverted images, Eden mirrors the . . . world and redeems its eter-nal potential through . . . art.

Perception flows both inward to the eye as a stream of sensory data entering the brain, and outward from the eye, as a projection of reality upon the sensory tumult beyond the body.

—MILTON: A POEM BY WILLIAM BLAKE
Kay Parkhurst Easson and Roger R. Easson, eds.,
pages 146, 147, 148, 150.

From the Explosion of Darkness to Enlightenment

THUNDER

5th Stage:
The Penetration of Light and the
Explosion of Darkness

When the light enters the unconscious and crosses the threshold of the ego, it makes the ego shaky and unstable. The sac is so full that it starts to rip and spill out its contents, projected on other people, and this bounces back to us. This is the first step of inner vision, provoked by outer darkness and by others. All that has been projected outward is returned, for it has been attracted to one's life by judging and condemning it. Thus it must be experienced personally to learn to distinguish what is true from what is false.

Everything that doesn't belong to the contents we have put in the sac. If we have no premature prejudices about something, it will not provoke a reaction in us. We accept certain behaviors in other people and don't try to correct them, even if we don't understand them. We don't react to a life experience that has no similarity to our shadow, for it doesn't seem close enough to our reality to provoke anything like a crisis. However, when we morally judge, deny, or try to correct something in others or in ourselves, we can provoke an experience that will define if our judgment is correct or not.

It is convenient to enter this stage around age 38; if we don't, it can indicate that we are stuck in the previous stage for too long. Often, people with an inquisitive spirit begin to enter this stage around age 30 and definitely at 40. Then, we realize that the whole of reality with its ups and downs depends on ourselves and not on the difficulties apparently provoked by the environment. Actually, it is the time of psychological and emotional growth where we encounter more conflicts either following our own path or that of others. If self-awareness and inner enlightenment is delayed past age 50, any psychological disharmony can jeopardize mental or physical health, due to an excessive permanence at the previous stage. No matter how many battles the environment may have presented, we remain constantly in these two stages. Although we might have controlled a hostile environment, at some point we have to begin to explore from within. When added to excessive control of the outer world due to a prolonged stay at the previous stage, the explosion and provocation of the shadow may cause illness of body or mind.

We enter into this stage when we look into the sac for the first time and realize we have repressed positive aspects of our energy, as well as negative ones. At first we only regret having given up some of our powers or gifts, and we know that the outside reasons were not strong enough to justify not following our individual creativity. Perhaps we only regret not using our potential because of something we cannot admit. We do not acknowledge that the substance of the shadow that has been growing inside the sac is also made up of other activities we greatly despise. We only have to look inside once to realize that it is we who have complicated the external situations and have attracted the experiences we are going through now, in order to start losing the control we had so arduously constructed before. In any case, we are already immersed in the turmoil, relationships, and commitments to the circumstances of our lives, and although we are not ready to recognize them entirely, we have chosen them ourselves. The projections continue, but now with such an after-effect that we have a hard time separating the consequences of our repressed inner activities from our intimate experiences, while the circumstances that made us fear and control them are taking place.

Somehow, the projection and its reflection has turned wild and violent to force us to take sides. We have to live the experience in order to know whether or not a part of us needs to excuse our weaknesses or if our weaknesses aren't so reproachable after all.

Somehow, things happen to break the clichés by which we have lived for such a long time, and we become more flexible and realize that everything is relative. Therefore, this stage is dangerous for elderly people who have had to do terrible things to gain social acceptance, because their conscience is troubled and they often cannot forgive themselves for what they did.

If a man wants to connect with his feminine side, he soon realizes the hostility involved when he sees the hostility aroused in his partner. Likewise, a woman may see the cruel tyrant's face in the man she loves. In some way, the feminine and masculine sides seemed to be bothersome excess energy and it was loaded on the partner little by little, but we get it back in one minute when its energy is returned to us. This scares us so much that we return to the previous stage of self-control and projection. Thus we damage the relationship with the partner again, or delay our own process of psychological growth.

The truth is that we enter into this stage in a series of phases that are marked at intervals by the unconscious control and projection of the previous stage. What is essential is the time it takes us to make the complete transition. Then, finally, we will have dominated all and everything and we begin to realize that the monster is not outside but inside, and, as brave warriors, we dive in at once to encounter the shadow, no matter how painful, and acknowledge it as our own. Most people have a shaky ego and can only accomplish this in small doses and without losing the control achieved in the previous stage.

The truth is that the monster, either through internal mental dialogues, inner emotional struggles, or repressed desires, robs us of most of the energy we have available to deal with other things. Some people face the shadow when they are provoked by an external agent, and they experience the catharsis as a battle they are sure to win. Others, however, being unsure of their own success, or fearing not to be able to control themselves if they let their monster show its head just a little, need small and frequent external provocations, either consciously staged through therapy or as they appear in their lives, but still avoiding a direct confrontation.

Sooner or later, some of the projections begin to rattle and disconnect the person; something doesn't fit in anymore. The reality we have created for ourselves no longer satisfies us. It bores us and we begin to sense catastrophes, defeats, and ruin around us and no longer have anyone to blame. From the time we begin to acknowledge our failures and errors, to acknowledge our deficiencies and weaknesses, something changes and suddenly all our relationships get worse and we ourselves increase our problems.

Others take advantage of our lowered defenses to complain about us, while we finally admit our inner monster by experiencing it. Whether we try to repress it or observe it, if we keep controlling it, it keeps growing. It becomes, then, an irreversible process, and we can only, to some extent, plan the confrontation if we don't run away from it. If, on the other hand, we try to avoid facing our own monster, it will personify itself in another person who represents the shadow, and will attack us when we least expect. This would increase the conflict and disharmony even more and prolong the individuation process. It is difficult to determine in each individual case whether this intensifies it by deepening psychological contact, or if it blocks it, causing damage in the overall health of the individual. All knowledge about the human being depends on the unknown state of the psyche, and, therefore, the process of psychological stages, and the result of these stages, is all the more mysterious, since each process is unique. The maximum differentiation occurs as a result of a number of more or less individualized psyches interacting at a certain point in time with the psyche of one specific individual, conforming the synchrony in the totality of each critical experience of life. It is impossible to take all this into consideration and decide whether the psychological explosion-enlightenment of an individual will be able to cross the threshold of maturity or not. Thus, it is unique and personal; no one can cure us, save us or guide us; we just choose a series of travel companions. This process almost always injures the vital, mental or astral body to some extent, producing certain damage, more or less serious, in the individual's physical body.

The process of the previous stage of throwing out the substances of the sac now becomes a process of reabsorbing all those qualities we have scattered all over the world, projected on other people of the same or different sex, on our parents, children, teachers, nation, or race. The explosion suggests they return it, or we run into a situation in which we would need to use those contained qualities again in order to defend ourselves. However, now they are untamed, in a raw and wild state.

A person sometimes seems to provoke in us all those feelings and actions we thought we had overcome. That person personifies the shadow and is usually of the same sex, for we accept more things from someone of the opposite sex than from someone like ourselves. The intensity of the explosion and provocation of the shadow will depend on the proximity and interaction among both people close to us. Most same gender people carry aspects of our shadow: mother, sister, friends, mother-in-law, sister-in-law, and at some point these aspects become evident and provocative. Caring and love help solve many of these close encounters.

When there are intense emotions, the catharsis is even greater. This happens when our love mate is attracted by another person or is having a relationship with someone else, who always represents our shadow, since he or she manifests all that we ourselves have repressed and have kept in a raw state. The person who loves us is always involved with our whole being, and somehow finds some elements missing, which he or she senses we have, but that we have repressed so much that they no longer make up our personality. If, at some time, his or her being needs them, the lover looks for them or finds them in another person. This happens as a result of projecting certain qualities on the partner, who needs to contrast them with another person to integrate them or dispose of them within his or her personality.

Our animal instincts are so connected with the shadow that we know and sense the tactics and manipulations that the person representing our shadow will employ. While our instincts are alert to defend from the extreme situations our shadow creates, we become aware of them because they are activities and patterns of action we have condemned and repressed in ourselves. Thus, we attract the kind of circumstances that make our experience more difficult, in order that we become aware of them.

From the moment the provocation begins through friends, associates, boss, or lovers of our spouse, it can take a long time for us to realize that they are reflections of our inner darkness. Otherwise, the contents of the sac may increase, and the circumstances we unconsciously attract into our lives can be aggravated, until we realize that they stem from our chronic thoughts and emotions.

We can remain in this struggle of cconsciousness and subconsciousness most of our lives in order to realize that the world we have created is due to the same things we perceived when we were babies. What is inside is outside, only now in individualized and independent form, but we must realize that we and our circumstances are one and the same.

This stage represents the period of cathartic violence, either mental, emotional, or physical. We all must go through it to re-own the power we have granted other people. It is not returned smoothly due to the amount of self-criticism and judgments projected on those issues. The more intense and radical the repression or denial has been, the more intense will be the experience provoking the catharsis and the re-owning of power.

After age 30, people begin to be individualized, leading to ruptures in couples formed before that time, due to a lack of space for their individual beings. The attempt to maintain the marriage structure in spite of the growth blockage it involves will only aggravate the situation further and lead to a greater catharsis. Likewise, any situation left unconscious and unsolved will repeat itself more intensely. Unfinished relationships of the past create complications for future ones. There's no sense in running away from confrontation for fear of the unconscious repercussions of letting the hidden inner monster out. In the world of the psyche, nothing can be repressed, but instead it should be allowed to come out spontaneously, observed and modified positively without judgments or criticisms. Afflicted people attract "moral intelligence" to ignore provocation, and this becomes a tool to continue unconsciously. The consequence of giving up power to others once provocation has begun, is to become more and more weakened and undervalued, for lack of the inner tyrant to yell out "Enough!" We even get to the point of blocking out the feeling of pain. Men become ever more cold and indifferent, enduring the games of their partners. Meanwhile, women let tyrant husbands turn them into slaves and let them take away their power so that relationships break up or they finally become independent of the patriarch they have projected. The only solution is to strip men of their tyrant-hero qualities, and the women of their witch-saint ones, both being endowed by the partner or associate. This is done by personifying and representing these qualities ourselves. This is frightening, for we sense the danger of overdoing it and letting out all the repressed reaction at once. It is usually easier to lose control and react irrationally and unproportionately.

This stage is essentially a time to clear up within ourselves all our psychological projections. The provocative return of our projections leads to conflict after conflict in relationships, until we acquire enough independence to become individualized, to look inside and slay our own monster, eat the shadow, or integrate those qualities into the personality. Instead of being negative, it is a painful but necessary growth process.

The success or failure of this stage stems from not being afraid to be oneself and acquiring a positive, transformative conscience. If our parents had passed on to us that positive sense of transformation or inner change, we could have modeled it after some archetypal historical character, as long as we could recognize that our process is individual and unique. We may have guides and counselors to transform us, but only we can decide to do it. So, all another person can do is show us how to contact that inner source of power. That source is found the moment we contact the power of our shadow, and the best a person can do for loved ones is to let us contact our monster without judgment, criticism, or rejection.

The most difficult thing to recognize in this process is that our emotions provoke the emotions of the other, and it is very painful when we express our monster and the other does not react with his or hers. This situation can only be salvaged by an age difference or by the higher knowledge of one of the individuals involved, by having gone through one of these stages and having grown psychologically from it. This creates a capacity of resistance to suffering caused by all those complications and misunderstandings. In all transitions there is the woe and strife of losing a part of ourselves and acquiring something new. Everything we receive must be transformed to become part of our consciousness; once inside, the agent object or subject is no longer necessary. True inner transformation comes when we are ready to look inside and penetrate the unconscious with the light of awareness, no matter how painful it may be.

Particularly, contacts with people of the same sex provoke the irrational reactions of the shadow. If a person is the shadow, one will also become its reciprocal one, although the difference in age, in psychological and emotional maturity, and in consciousness is obvious, and each provokes a different kind of reaction, consciously or not.

It usually happens as an impulsive act: before we realize it, an evil reaction or gesture happens and we have made the wrong decision, or have done what we wanted consciously to avoid. The shadow is not only what we repress or omit and deny personally; it is also shared as a collective infection with many other human beings. It is an inborn instinct that seems to be rejected among the same sexual gender or race. Even for people with a high level of consciousness, it is hard to integrate the qualities of the shadow, since it contains the passional impulses and the repressed energy of the past, which only manifests when the situation presses the right buttons. Then, unexpectedly and unwantedly, the irrational defense mechanism pops out. Even if the reaction mechanism is maintained in self-control, it will only turn more and more hostile.

The other person upon whom we have projected the shadow becomes more hostile and revengeful for being misunderstood and ignored. Although one may escape and go unconscious, the repressed instincts erupt in our mental attention even with violent physical gestures and acts, usually only for a few minutes before we control them again. By denying the facts, we enter into a soft and slow schizophrenia resulting from our duality, where we believe to have control over our lives.

The ego gets tired of controlling, or loses sight of the reason for it, letting the individual become aware of the hidden and evil side of the personality. This requires courage, defying ridicule, and an heroic act of persevering on a mission to an unknown destination. Often, hidden talents and positive powers are found inside the shadow, but for many, the risk of mental disorder is too high a price for it. So, most individuals keep on controlling this explosive stage of the individuation process, although the mental and emotional provocations end up attacking the nervous and digestive system, and may cause an illness.

People who can recall dreams will attain a higher degree of consciousness, but will always find themselves facing fearful crossroads in terms of the interpretation and symbolism of these dreams. Many ethical doubts arise when we attempt to give straightforward definitions to dreams revealing the shadow. It even shows up through creatures symbolizing deep unconscious impulses that can only be felt in the body. Part of the labyrinth of penetrating into the psychic inner world is making mistakes in the interpretation of the messages from the unconscious; we may continue to believe that we are right, but the situation almost always gets complicated with morality and behavior and ethics. There are people who harbor unconscious criminal thoughts that are affecting or hindering the destiny of another person. This can have an impact on the destiny of both parties involved, whether or not we are conscious of the meaning of our interaction and karma.

In many cases, it is convenient to repress crossing the barrier of the unconscious, especially with people who would unleash their criminal impulses. It has serious consequences and we have to be brave enough to look at the contents of our shadow when most people are too lazy to think in depth about the moral aspects of behavior; we may be aware, but delay processing them, disregarding the effect the unconscious has on what we attract to our lives.

Many ethical difficulties arise subtly in our lives, in addition to dealing with the shadow. This "inner figure" is represented by the opposite sex in dreams, like the animus for a woman or the anima for a man: the irrational capacity for feelings and for falling in love in the masculine unconscious and the rational capacity for judgment and independence in the feminine unconscious. The provocation of the negative animus or anima in real life can be provoked by both sexes: by a person of the opposite sex representing the projection of the negative animus or anima, or by a person of the same sex as the individual, characterizing aspects of his anima. In this case, reactions and confrontations are stronger since they are mingled with reactions from the shadow.

When the provocation of the shadow of the same sex mingles with misunderstandings of the projections of the negative anima-animus of the individual, the messages and interactions are much more difficult to integrate, because it is hard to distinguish clearly whether it is the inner Self or the shadow. This usually happens in extreme cases of non-integration of the contents of the shadow, since the shadow alters the characteristics of the Self and disguises itself to keep probing in its winding depths of riddles and puzzles.

This stage is a crucial crossroads where we can again connect with aspects of ourselves we believed we had outgrown. This fractures, separates, and damages many relationships, mostly because the shadow and the negative anima-animus mingle, reacting with people of any type and sex.

The personification of the negative anima begins in the relationship of a man with his mother. By denying these qualities, the result is impotence, boredom, or suicidal intentions, like a demon of death. Even being effeminate can be due to not recognizing the negative aspects of the anima and not being able to deal with the problems of life. The negative anima also appears in pseudo-intellectual and tactical male games. However, the most frequent manifestation occurs in sexual problems, by not wanting to satisfy his partner sexually due to a lack of generosity, aggression, or macabre eroticism. It also happens when a man does not cultivate his feelings in relationships or is emotionally immature.

It is easier to detect masculinity in women when it manifests. Her negative animus appears as an obstinate and unreachable part that will not acknowledge her mistakes. It can also be like a demon of death, with a side that destroys relationships, finding ever more absurd reasons for her behavior; a side full of malicious thoughts, calculations, and intrigue, even getting to the point of wishing someone's death. A woman's inner destructive attitudes can drive her husband or children to have accidents, illnesses, or to create bizarre situations where her children cannot find a companion. The psyche of a woman is so connected to that of her children, that at a certain stage of the individuation process, she can interfere dangerously in their lives, due to the messages of the negative animus. She is not aware of this; only through certain thoughts that arise and dreams she blocks out, forgets or misinterprets. The consequence is a greater personal negativity. Sometimes, the unconscious opinion of a negative animus can make her feel useless, unmotivated, apathetic, and insecure. "Why should I make an effort, if it won't change anything?"

All these thoughts, in extreme cases, begin to have their own identity, as if one were possessed, mostly when one has turned a certain age, disregarding the previous provocations of the shadow, continuing to project it outward. It is even personified in a psychic demon.

All this double psychic complication is usually due to a lack of true love or to a traumatic love experience and lack of understanding of the personal reasons for that experience, which makes one continue to blame the other. In these cases, there is a long period of suffering before one can find that love again inside oneself, which would be the reconciliation of the negative anima-animus. This might happen at an age where one can still experience a good love relationship, even in a temporary way. When this inner union takes place within the psyche, it begins to be ready to connect with the internal Self that is androgynous and contains both masculine and feminine characteristics, marking the entrance into the next psychological stage.

The fact is that instincts and unconscious reactions cannot be repressed, because it would only lead us to psychological, physical or mental illness, and we would lose contact with the true inner Self that contains the unique and whole unit of each of us.

We cannot bury the past either, because it turns into chronic images and traumas that try to emerge through other channels of expression. Artistic expression is the most healthy connection with the unconscious, although it does not soften the blows and provocations of the shadow. However, it acts as a guide for interpretation and helps in the search for meaning in the painful experiences of this psychological stage.

Somehow, sooner or later, we will have to deal with ourselves, although we might not have lived out this stage intensely or may have remained single or emotionally uninvolved. Often it is friends or other people who reject us and leave us alone. They have gotten tired of acting out our projections or their own in our presence. They leave us as if saying: "I don't like to play your game," since in their presence there is no other way of relating other than feeling and interacting with the different games of the shadow.

The goal is to recognize our inner disharmony, and if this is not done psychologically, the compensatory result is physical disharmony. So, we may have to deal with an illness that puts a whole new emphasis on being conscious, or we have to deal with our own imbalance. Since the polarity of Thunder is the Wind, these two stages are continuously interplaying, until we are able to enter the next one, where the individuation process is understood and acknowledged, and the monster of our own shadow begins to be assimilated.

FIRE

6th Stage:
The Revelation of Light and the
Centering of Darkness upon Recognition

This happens when we acknowledge the negativity within and how we attract the negativity of the environment from the center of our thoughts and our vibrations.

The light has filled us and we are now able to look inside and recognize the darkness and unconsciousness in which we were acting and reacting previously. The central Yin line is where our consciousness lies, and the unconscious is clearly visible through the Yang lower line.

We are ready to acknowledge errors and begin to attract people who resonate with the understanding of our psyche and according to the increased awareness of their subconscious.

We all radiate and absorb synergy, attracting people and situations that help us overcome negativity and understand mistakes. We understand ourselves and understand the effects of our lives. It is advisable to enter into this stage around age 50, because after 60 the astral, physical, and mental bodies are very damaged, and the individual has already gone through extremely intense and unbearable experiences due to an excess permanence at previous stages. Many people enter into this stage at their death-beds, and many even through violent or sudden death. This stage will happen after death, when we revise all the acts done during a lifetime.

When we evolve in consciousness, and enter into this stage at age 50, the peace and harmony flowing from those of us who are approaching the next stage of the Lake is evident to all, even though there might still be confrontations or we might still be subject to the projections of others' shadows or negative animus-anima. The trials keep coming, but we reduce the impact of the blows with our attitude of humility and courage in recognizing our own failures and mistakes. Therefore, we personify the contact with the Self, where the feminine and masculine merge, and the positive qualities of a man's anima or of a woman's animus merge with the qualities expressed in living physically the sensations of a single gender. However, we are able to express with vigor the positive powers both genders have granted us. The challenge now is to integrate the deep archetype of the animus-anima.

Within the Self, at the core of the psychological individuality, we have found the quality of being whole, not lacking anything, having to live physically one pole of the duality. The dynamics of personality contain the expression of courage and generosity of love that every human being looks for in another person.

For that reason, love relationships are a key element in the individuation process and in the development of the psyche. By restraining from getting fully involved in an intimate relationship for fear of conflicts, we hinder our illumination process and individuation process.

Before going into this stage, the Self might have appeared in dreams as a guide, as a special master, or even as a magical hermaphroditic animal. However, we do not yet personify the qualities of beauty and receptive firmness that are the behavioral characteristics of this stage.

Here, we begin to realize that many of the denied and condemned qualities are necessary for individual growth; we are ready to make friends with the shadow and this is reflected in everyday experience by making up with the person or persons who have personified the shadow and have even motivated painful provocations and confrontations in the past. This can be done because we do not feel endangered by the other's personality, nor are we afraid of being contaminated by the other's personality; we simply accept it, see its assets, and see as positive the things we used to consider negative.

Suddenly, it's as if we became exhausted after so many fights with the outside world and we feel even more confused and mixed up since we begin to see the projections and realize that we also sometimes behave the same way as those we condemned and judged.

This attitude of surrender puts us in contact with a new inner source which makes us feel more confident in our relationships. This is the time when we begin this stage of revelation and understanding of both ourselves and our external circumstances. Most of all, we have no more strength to fight, since all the energy has been invested outside and there is no more left inside.

The man who has passed on his good witch from his mother to other women is tired. At first he was not aware of what he wanted and was frightened; all seemed black or white and now he has no more energy left to make strong decisions from the bottom of his heart. So he needs to recover that power to know where he is and where he is going. He is aware that it was he who put up all kinds of obstacles and difficulties to keep himself from reaching his goals, because he was afraid of himself and of using his own power incorrectly.

The woman has projected her tyrant patriarch from her father to all the other men she has associated with, even at work, and now that she has won and vanquished all, she has no more energy left nor a clear direction forward. She becomes disoriented when there are no more external battles to fight. When she recovers the power of the shadow, as if swallowing it, she realizes that, in spite of all the willpower it has produced, it has no longer any purpose.

The true warrior is the one able to dive into his or her unconscious, acknowledge difficulties and not slay the monster completely, but tame it and pacify it, accepting certain instinctive qualities that grant renewed power and purpose to his or her life.

People who have had no physical contact with, or who do not know, their parents have a hard time understanding where their anima-animus characteristics come from, and they will often need outside help to reach this stage.

At this stage, we begin to retrieve that bad boy or girl inside and let it express itself little by little, becoming adults with distinctive differences in our rapport toward other people. We are happy with ourselves and with being different, and contrary to what we used to think, we seem to be better accepted by others and even attract circumstances in which we can share enriching experiences. Another crucial aspect of the karmic changes indicating the entrance into this stage of the psyche is experiencing the other side of what we once looked for in others. That is, when the roles are exchanged, we live out what we used to blame on others. It is as if we have to feel the deficiencies or attitudes we used to project outside and did not live inside. This means we are recovering part of our shadow or are allowing ourselves to experience some of its contents instead of projecting them outside. In some way, this slowly awakens us and reveals that the situations we attract are a reflection of our own mental and emotional obsessions. We begin to fear solitude, feeling shunned by the whole world, but learn to know the difference between solitude and individuality. Sleeping problems may appear, and trying to sleep only makes them worse. Involuntary situations (like sleep problems) spring from the center of our true Self, in order to force us to re-encounter that new Self we lost at birth.

When the Self begins to reveal itself, women begin to notice masculine qualities in themselves which they may have previously attacked, or they were victimized with by the men they lived with. They express this energy in a more moderate way because the energy is linked to their feminine side. Men feel and live out experiences that irritated them in the women they maintained contact with. These are indications that the Self is awakening although the shadow still provokes explosions from the previous 5th stage. It can take a long time to realize that everything is a reflection of our own psyche, and sometimes these indications happen for years while the Self is in the process of uniting its feminine and masculine qualities.

The Fire stage begins when we attach a strong shadow projection on a person we are able to surrender to and love in spite of all. The opening of the heart without judging is the crucial test to be able to enter this stage. Finally, we begin to feel comfortable with certain new attitudes. Somehow, it is no longer a matter of covering up or denying these new attitudes; we accept them and begin to fit them into our personality. The surprising thing is that they don't make us feel bad or uneasy as long as they haven't been repressed for a certain time. They don't become savage or excessive; in fact, when they are unleashed, they seem to add very convenient and enriching qualities to the personality, and surprisingly they are neither shocking to anyone nor are we rejected. Others relate to us in a different way.

Although it might seem so natural and others might not be aware of it, we can be more ourselves when we stop launching projections of our negative shadow on our social contacts. Others simply feel more at ease and they attribute it to a change in us or in themselves, depending on their own process of psychological evolution. We continue to test relationships and have frictions because, in a way, we are saved from the worst circumstance with that person or we experience it another way. We even help the other, or the situation is resolved the best possible way. That is to say, that when we integrate the shadow, we radiate peace and are more prone to sorrow than to anger. We even recover energy, which is essential to cure any illness and recover vitality. The senses begin to be more alert since they have been freed from the weight of the gag we imposed to prevent the unleashing of instincts.

The key to this stage is revelation through surrender of the war with the external world. In some way, the Self contains the two feminine aspects of the anima and the two masculine ones of the animus, leading people to the greatest balance and harmony they have ever experienced. The physical, vital, astral, and mental bodies are in the greatest harmony to regenerate health or to enable people to interact with the environment with greater harmony.

There are thousands of ways of retrieving the projection, of swallowing the shadow, or of integrating contents of the sac. One of the easiest ways is using language and words correctly, having mental clarity and clarity of speech. There are certain forms of conversation and internal dialogues that act like nets that throw out and scatter the substance. Writing, painting, and all artistic forms help us come in contact with our dreams and with the shadow, the inner tyrant or witch. It also helps us find the spiritual guide, our true center of the Self, within us, not as a passive experience of it through another person.

When we reach this stage, the light of the inner fire melts with the external environment (Yang lines above and below), while we accept the whole substance of the negativity spread out around us. However, the experiences of fusion and unity with the environment and the inner being soften the trauma and humiliation those circumstances provoke or have provoked in us.

Being able to be who we are is the most wholesome experience of all, because the fusion with the environment is love that pours out around us; it is the preparation for the mystical state our spiritual nature longs for, the same as the Aborigine way with nature.

It is the fusion with the cosmos, extrasensory experience that can happen before entering into this stage; it is working on ourselves through meditation, breathing, and silence techniques that do not extend in time until we enter the stage of psychological fire. It is like a beauty that emanates, a charisma, an acceptance of life we observe in certain elderly people, although in many it is mixed with resignation and resentment. This stage comes about from fighting against the continued distortion of consciousness as preparation for death, at whatever age.

If we attain this loving function with the environment and the cosmos at an adult age—50 to 60—we are leaders who attract people adequately and, although life continues to bring trials and crisis, we learn from them in a special way, with an attitude of humility that comes from recognizing what is. We begin to understand why we have done the things we did instead of lamenting about incorrect decisions, unfruitful efforts, or what could have been. We feel good and accept ourselves as we are.

We stop feeling like isolated entities while we realize that experience is unique and unrepeatable. We manage to reach an agreement with that center, with the limitless vacuum that we must explore and acknowledge in order to temper anxiety. That vacuum or void also creates an abysmal lack of communication, a duality of feeling, or the need to make friends because we feel an enemy. We can bear the solitude our psychic conscience provokes in us because it is no longer isolated the moment we recover our awareness of the umbilical cord that connects us to nature. Enjoying a good love relationship at this stage is one of the most transcendental realities of trust and the closest experience to unconditional love.

In dreams we may see symbols of transcendence in the form of sacred animals: dragons or horses, coiled serpents—messages from archetypes of initiation rituals. Initiation is a meeting point in the psyche; after a period of submission and surrender comes a moment of liberation. Everyone experiences this to a greater or lesser extent according to the circumstances, and the same happens with any relationship or even any human commitment or endeavor. Thus, every individual can reconcile with various conflicting aspects of personality.

By coming in contact with the subconscious, the shadow is no longer the enemy and starts to be a friend, asking us sometimes to give in, to resist, or to give it love. At times the power of the shadow is strong because the Self is pointing in the same direction and it is hard to recognize whether the messages come from one or the other. The confusion usually relates to a secret and reserved force within every human being that allows us to make great decisions at crucial times. Acknowledging the reality of the unconscious leads to self-analysis and to reorganizing goals, and it happens as a consequence of contact with the inner master and spiritual guide we sensed at times during childhood and whose guidance we felt through the first and most crucial decisions of life.

Often couples who reinforce the negative animus in one and the positive anima in the other (or vice versa) end up in divorce, with no negative effects on their karma. The one representing the positive anima suffers and matures too quickly, while the one indulging in the negative animus controls or unleashes emotions so much that no psychological maturation can take place. That person blocks himself by demanding and abusing others, expecting them to put up with him the same way his positive anima companion did. In order to enter the stage of Fire, these couples must separate or divorce. All the frustrations in love relationships from the Water stage must be solved in order to enter fully into this Fire stage.

The anima-animus of any individual, through a union with the Self, can contact inner values and open the way to psychic depths and the development of extrasensory capacities.

When we incorporate the qualities we have usually lived through the opposite sex, our personality becomes balanced, and we discover talents and gifts that open up untrodden paths. We discover new facets that enrich us.

The Self helps us realize that none of our past experience is worthless nor something to be ashamed of. This positive function of the unconscious occurs when we take feelings, expectations, and fantasies seriously. We can express them through artistic means. For women, this becomes a sacred conviction, and they may develop some forgotten talent or significant activity or social contribution. The animus joins with the Self through some creative activity.

Once the shadow is integrated and we have become friends with some of its qualities, we reach the negative anima-animus which is the threshold to the Self. By facing the reality they represent, a lot of suffering is also released. We find an inner companion with the qualities of love, initiative, objectivity, planned action, and inner wisdom.

This lends a new meaning to life, making us more receptive, even, to new creative ideas. The spiritual depth acquired is due to having the courage to question the feelings of the anima and the beliefs of the animus. The person in the Fire stage of the individuation process understands the qualities contained in the negative animus-anima and how these can be incorporated into the personality. This action can modify the structure of the psyche and even the genetic structure in cycles of 9 to 19 years.

When an we have struggled enough with the problem of the anima or animus, we no longer identify consciously with the negativity the unconscious projects outside. We are transformed when we find the Self at the core of our psyche. It is the Self that is active in the next stage of the psyche, for in this stage we are still going through the turmoil of distinguishing which messages come from the Self and which are colored by its predecessor, the negative anima or animus, causing fear and blame for the past.

Continuing self-criticism becomes an excuse for weakness and a tactic of humiliation, instead of the true humility the Self radiates. Solitary meditation and artistic activity are liberating experiences that help unite instinct and wisdom.

Sometimes this stage separates people from their families or from their past. In merging with oneself, life provides us with other new and significant contacts. The Self creates very specific emotional ties where there are no projections, envy, jealousy, or possessions as there were before.

If we are not at peace with ourselves, we cannot be at peace with anything else, since we cannot force ourselves to do anything against our own good, and when we have to make a sacrifice, we don't experience it as suffering but simply as just a greater effort. The most important thing is finding true inner meaning. That's why we give priority to the individuation process and do not allow distractions caused by desire or temptation, except when we cannot tell clearly whether they come from the Self or from the anima-animus. Now the unconscious wants to link the loose ends and no longer sees things in terms of dualities of shadow and light, God or devil.

We find compensation for this new reality when we discover that the Self points to new paths of social function and unites people who belong together. The inner light attracts, with synergy, people with the same integrity and maturity.

Although this is a stage of huge solitary reflection regarding the Self, each time there is real contact, a true and positive projection takes place in the direction of harmony, producing a mystical and creative fusion with the outer world.

This stage is also reached by less evolved people by living out everything they feared or denied during their youth, during the Water stage. Often the path to revelation passes through an illness or people experience great dissatisfaction.

However, this is a necessary threshold people must pass to let go of matter and discover that there is something that lies beyond physical reality. It isn't a pleasant way to reach this stage, which in itself can be of unequaled beauty, but the lack of consciousness with which we often live most of our lives forces us to acknowledge our errors in order to, at least, attain psychological maturity, or else enter into the next stage, even if it be in reflections on the past or in old age senility.

LAKE

7th Stage:
The Integration of Light and the
Expulsion of Darkness

For many people, this stage means losing the fear of death before it happens. Only a few people are granted, during this stage, the possibility to participate in life with the wisdom of a magician or miracle-maker who can use an inner illuminating power to cancel out external darkness. For the majority, it is a period of peace and acceptance for having forged their own destiny; they recognize their errors and feel neither frustration nor repentance for anything they have done. This gives them an indispensable wisdom and a means to participate in their world.

In the previous stage, inner solitary reflection alternates with participation in the external world. Here, the external world asks us to use our inner light to enlighten the outer darkness. The only frustration of this stage is the realization of a huge extension of darkness and how little we can do to illuminate it. We may feel like small light bulbs in the midst of a dark and stormy night.

The central Yang line represents the illumination of the Self, and upon entering the world of an ultimately positive personality, outer negativity and the darkness of the upper Yin line has no effect.

It may refer to becoming as children again and enjoying life as the Lake trigram represents. All experiences are valued, no matter how difficult they may be. The signs of having entered this stage are usually miraculous cures in elderly people and a joyful and peaceful personality with no signs of immaturity. And we become aware that this life is but a reflection of another life where we live with the experiences gained in this one. Finally, we can believe there is something more after death, and the memories of the past are lived intensely in the dreams of the fourth dimension.

To a greater or lesser extent, it is the mystical experience of being alive. This is a psychological liberation from the material world, although we are surrounded by it and may not yet be aware of physical limitations. Consciousness takes the lead and self-transforming perception makes us feel united to the infinite. We know that death is not the end, for there is something to immortality. Something happens inside that is beyond time and space.

From the center of the Self, the universe is perceived in its imperfection, for it is precisely this that stirs the loving union with the Whole of the Lake. This psychological maturity is a spiritual and significant goal of the individuation process. This is much more than getting on good terms with the individual germ of the whole and accepting external facts. An inner voice knows all and we recognize ourselves in that inner voice. The ego must be capable of listening and surrendering to its own Self with no motivation other than knowing that it is right for the enrichment of its inner life, which is where we shall live ever after.

The Self is the temple of the soul. It has no age or sex and it is represented in dreams as a magician, a god or goddess, a spirit of nature, or an important public character. It does not express itself with anything contained in time and so represents an incalculable and unsuspected source of power. This stage is represented by the joyfulness and peaceful happiness of the Lake, because it represents a crucial point in the basic attitude and the way of life of the individual. The Self is also characterized by the vision of a superior human being and by the unity of the double duality. The four aspects of the psyche become activated: the two aspects of the animus with the two of the anima, plus the integration of the physical, vital, astral and mental bodies becomes as harmonious as during childhood. We recover this radiant ball of energy and now know how to direct it slowly and safely. The physical body is a little worn out and no longer needs so much movement to express joyous energy. A unique flowing quality is experienced and with hardly any effort, things fall into place.

Time seems to stretch and, perhaps due to the slowing down of brain rhythms, the Beta rhythm progressively gives way very naturally to an Alpha rhythm. Even with no experience in meditation or relaxation, we might say that consciousness finally becomes conscious. It is the symbol of the inner light of the unity of all human existence. Another symbol of the Self is gold, quartz crystal, the metal that reflects the inside and the outside as in a mirror, just as the Lake in the I-Ching.

Cosmic human beings are more a psychic inner image than a concrete external reality. A part of every human being is immortal, and it is this one that manifests itself in this stage and redeems us of all personal suffering. This is not to say that we do not have enormous conflicts or reasons to suffer, but this is only in terms of other loved ones, not because of something lacking in ourselves. Already we know that the one thing we need is psychological fulfillment, listening to the inner voice of the Self. We realize that the only purpose of it all is to be human, with its weaknesses, flaws, and virtues. To feel, as a symbol of being alive, but not to suffer, which is a symbol of fear of death.

Some people don't reach this stage with good health, while many others start to live and experience a secret or special gift that grants their lives a unique feeling.

If, at a certain age, we have not contacted with the Self or acquired a rich inner life, an obvious symptom is losing our sense of humor and many human contacts. We are left alone and living becomes an effort. We vegetate instead of living. However, from the center of the Self, we become like a mirror where we can look at ourselves or reflect on ourselves if the psyche is sufficiently evolved. We can observe everything positively without getting personally involved in it, and we accept contact with the Earth, and suffering becomes a vehicle for the human soul to transform and perfect itself. Thus, many barriers that hid our divine potential are demolished.

If we do not fear death, we fear nothing. Unfortunately for many people, this stage only occurs days, hours, or even minutes before death, or it can even happen after death.

However, if we attain this inner peace in our maturity, we are magicians, healers, and transformers. Knowing people who are in this stage leaves an unforgettable impression, especially because it helps the rest of us lose our fear of death. These people become spiritual guides. He or she is not afraid of loneliness and spends little time alone, because people feel attracted to an innate charisma.

The fear of death and the reason for taking on a material existence are revealed and life becomes meaningful. There is really a direct relationship with the stage of the infancy of the Mountain, because we have lived out what we have chosen as well as what we have repressed and feared during that stage. We have, in some way, lived out all those fearful thoughts and fantasies.

The psychological reality of each individual is oriented toward the symbol of the Self. It is funny that, psychologically, we only enjoy life at its end, perhaps being the time when we truly learn to live.

The previous psychological distortion is that we fight to be alive by giving in to the indulgence of matter, of desire, and we only appreciate the satisfied appetites. It is as if we were looking for a reward for the suffering we experienced at birth and throughout life. On the other hand, before dying, we realize that it was all worth it, and with those experiences we live in eternity after death.

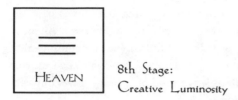

HEAVEN

8th Stage:
Creative Luminosity

This represents life after death, life as a spirit, the light of understanding and the awareness of all we have lived. Many people do not enter this stage even at the time of death, because their astral body is stuck to matter and blocks them from the spiritual light and eternal fusion with the Whole.

This period, long or short, is unknown to our physical conscience, and is, therefore, inexplicable. It redeems us of all our creations, of all duality of errors and, above all, of suffering, since death is less painful than birth.

The peaceful expression on the faces of some people at the moment of death induces others to accept death also, and indicates that the deceased enters this stage early after death. Many others make this revision and reflection of their life in the previous stage of the Lake when they die, and it takes them several years to enter this 8th stage after death.

People with heightened consciousness experience astral journeys, and beings who are evolved on the transcendental extrasensory plane enter this stage temporarily when they travel through the cosmos to receive spiritual teachings to help the beings under their spiritual care. This does not happen because of individual spiritual needs, but because the individual merges with the collective and with the universe itself.

It is called creative luminosity because from this place things can be created anew whenever there are no personal motives. From this place we return or influence other incarnate spirits to resolve what has been left unsolved in human experience and all that resonates with what we have been part of in a global consciousness.

This stage represents total happiness. We cannot fathom this from the standpoint of our physical existence. We can only imagine it in its similarity to the world of dreams when there is no anxiety of the kind that sometimes appears in dreams due to their connection with emotional references in the sphere of physical experience.

We exist in a body of light of greater or lesser intensity based on our happiness and our detachment from physical experience. The consciousness of the spirit relates to our creativity, since it is from this state that all we experience is created.

Life takes place inside time and there is no delay between thought and its realization. Thought is all that is. Our individual consciousness is aware of the movement within the thoughts themselves. Our individuality is translucid and transparent, and allows an immediate understanding of any error or distortion.

If there is such a thing as individuality, it is so fused with the all and all existences that there are no differences, only equality. The individual psyche continues to feed on its experiences in matter, but also begins to understand how all human beings have lived similar experiences. The individual eventually sees the unity of human experience.

The void can fill all voids and can incorporate all experiences into its individual experience. Our new entity is like a holon, a piece representing the whole and similar to it. It is part of a giant hologram, but it maintains an identity that cannot be imposed upon another entity. This stage represents that inexplicable dimension, so infinitely eternal that we are terrified to decipher or define it with our dualistic minds, or from our sphere of ordinary experience.

If we have trouble understanding the 1st stage of receptive Earth—which should be easy to grasp because of its closeness to this reality—how can we dare define this 8th stage, which is farther from our extrasensory perception and much less intellectual?

We can only say that karma is nonexistent there, that there is no action or reaction, that all movement finds an immediate compensation and that we go on existing although we cannot understand how. Just as we cannot understand the material density of light and its microscopic photons, it is useless to define with words the existence of eternal silence. From there we do not communicate with words; only the voice of our individual Self comes into contact with the void, and, once in a while, with a dimension that transfers some sensation from the inner voice to our physical life.

Perhaps the only time that counts here is that which has been lost in matter because of our involvement in spiritual and creative things, or in doing nothing, not even thinking. The time spent sleeping and not remembering our dreams has not helped us contact this unknown dimension. It pertains to resonance frequencies of ultrasonic speed, although, when entering into them, our brain reduces its rhythm to the initial ones. The three pulses stop: the cardiac, the respiratory and the cranio-sacral—the slowest of all—which is the first to enter matter and the last to leave it. It is another rhythm of vibration imperceptible to our senses, since it does not belong to earthly and gravitational reality, nor to the electromagnetic reality of Heaven.

In fact, sooner or later, all humans go to live in Heaven, but some become attached to emotions with their astral bodies and maintain contact with the terrestrial and the darkness—that is, what Christians call hell or purgatory—to understand all that happened in the material dimension. This is like swallowing the shadow when it is no longer there, for the dark sac was so large that these people have not had time to review all its contents and are staying in the realm of no-time. That dissonance of frequencies must be hell, when people are so close to dissolution in the vacuum of the Whole, and fail to do it. They fail to share personal responsibility with cosmic love, or cannot share personal responsibility with cosmic love while disintegrating into the collective.

Perhaps the torture called purgatory or hell is maintained after death with a certain amount of psychic individuality. The Self has certain qualities of Heaven during its life in Hell, since liberation is complete when we eventually merge with the cosmos.

William Blake speaks of seeing an upside-down world or a world in which what is far becomes close and what is close, far. Thus is the interaction of that other dimension with our own.

The Luminosity of the Self

The Self has some qualities of Heaven during this life. Pain and suffering are needed to crack open the shell around the crystal of light at the center of our brains. Many individuals have deep experiences with the Self at least once in life. Once the Self has been known and contacted, it can be kept as that inner companion whose attention is continuously inspiring. It is understood that the psyche and matter are one and the same, but are seen from different observation points: one from the inside, as a convex reality, and the other, from the outside, as a concave reality.

This contact, this constant, irregular, and sporadic attention to the Self from the most intimate core, produces the radiation that connects Heaven and Earth through each one of us. This inner spark of light penetrates through the crown of the cranium and, by igniting the pineal crystal, penetrates the body through the spine and merges with the Earth in the center of gravity. It ascends the body again and, forming a Lemniscate (a figure 8) in our bodily, emotional, and mental senses, synchronizes and tunes them with the right time and place, and the right people to accompany us in our journey through the magic of synergetic synchronicity.

The significant coincidences outlined by Dr. Jung under the name of synchronicity penetrate deeply into the relationship of the psyche with matter. More synchronistic events occur during the crucial phases of the individuation process, especially when we are already capable of noticing these coincidences, sometimes insignificant, sometimes of great magnitude. If we have become trained in their interpretation through the I-Ching or other methods of symbolic association, we can grasp their essential meaning through which our Self is manifesting itself. There are no discontinuity zones except when we question what we do. Each nerve cell is connected to all nerve cells and each atom to all atoms of the universe.

By giving daily attention to the reality of the Self we are attempting to live simultaneously in two different worlds or on two levels of existence or in several dimensions. We are alert to daily chores, while being open to the clues and messages synchronicity brings when living in the here and now. We are aware, thus, of the relationship it all has with the Whole and with life in the dream body.

We can develop an inner perception of the Self fully integrated with all circumstances and creatures of external life, but watered down to the point where it allows us to stay in contact with external reality, not letting thoughts interfere with the inescapable reality of all the perceptions synchronized in unison. Everything that we experience can produce a revelation, an awakening, or an inner illumination that erases doubts about self and happiness in this terrestrial existence.

In normal experiences, we feel charged with an exciting adventurous energy where everything fits our unique individuality. This energy can only be lost by an instinctive urgency or by an ego-centeredness that would lead to a loss of balance. That unilateral egocentric vision is what primitive people once called "the loss of the soul," referring to a loss of physical and mental sanity.

When we undertake a true search in our own inner world, we know ourselves not only because we become aware of stagnant thoughts or emotions but also because we acquire subjective knowledge about the complexity of existence. We also learn to listen to ourselves. We express ourselves through dreams and life flows like a stream that already knows the way to the ocean. The Self will soon emerge and will find a power that contains all possibilities of renewal and transformation. We also feel as part of something much larger and complete, belonging to a transcendental whole.

The Self has an individual, a transpersonal, and a universal aspect. In order to understand the symbolism through which our Self expresses itself through the unconscious—and that center is a tornado of spirals from Heaven and Earth—one must be careful not to be "out of oneself" or "close to oneself" but to be "within oneself." Only with that totality can we unite the eternal contradictions without falling into either of the two extremes. It is finding the perfect polarity. The Self is the center of the sphere of all that exists around us, since it has been created by our inner self. Perhaps it already existed before birth and will continue to exist after death.

Just like the anima or animus, and the shadow, the Self has its uncontrollable dangers when we are aware of how everything arises from the depths of our unconscious; it can even create the difficulties and hardships we unconsciously ask for, pushing us to grow. It has aspects of darkness and light, ambivalent and indefinite, for it is from that tornado-center that the positive becomes negative and the negative, positive. It has such a transformation potential that it puts us in contact with the forces of the universe, creating never-ending circles. Once the Self has awakened and it has been driven to guide us, it takes hold of us, and if we are not awake and have not united the masculine and feminine poles, animus and anima, and integrated the shadow, there is great risk involved for the conscious ego. There is the risk of falling into schizophrenia or of being possessed by paranormal forces as a result of the contact established, through the Self, with forces from other existential dimensions. That's why the contact with the Self is a danger for the ego when we have not regenerated the negative parts of our psyche. Then the Self acts like an evil spirit that can psychologically petrify us in a state of imbalance. In a normal individuation process, this is the last stage of evolution from where everything can be regenerated.

The Self can also be contacted through admiration of a spiritual guru that moves us to follow in the guru's footsteps. While the need of the Self provokes this cause, this would constitute a failure of true individuation for we look for examples to imitate outside ourselves. The Self initiates the need, but this is only a learning step when we still don't trust the inner guidance of our own Self.

Reaching psychological maturity is an individual task and it is much more difficult when individuality is threatened by conformity to social standards. One of the reasons for the rebelliousness we see in artists is that they have come in contact with the Self to some extent. Due to that source of inner guidance, they are suspicious and distrusting of staid social groups. Although they contact the Self, they may not reach psychological maturity, or may not able to cooperate as conscious individuals because they feel threatened by the social spectrum of the Self.

Artists often see their works in dreams and materialize them during sleep; the Self is always inspiring and revealing itself to us, but it is in the conscious state that it puts us to tests and hardships so that we return to our inner self. The fact that progress depends on the individual becomes clear in dreams. At times it is like a call from a divine being that asks us to do a special task and gives us the strength to go against the social environment. Artists take the petition of the soul completely seriously and overcome social prejudices and shackles in order to accomplish their goals.

The life in dreams allows us to experience our perceptions as well as see how they really affect us, and how they affect others. That's why Native Americans and Tibetans know how to go into dreams and recognize what is happening in their lives and what the future has in store. Their meditation practices teach us how to penetrate into that world and change personal aspects and aspects of our immediate environment. The first thing they do in the morning is sing and share their dreams with the other members of the family or clan. This reveals aspects of both the personal and collective psyche.

There are no infallible rules or methods to interpret dreams, but only a constant practice and self-confrontation that helps adjust the needs of the individual. Social conscience maintains its autonomy just like individual conscience. An honest intention is required for its interpretation.

The Self regulates our relationships, both with others and with ourselves, and from that center, it radiates outward, or else the outside has an impact on that center. The ego, when in contact with its conscious Self, learns to detect projections, false illusions, and knows how to deal with them from the inside instead of from the outside. That's why all the characters we dream about actually represent aspects of ourselves that take on the symbolic form of people or groups of people that signify our social consciousness.

Activities and obligations belong exclusively to the external world of the ego. They damage the activities of the unconscious and the contact with the Self, causing us to react. They represent external situations that have provoked and irritated them through these unconscious ties. When we join the people we are to learn with, our paths resonate and attract each other from the Self so we can repeat a karmic pattern. That's why relationships are karmic ones, for they are repeating and resolving patterns of the collective human unconscious.

The individuation process definitely changes all our relationships to others by radically altering our relationship to ourselves. From the deepest fiber of the Self sprouts the call to participate in the lives of others. When this happens, the union with the outside through the Self leaves us with the feeling of having lost contact with our own Self. The result is a combination of external participation and inner recollection until they combine in psychological maturity.

The Self has a profound effect on love, for it is the Self that surrenders to the other or avoids surrendering. When we are in contact with our Self, we fall in love with the other, not because of physical attraction, but because of how that person relates to us. It is as if the loved one helps us feel a greater and more intimate contact with our own Self. The loved one would then be a person who helps us come in contact with ourselves, and falling in love with this person is like falling in love with our own Self, without selfishness or conceit. Through contact and intimacy with this person, we dive into ourselves intimately, and with such cosmic depth we feel united to everything. In the moment of true love, we are in love with life itself, which means truly unequaled emotional growth. Thus, a detectable indicator of emotional and psychological maturity is our record of relationships. Having been able to choose well and to solve the problems that may have come up with a partner indicates that we are in touch with ourselves. Relationships are the most enriching aspects of the process of psychological growth and sanity. It is also an arduous task to succeed in them without losing contact with the Self.

A lack of intimate relationships delays the individuation process. It affects certain emotional and psychological conflicts that are absolutely necessary for mental balance and for recognizing the inside-outside pulsation of the Self's messages. In the interaction between two people, the electromagnetic interhemispheric coherence merges and the one with the higher consciousness affects the other, though at the price of lowering one's harmonic state temporarily.

The Self is the window that closes, opens, radiates, absorbs, or merges with the most intimate relationship we create with the world and its external relationships. The Self is the nucleus of the atom that has the power of altering the spin of the electrons around it. To know the Self is to know that invisible player that moves the pieces of each individual life. To come in contact with the Self means recovering free will with responsibility toward the whole.

Advice From the Self*

Clarify your Intentions • Have Intentions without being Goal-oriented • Being Centered • Sensitivity • Awareness • Really Listening • Really Observing • Respect • Honor • Humility • Dignity • Practice Curiosity • Vulnerability • Receptivity • Openness without Expectations • Patience with your own Process and with others • Know what you Know • Know your Limits.

---

*W.O.H.C. Shiatsu Group, Merry Witty, 3985 Wonderland Hill, Boulder, CO 80304.

Bibliography

Argüelles, José. *Earth Ascending: An Illustrated Treatise on the Law Governing Whole Systems*. Santa Fe: Bear & Co., 1988.

———. *The Mayan Factor: Path Beyond Technology*. Santa Fe: Bear & Co., 1987.

———. *The Transformative Vision: Reflection on the Nature & History of Human Expression*. Muse Publications, 1992.

———. "Trends in Modern Thought," in *Main Currents in Modern Thought*. New York: The Center of Integrative Education. January, 1969.

Argüelles, Miriam and José. *The Feminine: Spacious as the Sky*. Boston: Shambhala, 1978.

———. *Mandala*. Boston: Shambhala, 1974.

Capra, Fritjof. *The Tao of Physics: An Exploration of the Parallels between Modern Physics & Eastern Mysticism*. Boston: Shambhala, 1991.

Cheng Man Chi'ng. *Cheng's Thirteen Chapters on Tai Chi*. Berkeley, CA: North Atlantic Books, n.d.

Cheng Man Chi'ng and Robert Smith. *Tai Chi: the Supreme Exercise for Health, Sport & Self-Defense*. Boston and Tokyo: C.E. Tuttle, 1967.

Chu, Wen Kuan and W.A. Sherrill. *Astrology and the I Ching*. York Beach, ME: Samuel Weiser, 1980.

Cleary, Thomas. *The Buddhist I Ching* (Chih-hsu). Boston, Shambhala, 1987.

———. *The I Ching Mandalas: A Program of Study for the Book of Changes*. Boston: Shambhala, 1989.

———. *The Taoist I Ching*. Boston, Shambhala, 1986.

———. *Zen Essence: The Science of Freedom*. Boston, Shambhala, 1989.

Clifford, Terry. *Tibetan Buddhist Medicine & Psychiatry: The Diamond Healing*. York Beach, ME: Samuel Weiser, 1984.

Connelly, Diann. *Traditional Acupuncture: The Law of Five Elements*. Columbia, MD: The Centre for Traditional Acupuncture, n.d.

Da Liu. *I-Ching Numerology*. London: Routledge & Kegan Paul; New York: Harper & Row.

———. *The Tai-Chi Chuan and I Ching: A Choreography of Body and Mind*. London: Arkana, 1990.

———. *The Tao of Health & Longevity*. New York: Paragon House, 1991.

Damian-Knight, Guy . *Karma & Destiny in the I Ching*. London: Arkana, 1987.

Dhiegh, Khigh. *The Eleventh Wing: An Exposition of the Dynamics of I-Ching for Now*. New York: Delta, 1973.

Easson, K.P. and R.R. Easson, eds. *Milton: A Poem by William Blake:* Boulder: Shambhala, 1978.

Ferguson, Marilyn. *The Aquarian Conspiracy: Personal & Social Transformation in the 1980s.* Los Angeles: J.P. Tarcher, 1981.

Govinda, Lama Anagarika. *The Inner Structure of the I-Ching: The Book of Transformations.* New York: Weatherhill, 1981.

Harner, Michael. *The Way of the Shaman.* New York: Bantam, 1982.

Heckler, Richard. *The Anatomy of Change: East-West Approaches to Body-Mind Therapy.* Boston: Shambhala, 1984.

Hook, Diana Ffarington. *I Ching and Its Associations.* New York: Viking/Penguin, 1988; London: Routledge & Kegan Paul, 1980.

———. *The I Ching and You.* London: Routledge & Kegan Paul, 1973.

———. *The I Ching and Mankind.* London: Routledge & Kegan Paul, 1975.

Jaffé, Aniela. *From the Life & Work of C.G. Jung.* Santa Rosa, CA: Daimon Verlag, 1989.

Jung, C.G. *The Collected Works of C.G. Jung, No. 6. Psychological Types.* G. Adler et al, eds. R.F. Hull and H.G. Baynes, trans. Bollingen Series XX. Princeton, NJ: Princeton University Press, 1971.

———. *The Collected Works of C.G. Jung, No. 12. Psychology and Alchemy.* G. Adler et al, eds. R.F. Hull, trans. Bollingen Series XX. Princeton, NJ: Princeton University Press, 1968.

———. *Jung Extracts: Dreams.* R.F. Hull, trans. Bollingen Series XX. Princeton, NJ: Princeton University Press, 1974.

———. *Jung Extracts: Mandala Symbolism.* G. Adler, ed. R.F. Hull, trans. Bollingen Series XX. Princeton, NJ: Princeton University Press, 1973.

———. *Jung Extracts: Psychology and the Occult.* G. Adler, ed. R.F. Hull, trans. Bollingen Series XX. Princeton, NJ: Princeton University Press, 1976.

———. *Man and His Symbols.* New York: Doubleday, 1964; London: Aldus Books, 1964.

———. *Modern Man in Search of a Soul.* Orlando: Harcourt Brace, 1955.

———. *The Spirit in Man, Art & Literature.* G. Adler, et al, eds. R.F. Hull, trans. Bollingen Series XX. Princeton, NJ: Princeton University Press, 1966.

———. *Synchronicity: Synchronicity & a Causal Connecting Principle.* G. Adler, ed. R.F. Hull, trans. Bollingen Series XX. Princeton, NJ: Princeton University Press, 1966.

Kimmelman, Susan and Tem Horwitz, eds. *Tai Chi Chu'an: The Technique of Power.* Chicago: Chicago Review, 1980.

Kushi, Michio. *The Book of Do-in: Exercise for Physical & Spiritual Development.* Briarcliff Manor, NY: Japan Publications, 1979.

Lao Tzu. *Tao Te Ching.* Gia-Fu Feng, ed. Jane English, trans. New York: Vintage/Random House, 1989.

Liang, Master T. T. *Tai Chi Ch'uan for Health & Self-Defense: Philosophy and Practice.* New York: Vintage/Random House, 1977.

Ouspensky, P. D. *The Psychology of Man's Possible Evolution.* New York: Random House, 1973.

Rawson, Philip, and Lazlo Legeza. *Tao: The Chinese Philosophy of Time & Change.* New York & London: Thames & Hudson, 1984.

Riencourt, Amaury de. *The Eye of Shiva: Mysticism and Science.* London: Souvenir, 1980.

Rimpoche, Chogyam Trungpa. *Cutting through Spiritual Materialism.* Boston, Shambhala, 1978.

Schonberger, Martin. *The I-Ching & the Genetic Code.* Santa Fe, NM: Aurora Press, 1992.

Shima, Miki. *The Medical I Ching: Oracle of the Healer Within.* Boulder, CO: Blue Poppy Press, 1992.

Suarès, Carlo. *The Cipher of Genesis.* York Beach, ME: Samuel Weiser, 1992.

Talbot, Michael. *The Holographic Universe.* New York: HarperCollins, 1991.

Toben, Bob. *Space Time & Beyond.* New York: Bantam, 1983.

Tulku, Tarthang. *Gesture of Balance: A Guide to Awareness, Self-Healing & Meditation.* Berkeley, CA: Dharma Publishing, 1976.

van Franz, Marie-Louise. *Alchemy: An Introduction to the Symbolism and the Psychology.* Toronto: Inner City Books, 1982.

———. *Individuation in Fairy Tales.* Boston: Shambhala, 1991.

———. *On Divination and Synchronicity: The Psychology of Meaningful Chance.* Toronto: Inner City Books, 1980.

Wilhelm, Hellmut. *Change: Eight Lectures on the I Ching.* C.F. Baynes, trans. Bollingen Series LXII. Princeton, NJ: Princeton University Press, 1960.

Wilhelm, Richard, trans. *The Secret of the Golden Flower: A Chinese Book of Life.* Foreword by C.G. Jung. Orlando: Harcourt Brace, 1970.

Wing, R.L. *The I Ching Workbook.* New York: Dolphin/Doubleday, 1979.

———. *The Illustrated I Ching.* New York: Dolphin/Doubleday, 1982.

Ywahoo, Dhyani. *Voices of Our Ancestors: Cherokee Teachings from the Wisdom Fire.* Boston: Shambhala, 1987.

Index

Santiago Gómez Esteban

About the Author

Marysol González Sterling lives and works in Madrid, Spain. She is a self-taught artist, painter, sculptress, and innovator of environmental art forms. She has a passionate interest in the integration of mind, body, and spirit, and studied astrology in order to use it as a psychoanalytic technique. This book about the use of the symbolism inherent in the I-Ching, and how these symbols can be used to understand the transformative process of a lifetime, developed because of her friendship with José Argüelles and the study of his book *Earth Ascending*. Sterling has studied Tibetan Buddhism at the Naropa Institute in Colorado, and is the founder of Planet Art Network with her partner, Geraldyn Waxkowsky, in Spain. She is presently investigating octaves in light and sound, and is working on a book combining color and sound harmonics, crystals, iridology, astrology, and the I-Ching called *Photonics: Cromodynamics and the I-Ching*.